BISHOP JOSEPH HALL

AND PROTESTANT

MEDITATION

medieval & renaissance texts & studies

1. Frank Livingstone Huntley, *Bishop Joseph Hall and Protestant Meditation in Seventeenth-Century England: A Study, With the Texts of The Art of Divine Meditation (1606) and Occasional Meditations (1633).*

2. *Johannes de Alta Silva, Dolopathos: or The King and the Seven Wise Men.* Translated by Brady B. Gilleland.

3. Albert Rabil, Jr., *Laura Cereta: Quattrocento Humanist.*

Bishop Joseph Hall

and
Protestant Meditation
in Seventeenth-Century England:
A Study
With the texts of

The Art of Divine Meditation (1606)

AND

Occasional Meditations (1633)

BY

FRANK LIVINGSTONE HUNTLEY

medieval & renaissance texts & studies
CENTER FOR MEDIEVAL & EARLY RENAISSANCE STUDIES
Binghamton, New York
1981

Publication of this book was generously aided by a grant
from the Horace Rackham School of Graduate Studies,
University of Michigan

*This book is published in both
clothbound and paperbound editions.*

ISBN 0-86698-000-8 *(cloth)*
ISBN 0-86698-005-9 *(paper)*

For Katherine
Again

Preface

For the history of meditation as a religious exercise and its impact upon the literary mind of the seventeenth century we are all inescapably and fortunately beholden to Professor Louis Martz of Yale. He drew our attention, in this respect, to the influence of St. Ignatius of Loyola. In teaching "metaphysical poetry," however, many of us and our students have had difficulty in descrying the rather exacting formula in the poems of Donne, Herbert, and others.

Though scholars have not overlooked Hall, no one has yet shown how crucial Hall was in preparing the way, from the "Gunpowder Plot" on, for a non-Jesuitical, Protestant, and English mode of meditation. I hope, then, that the present work will complement that of Professor Martz by presenting a different point of view and by furnishing two of Hall's basic texts, for the first time according to modern editorial practice, as a contribution to our better understanding of seventeenth-century English literature and religion.

FRANK LIVINGSTONE HUNTLEY

Ann Arbor, Michigan
January, 1981

Contents

Certainly it is heaven upon earth to have

a man's mind move in charity, rest in providence,

and turn upon the poles of truth.

— *Francis Bacon, "Of Truth" (1625)*

Introduction

I

Protestant Meditation and the "Three Books of God"

The words "Renaissance" and "Reformation" imply a revolution against a previously established mode of thought and action accompanied by a return to preceding models for inspiration. The Italian rebirth of culture went back to classical models of Greece and Rome; and the protest against the Roman Catholic Church "returned" to the Bible, the early Church fathers, and the "Pre-Reformation Reformers" of the thirteenth and fourteenth centuries. Quite apart from the necessity Martin Luther saw of ridding the Church of certain illegal and sometimes immoral practices, Protestantism meant a freeing of the individual believer from doctrinal and ecclesiastical confinement. One of the responses to the great "schism" was the Roman Catholic Counter Reformation and the founding of the Society of Jesus by St. Ignatius of Loyola. In England, Elizabeth maintained an even though at times precarious peace among the Roman Catholics, the Anglicans, and the growing number of dissident "Protestant" sects.

Although in her reign there had been an Anglican and Puritan tradition of meditation in England,[1] the militantly Protestant mode in theory and practice came into being at the beginning of the seventeenth century in direct conflict with the *Spiritual Exercises* of St. Ignatius when fear and hatred of the Jesuits was at its height. Thus Richard Rogers' *Seven Treatises leading and guiding to true Happiness*

(London, 1603) is a good place to begin. Dedicating the volume to the newly crowned King James, Rogers writes in his preface:

> I was moved hereunto by this reason, that the Papists cast in our teeth, that we have nothing set out for the certaine and daily direction of a Christian, where yet they have published (they say) many treatises of this argument . . . . they cannot deny (but they care not what they say, to bring the people out of love with our religion) . . . that both in catechisms, sermons, and other treatises, there is set forth by vs that which may clearly direct Christians, and stirre vp Godly devotion in them.

As for Jesuit devotional books, he has read two: one by Robert Parsons, "the King of Spaine's confessor"; and the other by "Iasper Loarte, an Italian Iesuite Doctor in Diuinitie and translated into English by some fauourite of Poperie." The first, Rogers declares, merely persuades men "to leaue some grosse euills," and the second "is a ridiculous tying men to a daily taske of reading some part of the stories of Christs passion, and saying certaine prayers throughout the weeke everie day." There follows a long paragraph of unrestrained anti-Jesuit invective characterizing their worship as "a confused heape of superstitions, and outward dead worship, even Iewish and Heathenish ceremonies."

His own meditations, Rogers believes, combine the understanding and the affections: "they set our minds on worke about the cogitation of things heauenly, by calling to remembrance one or other of them which we knowe and so debate and reason about the same, that our affections may thereby be moued to loue and delight in, or to hate and feare, according to that which we meditate on" (p. 235). He calls attention to the great variety of subject matter (p. 236): any part of God's word, any attribute of God, any of His works and judgments, any affliction of this life, our own sins, and our mortality. He ends his treatise with a list of twenty subjects for meditation, including two which Joseph Hall was soon to use in his *Art of Divine Meditation*: no. 7, on God's saints, and no. 13, on death.

Protestant and Roman Catholic meditation have much in common, since they are both Christian; and yet, as Protestant meditation came to be more and more opposed to the *Spiritual Exercises* of the Jesuits, it may be recognized by five major characteristics: philosophically it is Platonic, not Aristotelian; in psychology it is

Augustinian, not Thomistic; its theology is Pauline-Calvinist; though starting with the individual it finally becomes more public than private, and bears a greater similarity to the sermon than to penitential prayer; and it finds a greater variety of subject matter in God's "three books." Each of these characteristics demands some exposition.

Platonic Philosophy. The Renaissance in Italy may be thought of as the victory of Platonism over Aristotelianism, due mainly to the outpouring of translations and commentaries on Plato and his followers that issued from Marsilio Ficino's Platonic Academy in Florence. The victory was important for modern science and for religion. Galileo's proof that Copernicus was right is an example of the victory of the mind over the senses, for our senses tell us that the earth and not the sun is the center of the universe. In religion, whereas most of the Roman Catholic writers got their Aristotelianism from St. Thomas Aquinas, the Protestants became imbued with the Platonism of SS. Augustine and Bonaventura. The distinction has been made so clearly and importantly by Etienne Gilson for Bonaventura, that his words bear quoting in full:

[There are] two irreducible mental attitudes, from which flow two absolutely irreconcilable interpretations of the universe. Aristotle's universe, born of a mind that seeks the sufficient reason for things in the things themselves, detaches and separates the world from God. Plato's universe—at least if we may take St. Augustine's interpretation as true—inserts between God and things ideas as a middle term: it is the universe of images, the world wherein things are at once copies and symbols, with no autonomous nature belonging to themselves, essentially dependent, relative, leading thought to seek beyond things and even above itself for the reason of what they are. If, then, we penetrate to what is fundamental in the doctrines in order to lay bare the spirit which animates them, it is clear that the human mind has already long since chosen between the two perspectives, one facing towards Christianity, the other turning its back upon it. Essentially pagan, because it sees things from the point of view of the things themselves, it is no marvel if Aristotle's philosophy has succeeded in the interpretation of the things of nature: from its first moment it was turned towards the earth and organized for its conquest. Plato's philosophy, on the other hand, was in its very first intention a philosophy of what is beyond, placing the reasons of things outside the things themselves, even sometimes going too far in denying them all subsistence of their own; it was, then, a philosophy directed from its very origin towards the supernatural, a philosophy of the insufficiency of things and the knowledge of them.[2]

There has been a tendency to believe Yeats' famous line in "Among School Children"—"Plato thought nature but a spume that plays / Upon a ghostly paradigm of things"—and to conclude that Protestant meditation, being ultimately Platonic, disassociates itself from images that derive from the senses as does the Ignatian *compositio loci*. From Plato's "twice-bisected line" in the sixth book of the *Republic*, however, there emerges not a total rejection of things but a hierarchy in which things and their shadows are at the lower end of the scale, acquiring their shapes from and participating in the "hypotheses" and "IDEAS" at the top. To the biblically-minded Protestant, two important Platonic verses in the Greek New Testament are: "In the beginning was the Word [*logos*], and the word became flesh" (John 1:1), and "Be ye therefore perfect even as your Father in heaven is perfect" (Matt. 5:48). In fact, Hall seems to be quoting the key passage from Plato's *Republic* when he writes: "It is a good thing to see this material world, but it is a better thing to think of the intelligible world. This thought is the sight of the soul whereby it descerneth things like itself, spiritual and immortal, which are so much beyond the worth of these sensible objects as a spirit is beyond a body, a pure substance beyond a corruptible, an infinite God above a finite creature" (*Oc. Med.*, no. LXXXVII).

Thus, like Plato's twice-bisected line, Protestant meditation is filled with bifurcations. With Ramistic logic and rhetoric intervening, the English Protestant of the seventeenth century often divides his lucubrations into oppositions as bold as Plato's visible versus invisible worlds, the true versus the false, the beautiful versus the ugly.

Augustinian Psychology. As Ignatian meditation rests upon St. Thomas Aquinas' belief that all knowledge initially comes from sense-data, so its Protestant counterpart follows the psychology of St. Augustine in binding together the three powers of the soul. This distinction has been made most succinctly by Professor Martz in his chapter entitled "The Augustinian Quest" of *The Paradise Within*. Among the Protestants, he writes,

The hint of the presence of something like innate ideas in the deep caves of the soul leads directly to a long account of what might be called the dramatic action of Augustinian meditation. It is an action significantly different from the method of meditation later set forth by Ignatius Loyola and his followers; for that later method showed the effects of medieval scholasticism, with its powerful emphasis upon the analytic understanding, and upon the Thomist principle that human knowledge is derived from sensory experience. Ignatian meditation is thus a precise, tightly articulated method, moving from the images that comprise the composition of place into the threefold sequence of the powers of the soul, memory, understanding, and will, and from there into the affections and resolutions of the aroused will. But in Augustinian meditation there is no such precise method; there is, rather, an intuitive groping back into the regions of the soul that lie beyond sensory memories. The three powers of the soul are all used, but with an effect of simultaneous action, for with Augustine the aroused will is using the understanding to explore the memory, with the aim of apprehending more clearly and loving more fervently the ultimate source of the will's arousal.[3]

A by-product of this Augustinian simultaneity of psychological action is the Protestant's rejection of the Ignatian formulaic structure into the three parts: (a) the reconstitution of a scene, let us say, in the Passion of Christ, (b) baffling the mind through a series of questions, and (c) the colloquy with God. A favorite form for the Protestant is a division into two large parts which in themselves form an opposition and a balance. Such, for example, is Isaac Ambrose's *Prima & Ultima, Meditative Sermons on two treatises* (London, 1640). The "prima" is the necessity to be born again (from John 3:3), and the "ultima" is the four last things. The pairs are even set out in the engraved frontispiece: "Life's Lease" and "Death's Arrest," "Doom's Day" and "Hell's Horrour," "Right Purgatory" and "Heaven's Happinesse," requiring four hundred pages to exhaust. But actually there is no one shape to Protestant meditation, and even Joseph Hall in his own practice rarely followed the "steps" he set down in *The Art of Divine Meditation*.

Pauline-Calvinist Theology. Medieval theology stressed the relationship of man to God, even using human reason to argue His existence, whereas Luther, beginning the great revolt by embracing St.

Augustine's assumptions, starts with God in all His attributes and comes down to man. Man is a sinner and only God's loving mercy can save him, totally undeserving though he may be. So Luther often cried, "Let God be God" and derided the attempts to placate or bribe Him through good works. Faith is all-sufficient, particularly faith in the Bible, which contains everything necessary for salvation. So Luther spent much of his genius on translating the Vulgate into simple (and beautiful) German, and in his commentaries emphasized David's outpourings of his soul to God in the Psalms and the theology of St. Paul. For Luther, writes Roland Bainton,

The center . . . was the affirmation of the forgiveness of sin through the utterly unmerited grace of God made possible by the cross of Christ, which reconciled wrath and mercy, routed the hosts of hell, triumphed over sin and death, and by the resurrection manifested that power which enables man to die in sin and rise to newness of life. This was of course the theology of Paul, heightened, intensified, and clarified. Beyond these cardinal tenets Luther was never to go.[4]

After Luther, of course, came Calvin, a better theologian and more skillful organizer. Many of the English Protestants exiled by Mary I, Queen from 1553 to 1559, were gathered in Geneva; upon their return under Elizabeth they gave to English Christians, both Anglicans and Puritans, a strong bent of Pauline-Calvinist theology.

The Homiletic Thrust of Protestant Meditation.[5] Given the "church of all believers," the Protestant bias against the cloistered practices of the Roman Catholic church, and the central position of the hermeneutic sermon in Protestant worship, meditation became closely allied to the sermon. The once brief homily gave way to longer and longer sermons. At one point John Donne at St. Paul's pauses to turn over the hour glass before him. And though the following story has been told of several divines, George Lewis, in his *Life of Joseph Hall*,[6] tells it of Dr. Chaderton, Master of Emmanuel College and Hall's Cambridge tutor. Having preached for two hours, Dr. Chaderton said he would stop for fear of tiring his listeners, but they cried out, "For God's sake, Sir, go on, we beg you, go on!" Accordingly, he went on for another hour.

Joseph Hall's Protestantism combines the Anglican's learning and sense of style with the Puritan's "common touch" and zeal in preaching. He must have mined his sermons in order to publish book after book of meditations. In his autobiography he tells us that he was accustomed to give three sermons a week, writing each one by hand. Over an active ministerial life of fifty years this would mean seven or eight thousand sermons, and yet only forty-two of them, mostly of a celebratory character, are extant. In Hall's meditations one can often hear the voice of the preacher and detect the various rhetorical devices by means of which he gains the ear of the listener. Many of them share their purpose and structure with the sermon, including the exposition of a text and theme, the application, and the final short prayer. Thus Protestant meditation is as public as it is private, intended not for the individual alone but for large numbers of people, congregations perhaps, of the devout.

Variety of Subject Matter in the "Three Books of God." Finally, Protestant meditation as opposed to Ignatian has a far greater variety in subject matter and procedure since it is more widely based on the "three books of God." In meditation the Protestant is not confined to the passion of Christ and the four eschatological "facts." He is free to roam through all the majesty of God's creation, through the Old and New Testaments of the Bible, and into his innermost soul's perception of God Himself. Two of the "books" have been made familiar through such confessions as this one of Dr. Thomas Browne: "Thus there are two books from whence I collect my divinity: besides that written one of God, another of his servant nature."[7] As soon as the "I" is mentioned or even thought, a third "volume" is added for the Protestant, that of the ego, the conscience, the soul—through which, even were the creatures and the Bible unavailable, one can still know God. In 1623 Owen Feltham recognized the "three books" in his *Resolves*: "God hath left *three bookes* to the *World*, in each of which *hee* may easily be found: The *Booke* of the *Creatures*, the *Booke* of *Conscience*, and his written *Word*."[8] Thus Professor Martz summarizes "the Augustinian Quest" for Henry Vaughan by saying: "Such is the paradise within, compounded of the Bible, of Nature, and of the Self, which lies at the heart of Vaughan's *Silex Scintillans*, 1650. . . ."[9] For Protestant meditation in seventeenth century England, perhaps it took Joshua Sylvester's translation of the French Huguenot poet's *Les Semaines* to popularize the book of the creatures, King James' committees of Anglican bishops and Puritan divines for a new translation of the Bible to lend impetus to the book of Scriptures, and St. Paul, St. Augustine, and Calvin to stimulate the individual's soul-hunger for God.

Of the "three books," that of the Scriptures is central; and for meditation, if one book of the Bible were central to this, it would be the Psalms, a supposition strengthened by the incredibly fruitful custom, from Sydney to Milton, of putting psalms into English verse for singing. In the King James version of the Bible, the term "meditation" occurs more often in the Psalms than in all the other books of the Bible put together, and in the biblical mind of the Protestant the act of meditation is linked more closely to poetry and fervent ejaculatory address than to mental discipline. The Psalmist's most famous religious address (Ps. 19:14) does not mention paradigm or even intellect: "Let the words of my mouth and the meditations of my heart, be acceptable in thy sight, O Lord, my strength and my redeemer." Joseph Hall had sung the Psalms from his boyhood, and while writing on meditation tried his hand at "metaphrasing" a few of them. "Indeed, my Poetrie was long sithence out of date," he writes in the 1607 publication of the result, "and yielded hir place to grauer studies; but whose vaine would it not revive to looke into these heauenly songs? I were not woorthy to be a Diuine, if it should repent me to be a Poet with DAVID, after I shall haue aged in the Pulpit."[10] David's psalms contain all "three books of God": some praise the Lord for his "creatures" (Pss. 33, 104, 148); others cogitate His written commands (Ps. 119, no. 5); and still others seek God by looking into the poet's soul (Pss. 6, 22, 38, 42). One of the psalms that combines all three "books" is Psalm 19, which ends with the phrase "the meditations of my heart." The Psalm is divided into three parts: the first six verses meditate on "the Book of the Creatures"; the next four verses, on "the Book of Scriptures"; and the last four verses open up "the Book of the Soul," that is the individual's conscience. The Psalms of David, as well as the whole Bible from Genesis to the Revelation, provide literally for the Protestant "God's plenty" in varied subjects on which to meditate.

Certain metaphors cling to such a reading about God in the "three books." The most obvious one is the book metaphor: "writing," "alphabet" (as in Gerson's *Alphabetum Divini Amoris*), "God's

A.B.C.," "Abecedarium," "hand-writing upon the wall," "emblems," "hieroglyph," "characters," "volume," "lessons," etc. Of the "Book of Creatures," for example, Hall writes (*The Art*, end of chapter III): "God is wronged if his creatures be unregarded; ourselves most of all if we read this great volume of the creatures, and take out no lesson for our instruction." And in the Proem to *Occasional Meditations* he desires and charges his "reader, whosoever he be, to make me and himself so happy as to take out my lesson, and to learn how to read God's great book by mine."

Another metaphor, brought forward from the Middle Ages, is that of the glass as both a mediating instrument and a reflector. The medieval term was *speculum* or mirror, which mediates between man and the sun, whose radiance is too bright for mortal eyes. The glass is also a condition of our mortality, as in St. Paul's words: "Now we see through a glass darkly. . . ." Donne wrote in his last sermon, *Death's Duel*, "Our medium, our glass, is the Book of Creatures, and our light, by which we see him, is the light of Natural Reason."[11] In an *Occasional Meditation* on his own spectacles (no. CIV), Hall wrote: "Many such glasses my soul hath and useth: I look through the glass of the creatures at the power and wisdom of their Maker; I look through the glass of the Scriptures at the great mystery of redemption and the glory of an heavenly inheritance; I look through God's favours at His infinite mercy, through His judgments at His incomprehensible justice"—a one-sentence "mirror" reflecting the "three books" of creation, Bible, and conscience.

The most common metaphor for the "three books" in seventeenth-century Protestant meditation is that of "digestion," familiar to most of us in a secular setting from Francis Bacon's words: "Some books are to be tasted, others to be swallowed, and some few to be chewed and digested." In its religious parallel, as the body needs daily sustenance from real food, so the soul must "feed" daily by "ingesting" the "three books." In the Collect of *The Book of Common Prayer* for the second Sunday in Advent ("Bible Sunday"), the people ask God to grant that they may "hear, read, mark, and inwardly digest" the Holy Scriptures. Hall wrote in *The Devout Soul* (1643): "The food that is received into the soul by the ear is afterwards chewed in the mouth thereof by memory, concocted in the stomach by meditation, and dispersed into the parts by conference and practice,"[12] which is pretty complex alimentation, and yet the Biblical manna, symbol of Grace, is heavenly food. "What delights hath the taste in some pleasant Fruits, in some well relished meats, and in divers Junkets!" writes Baxter in *The Saint's Everlasting Rest*; "O what delight then must my soul needs have in feeding upon Christ, the living bread, and in eating with him at his Table in his Kingdom!"[13] And Edmund Calamy, whose title *The Art of Meditation* comes directly from Joseph Hall, tells us that the reason why sermons do us less good than they should is that we do not meditate on them: "for it is with Sermons as it is with meat, it is not the having of meat upon your table will feed you, but you must eat it; and not only eat it, but concoct it, and digest it, or else your meat will do you no good."[14] Again, this metaphor comes directly from the Bible, particularly from that verse in St. John's *Revelation* in which the angel commands John to eat the little book: "And I took the little book out of the angel's hand, and ate it up; and it was in my mouth sweet as honey: and as soon as I had eaten it, my belly was bitter" (10:10). Memorable is Dürer's great print of John eating the book as the tall angel stands at his side. The metaphor of ingesting goes deeply into the mythopoeic, magic, and religious human subconscious: Persephone's pomegranate, the rich viands of Keats' "The Eve of St. Agnes" and the roots served to the ailing knight by *la belle dame sans merci*, Coleridge's honeydew and milk of paradise, the savage's eating a bit of the sinew of his conquered enemy, and, of course, the bread and wine in the Holy Eucharist.

When the three books are put into the order of Creatures—Scriptures—Soul, the inevitable habit of dichotomizing often puts two of the books on one side, opposed to one on the other. Thus the first two books are means; the third, end. The first two books are past tense in that God did create the universe, and Christ did die to free men from the bondage of the law; but the third book is present tense or even future since the soul attains its real sanctity when it leaves the body. Again, the first two books are "read" in time and in this world; the third is "read" out of time and in the next world as the self realizes its immortality. Finally, the first two are *outer*, the eye being used for the creatures and the ear for the Scriptures; these take us to the *inner* eye and ear of our own consciences.

We shall see that Joseph Hall's meditations written over a period of fifty years are Protestant in that they are Platonic, Augustinian, Calvinistic, homiletic, and richly varied in their form and content since they directly grow out of reading all "three books of God."

II

A Brief Life of Joseph Hall;

the Journey to the Lowlands in 1605

Joseph Hall was born on July 1, 1574, near the town of Ashby-de-la-Zouch, Leicestershire, where his father was steward on the estate of the third Earl of Huntingdon.[15] The Earl's great-grandfather, William Lord Hastings, had built the great Ashby Castle, which played so important a part in English history that Sir Walter Scott made it the scene of the climactic tournament in *Ivanhoe*. The senior Hall's employer, as "President of the North," was the official guardian of Mary Queen of Scots; young Joseph must have inherited a suspicion of the Roman Catholic queen and an admiration for her staunchly Protestant son, James VI of Scotland. Ashby-de-la-Zouch is different now. During the "Great Rebellion," Cromwell's forces destroyed the castle with gunpowder and only the tall Hastings tower remains, looking very much as it did in 1850 for Turner's painting. The famous Ashby Grammar School is now a bustling "comprehensive," but between the ruined castle and the school still stands St. Helen's church, which Joseph attended as a boy.

The rector of this church during Joseph's boyhood was the Reverend Anthony Gilby, a preacher of extreme Calvinistic beliefs. At the beginning of Queen Mary's reign, Mr. Gilby had fled to Frankfort, where he translated some of the treatises of Beza and lent his knowledge of Hebrew to the translators of the Geneva Bible. Young Joseph, however, resisted Mr. Gilby's stern views of predestination and rabid enthusiasm for presbyterian polity. He became a moderate "Puritan" within the Church of England.

In 1589, when he was fifteen, he left Ashby Grammar School for Emmanuel College, Cambridge, founded only five years before by Sir Walter Mildmay and called by Queen Elizabeth "Sir Walter's Puritan settlement."[16] Hall was convinced he got there by the grace of God. The Reverend Mr. Pelset, a powerful persuader by his learning and oratory, had lately come to Ashby's church as visiting preacher. Noticing the brightness of young Joseph Hall, he offered to take the boy home with him and in seven years train him to become a minister with the same degree of skill in languages and divinity as any college could. Joseph's father, having twelve children to support, gladly agreed. Providentially, one of Joseph's brothers on a trip to Cambridge called upon Mr. Gilby's son Nathaniel, then a Fellow of Emmanuel College. Upon hearing of the plan for Joseph's private education, Nathaniel pleaded that the boy might be allowed instead to acquire a university experience. At the very moment that the elder Hall relented and gave his permission, a messenger came from Mr. Pelset with the indentures ready to be signed—too late. "O God," cries Joseph Hall in his autobiography, "how was I then taken up with the thankful acknowledgement and joyful admiration of thy gracious providence over me."[17] After two years an uncle offered to furnish one-half of the boy's expenses through the M.A. degree, and Joseph proved such a model student that he was soon elected a fellow at Emmanuel.

At Cambridge, Hall became steeped in Ramistic logic and rhetoric. Embraced upon the continent by Protestant theologians, the system of the French Protestant Pierre de la Ramée, writing in Latin under the name of Petrus Ramus, had been introduced to Glasgow University by the great Scottish Calvinist Dr. Andrew Melville. From there it came to Cambridge, especially to Emmanuel College, where it was taught by its master, Dr. Lawrence Chaderton. Ramus makes the complexities of Aristotelian logic simple through a reduction to disjunctive and complementary pairs. We saw such a disjunction in the plan of Ambrose's 1640 book of meditation—"Life's Lease" versus "Death's Arrest." Very often an opposing pair of terms creates a new whole as the initial units are of a lower and a higher value. Thus Milton learned at Cambridge how to write a poetic work like "L'Allegro" and "Il Penseroso," direct opposites but together forming a whole as we "rise" from the first poem to the second. Among the many oppositions that separate and bind the two poems is the reading matter of the two "types": the joyful man reads Jonson and Shakespeare (Allegro 132–33), whereas the contemplative man soars with Plato and Hermes Trismegistus (Penseroso 88–89).

At Cambridge, Hall was particularly brilliant in spoken and written rhetoric, which he taught for two years. So adept did he become at speaking and writing both prose and poetry in Latin and English that at one time it appeared he would not become an ecclesiastic at all, despite the fact that his parents had singled him out for the ministry and Emmanuel College had no other purpose. In 1597–98 he published two volumes of satires, so excellent that Francis Meres mentioned him in *Palladis Tamia* (1598) as one of England's foremost satirists.[18] He also wrote a satirical semi-bawdy *voyage imaginaire* in Latin called *Mundus Alter et Idem* (The World Different and the Same) which was published anonymously in 1605 and translated in 1609 into rollicking English by John Healy.[19] Furthermore, there is evidence that he had a great deal to do with composing a play, the second part of *The Returne from Parnassus*, acted at St. John's College in 1602 and printed in 1605.[20]

In the ordinary course of study at Emmanuel College Hall became ordained, at Colchester, on December 14, 1600.[21] One may wonder whether or not his heart was in it, for he had gotten to know many poets and had taken part in their quarrels. He may well have dreamed of an exciting literary and secular future. Not many, however, could make a living by the pen. In order to support himself, exactly one year after his ordination he became chaplain on the estate of Sir Robert Drury in Hawsted, Suffolk, while one of his best friends at Emmanuel, William Bedell, was rector at Bury St. Edmund's, only four miles away. At Hawsted, Hall developed a great affection for Lady Drury and little Elizabeth, but he chafed under the salary of only ten pounds per year (the very sum he had written bitterly about in his early satires). He tells us he had to write books in order to buy books.

The year 1603 was climactic for England and for Joseph Hall. In the general surge of enthusiasm for the new king, James I, Hall published an encomiastic poem of some three hundred lines welcoming James to England and prophesying a strong English church under his royal support.[22] Also, in that year he married Elizabeth Wynnyf, of a good Suffolk family, thus taking on the responsibilities of family life. In that year, too, he received his doctorate in divinity from Cambridge; and finally, in 1603 he was thirty years old, a year to decide where his true ministry lay: he would pursue an ecclesiastical career under the Establishment, and devote his skill in writing to promote the devout life. His first book of this kind was *Meditations and Vows*, written at Hawsted and registered on February 12, 1605. Its two "centuries" consist of brief, aphoristic, self-admonitory observations, written (as he would say himself) "without rule." He also published *Heaven upon Earth*, in which as a Christian he goes beyond Seneca in seeking true tranquillity of mind. "Not *Athens*," he concludes chapter 1, "must teach this lesson, but *Jerusalem*."[23]

About two months later, Hall was invited by Sir Edmund Bacon, Lady Drury's brother, to accompany him as chaplain on a mission to escort the English ambassador to the court of Archduke Albert in Brussels. Since it was on this trip, his first to the continent, that he received his initial idea for a theory or "rule" of Protestant meditation, an account of the sojourn will come a little later, closer to *The Art of Divine Meditation*.

Meantime his *Meditations and Vows* caught the attention of Baron Edward Denny at Waltham, later Earl of Norwich, who invited Hall to become rector at Waltham Holy Cross at ten times the salary he had been getting in the Drury household. Here, only twelve miles from the center of England's political and ecclesiastical power, Joseph Hall found himself in his element. Within a year he was invited by Prince Henry, heir to the throne, to become one of his twenty-four chaplains to serve, two at a time, as the custom was, for one month each year. He became acquainted with many of England's most influential men, including those within the royal circle, present and future bishops, scholars, and writers like Joshua Sylvester, Groom of the Chamber to Prince Henry. Still preaching three times a week, Hall poured his energy into writing books. In honor of King James, "England's Solomon," he published *Solomon's Divine Arts*, a compendium of the Canticles, Proverbs, and Ecclesiastes. Possibly inspired by the King's admiration for the French scholar Casaubon, editor of Theophrastus, Hall wrote the first book of *Characters* in England (1608).[24] In the following two years he published his *Epistles*, most of them to people of quality, the first man in England to publish letters in English. Here at Waltham, he began his twenty-year accomplishment of the *Contemplations*, which are meditations on the principal stories in the Old and New Testaments.

Often preaching before King James, Hall was sent on three separate trips as royal representative: in 1616 with Viscount Doncaster to France; to the Council of Perth (1617) in the king's effort to bring the Scottish and English churches closer together; and as one of the King's five representatives at the Synod of Dort in 1618. James had rewarded him with the Deanship of Worcester, and in 1624 offered him the Bishopric of Gloucester, which Hall turned down. Though his writings are brimming with admiration of James, who died in 1625, Hall is strangely silent on King Charles. Perhaps he was suspicious of high church leanings, particularly as William Laud was gaining power within the church. Hall did, however, accept from Charles the Bishopric of Exeter in 1627.

It was from Exeter that he yielded to Archbishop Laud's entreaty to write for episcopacy as the clouds of the Civil War were about to close in. Laud thought Hall too Puritanical and had even set some of his men to watch the new bishop, but he recognized a good debater. The result, *Episcopacie by Divine Right* (1640), got Hall into controversy with the Smectymnuuans and even with Milton. I have argued elsewhere[25] that it was Milton, not Hall, who began the game of "grim laughter" and who went far beyond Hall in personal abuse. And I think I have made a good case for the Reverend Robert Dunkin, an Anglican rector in Cornwall from Hall's diocese, as the author of *A Modest Confutation* (1642), the pamphlet that begot Milton's angriest prose, and not Hall himself.[26] But Professor Christopher Hill contends that "Hall had sacrificed his principles to careerist ambitions in becoming the spokesman for a divine-right episcopacy in which there is no evidence that he had hitherto believed."[27] There is evidence of "divine right" in his early and frequent praise of James I. In 1640 Hall must have recognized that the English Church was in greater danger, and having been a man of "order and degree" in church and state all his life, he came to its aid.

As if to defy Commons and the growing Puritan strength, Charles I translated Hall to Norwich while Hall was still in the Tower. But after he had been Bishop of that important diocese for only eleven months, Cromwell's forces sequestered the office and its emoluments. Bishop Hall tearfully watched a band of soldiers desecrate and destroy the whole inside of Norwich Cathedral, one of the most beautiful churches in England. Forced out of the Bishop's Palace, he moved into a small house in Higham, a mile or two away, and for the next thirteen years kept on writing, signing his books "Joseph Norvic." or "J.H.B.N.," still the Bishop of Norwich though his office was gone. In Higham, on September 8, 1656, he died, attended by a faithful fellow Anglican, the city's most eminent physician, Dr. Thomas Browne.

Fifty years before this, we left the young Reverend Joseph Hall accepting an invitation from Sir Edmund Bacon to accompany him as chaplain on an ambassadorial mission to the Lowlands. The trip was a turning point in Hall's thinking on the Christian duty of meditation. Hall accepted the invitation, he tells us in his autobiography, "for the great desire I had to inform myself ocularly of the state and practice of the Romish church, the knowledge whereof might be of no small use to me in my holy station." On this first journey abroad (he left his clericals behind) Hall began to think deeply about meditation, particularly for Protestants, as he became aware of the superior discipline in this genre maintained by the Jesuits he met on the continent, a discipline stimulated by the *Spiritual Exercises* of St. Ignatius of Loyola.

Sir Edmund Bacon's entourage landed at Calais and went by coach to Gravelines, Dunkirk, Winnoxberg, Ypres, Ghent, Courtray, and Brussels. In the Lowlands Hall saw farms, villages, and Protestant churches recently ravaged by war, but Jesuit colleges springing up everywhere. He and Sir Edmund went from Brussels to Namur, up the Meuse River to Liège, and thence to the hot springs at Ardennes.[28] Resting there, Hall added another "century" to his *Meditations and Vows*. Compared with the practical and often secular meditations of his first two "centuries," they seem imbued with real religious experience as though he had had, at last, leisure to think through some of its problems. He dedicates the small addition to Sir Edmund Bacon, Knight, because "they are part of those Meditations, which in my late peregrination with you, took me up in the solitary hills of Ardenne" (a veiled allusion to Psalm 121). Hall wishes "to be vouchsafed to bring but one sin towards the decking of the spouse of Christ; while others, out of their abundance, adorn her with costly robes, and rich medals. I commend [these meditations'] success to God, their patronage to you, their use to the world." Here lies the hint of a new grip on the art of religious meditation. As early as the second meditation (in this third "century") he introduces the lives of the saints which becomes his first long example in *The Art of Divine Meditation*. The new meditations have more biblical quotations, especially from the Psalms; he concludes no. 17 with "Every true Christian, then, must learne to sing that compound dittie of the Psalmist, *Of mercie and judgement.*"

In this "third century" of meditations he condemns the Roman Catholics for clinging to things rather than to ideas, to sensibly perceived objects rather than to the intuited "realities" that lie behind them:

Those that travel in long pilgrimages to the holy land, what a number of weary paces they measure! What a number of hard lodgings and known dangers they pass! . . . and when they come hither, what see they but the bare sepulchre wherein their Saviour lay, and the earth that he trod upon, to the increase of a carnal devotion? What labour should I willingly undertake in my journey to the true land of promise, the celestial Jerusalem, where I shall see and enjoy my Saviour himself! What tribute of pain or death should I refuse to pay for my entrance, not into the sepulchre, but his palace of glory, and that not to look upon, but to possess it![29]

The kind of "labour" he would "willingly undertake" to achieve this goal, thoroughly Platonic in its placing an idea between the Creature and the Creator, was the art and practice of meditation. His first theoretical work in the genre was entitled *The Art of Divine Meditation* (1606), written at Hawsted immediately after this trip. It was conceived in a Protestant continental setting at a time of high anti-Jesuitical feeling in England, and registered in London three days after the first anniversary of the Gunpowder Plot.[30] That year Hall wrote a eulogistic poem on William Bedell's *A Protestant Memorial or the Shepherd's Tale of the Pouder Plott.*[31] In the earliest printed sermon by Hall (1608), preached at St. Paul's Cross, he denounced, after the name of their founder, "those Loyolists" as enemies of English church and state.[32] Throughout his life, like most Englishmen of his time, he characterized Roman Catholics as "Romish," "papisticall," "idolatrous," "superstitious," and scoffed at their "hugging their crucifixes" and "tossing their beads."

Thus, after the journey through Holland and Belgium in 1605, Hall's view of meditation is instinct not with the Counter Reformation but with an older tradition: the Bible, the spirit of *devotio moderna*, the medieval naivete of the Augustinian monks, and Christian Neoplatonism in Ramistic dress. As soon as he returned to Hawsted from the Lowlands, he set to work on *The Art of Divine Meditation*.

III

The Art of Divine Meditation and its Sources

In the dedication of *The Art of Divine Meditation* to Sir Richard Lea, Hall refers to his two previous Hawsted religious books: the *Meditations and Vows*, which were "sudden," is to be followed here by a "rule" of meditation; and "after my Heaven upon Earth" he will discourse here "of Heaven above." His mention of *Heaven upon Earth* should give us the key to the organization of *The Art of Divine Meditation*, for the former book, earlier by only a few months, is an arch example of exposition by means of Ramistic bifurcations. Hence a glance at the frontal matter of *Heaven upon Earth* reproduced here conveniently gives us the clue to how he organized the present work. Whether the Ramistic "analysis" comes first or last makes little difference; probably, as most of us mesh a tentative outline with the finished composition, Hall worked back and forth between them. Why he gave us a "Table of Contents" instead of the series of pairs enclosed in brackets we do not know. Since his "Table of Contents" is, however, a series of dichotomies, I have turned it into just such an "analysis," which includes every one of the thirty-seven chapters, and this we must follow in order to understand *The Art of Divine Meditation*.

THE ANALYSIS OR RESOLVTION
of this Treatise concerning *Tranquillity*.

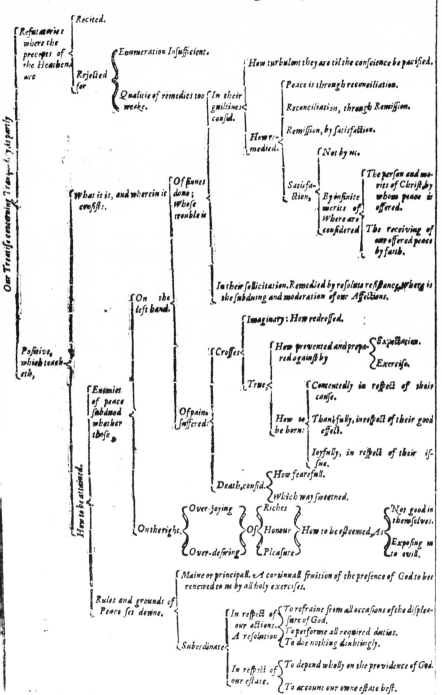

An Analysis or Resolution Concerning the Treatise on Meditation

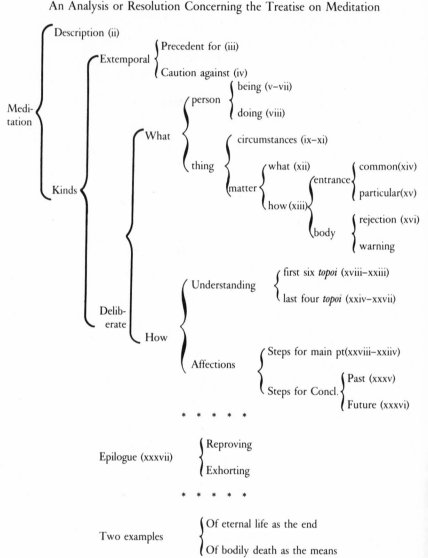

A Ramistic Analysis of the Art. After asserting (a) the benefits and
(b) the uses of meditation (chapter I), Hall divides his main subject into (a) a description of it and (b) its kinds (chapter II). The two major
kinds form an opposition between (a) "Extemporal meditation" and
(b) "Deliberate," an opposition Hall maintains for the rest of his life,
although the adjectives may change. His son Robert, in the preface to
Occasional Meditations (which are "extemporal"), makes the distinction
between "sudden thoughts" and "fixed meditations," and in *The
Devout Soul* (1643) Hall refers to the "outward" and "inner monitors"
of his meditations (Wynter 1:510).

In *The Art*, since his major purpose is to discourse on "deliberate
meditation," he spends little space on the other kind, merely dividing
his thoughts between (a) precedents for that kind and (b) cautions
against (chapters III–IV). Deliberate meditation takes up the rest of
the book, as first of all he divides it into (a) what it is and (b) how to
practise it. Under the definition he treats (a) the person who is
meditating and (b) the meditation itself. The person not only (a) is,
but also (b) does. In character (a) he should be free from sin (chapter
V) but also free from worldly thoughts (chapter VI). Apart from (a)
his being, he must (b) act also; that is, he must be constant and this in
both (a) the time he sets for meditation (chapter VII) and (b) its continuance (chapter VIII). The person (a) being out of the way, Hall next
describes (b) "other" necessary circumstances, such as the best place to
meditate (chapter IX), the best time (chapter X), and the best gesture
of the body (chapter XI). In all these he allows the individual through
experiment to find his own best way. Some like to meditate in the
study, others outdoors; some meditate best in the morning, others in

Figures

Facing page 20: Bishop Hall's "Analysis or Resolution," from
          Heaven upon Earth, in *Works* 1634, p. 64v (STC 12639).

Opposite: A parallel "Analysis or Resolution" for *The Art.*

the evening; depending on the subject matter meditated upon, some raise their eyes and hands to heaven, others may walk with head bowed. Hall prefers Isaac's way (Gen. 24:63): he meditates best while walking outdoors in the evening.

Still describing what deliberate meditation is as far as the *thing*, apart from the *person*, is concerned, Hall next takes up the *matter* of meditation in two segments: (a) the subject and (b) the method of dealing with the subject (chapters XII and XIII). The latter point, procedure, again, is divided into (a) the entrance into the meditation and (b) the body of the meditation. We may expect two kinds of "entrance": (a) the common entrance, which is usually prayer (chapter XIV), and a particular or special "entrance" depending of course upon the person and the subject matter (chapter XV). After (a) the entrance comes (b) the main body of the meditation, and, for purposes that will soon become apparent, this will first of all be negative; that is (a) a method, found in an anonymous book, to be rejected (chapter XVI), and (b) a warning or "premonitions" (chapter XVII) concerning the whole first part, that is, "what deliberate meditation is" or its definition (the "a" of chapters V–XVII).

Now he is ready to take up the second part, that is (b) "How to practise it," which demands the rest of the book. The practise of deliberate meditation is again divided into (a) a procedure or "steps" for the *understanding*, and (b) the same for the *affections*. Although the disquisition on the "understanding" is longer, that being the knottiest part and the most difficult for the beginner, it is the "affections" which are the more important. We are all born logicians, Hall says; logic is "natural." But it takes more than "nature" to be a Christian; it requires arousing the feeling of love and trust to make a commitment in terms of *either:or*.

Here come the *topoi*, topics, or commonplaces for "invention" memorized by every school and college boy in Hall's time. They are somewhat like the questions a journalism student learns to ask in order to become a newspaper reporter: *Who? What? Where? When? and Why?* Thomas Wilson, in his *Rule of Reason* (1553), one of the best-selling textbooks, lists eight *topoi*: whether it is or no, a definition, its parts, causes, effects, similarities, contraries, and witnesses to prove it.[34] Hall omits the first: why argue whether heaven, let us say, exists or not? And he adds to Wilson's list "appendances" or qualities, and "names," both of which allow the "inventor" more room for the imagination.

Hall does something else. Since he has ten commonplaces which will enable the neophyte to "spin out" a meditation on any given subject worth meditating about, he divides the ten, as Jesus divided the Ten Commandments, into the first six and the last four. The first six commonplaces to help the understanding have to do with the subject in respect to itself: (1) describing it; (2) dividing it into smaller parts; (3) discovering its causes; (4) weighing its effects; (5) finding how it is employed; and (6) listing its major qualities. These six are like the downward movement in making the sign of the cross to symbolize the relationship of God to man and man to God – Christ's bowed head.

Christ's second commandment, symbolized by the horizontal movement in "signing" the cross, intends man's relationship to his fellow man – the out-stretched arms. Like the last four of the Ten Commandments, the last four of Hall's ten *topoi* for the understanding have to do with things other than the thing itself: (7) contraries to it; (8) similitudes – nos. 7 and 8 being opposed; (9) names that may be applied to it; and (10) testimonies from Scripture. These ten *topoi* in this order take up ten chapters between XVIII and XXVII. The division of the ten *topoi* into two classes is made clear at the beginning of chapter XXIV. So much for the "Understanding."

The following chapter (XXVIII) is entitled "Of our Second Part of Meditation, which is in the Affections." The first part is of the mind; the second, of the heart. Here Hall gives us seven steps for (a) the main part, and two steps for (b) the conclusion. The latter two steps are again dichotomized into a thanksgiving for what is (a) past; and a recommendation for what must come in (b) the future. The seven steps for the affections take up chapters XXVIII to XXXVI, leaving only one more chapter, XXXVII for the Epilogue, which consists of a final opposition between (a) reproving the neglect of meditation and (b) encouraging the reader to practise it. This exhausts Hall's "theory of Protestant meditation" – amazingly simple and easy to grasp.

But one must not overlook his two examples, which are a final overpowering dichotomy: "The one of eternal life, as the end; The other of Death, as the way." Reducing theory to practice better than anything else could, they are among the best pieces of prose that came from Hall's eloquent pen. Explaining a *topos* is ratiocinative and abstract. The example that follows functions like the parable, let us say, of "The Good Samaritan" to "define" what one means by the word "neighbor." The first example was included in the first edition of 1606, and is divided as illustration of each chapter heading from chapter XV (immediately before his rejection of Mauburnus' "scale" for the "Understanding") to chapter XXXV, that is, nineteen separate segments starting with the "particular" entrance into the meditation and ending with the "thanksgiving."[35] The second example, all in one piece, was added to the folio edition of *Collected Works* in 1614. At the end of chapter XII in the first edition he had anticipated two examples among possible subjects for meditation: one being "the glory of God's Saints above" and the other, "the certainty and uncertainty of our death." We have already seen how swiftly *The Art* was composed at Hawsted after his return from the Continent, and he may have wanted to publish it while the Gun Powder fervor against the Jesuits was at its height. For this reason he may have skipped writing the second example.

A possible reason for his adding it to his treatise in 1614 may have been the death of Elizabeth Drury a few weeks before she was fifteen, and John Donne's writing of the two *Anniversaries*, one on the first anniversary of her death, 1611, on death; and the second in 1612 on the immortal life of the soul. To these poems Hall contributed the introductions in verse—surely another and forceful reminder of the death-life dichotomy. Hall had already written in prose of the "eternal life" of the saints; in 1614 he added the second example to his theory of meditation, a meditation on bodily death as the gateway to that blessed end. Hall's two examples complement one another as Donne's dichotomized *Anniversaries* do.

All of his illustrations of the *topoi* should be read carefully as models of spinning or weaving (my metaphors) a meditation, but one that stands out as a superb example of seventeenth century "invention" is the one on "Contraries" (chapter XXIV).

At some risk, one might try to "invent" a meditation by following Hall's *topoi*—this to test the theory, not to attempt to match the style. So, I will choose the subject of "My actual meeting with God." First I would stretch my imagination in a description of that meeting: biblical pictures come to mind, an entrance through pearly gates, a long avenue of alabaster walls, at the end a majestic figure seated on a golden throne, the slow approach between files of singing angels. How shall I "divide" my subject? Perhaps as Shakespeare, from just such *topoi* as these, "divided" his sonnet no. 129: *before* the meeting, *during* the meeting, and *after* the meeting. And what caused all this? God's promise for one thing, my own desire instilled from boyhood, the expressed wishes of some of my friends, etc. Causes bring their effects, such as ineffable joy, freedom from personal inadequacy, assurances of eternal life. How can this subject be employed? And what "qualities" pertain to it? Fortunately, my teacher told me that I don't have to try to fit every *topos* to my subject, lest I be guilty of "racking the invention" (chapter XVII). So I shall go on to "Contraries." What is the opposite of such an expectation? Like going to the airport to meet a dear friend only to hear over the public address system that his flight has been cancelled? This leads "naturally" (Hall would say) to "similitudes" (a category which happens to be the only one Hall included from Mauburnus' parallel scale). I would have to think of several comparisons from real life to fit my imagined meeting with God. Next, can I give this imagined experience "Names"? What's in a name? Answer: nothing and everything. Nothing if by any other name a rose would smell as sweet; everything if we contemplate the Tetragrammaton or Christ's insistent query, "Who say ye that I am?" I can't come up with any good names. But the end is here: quoting scriptural authority—St. Paul on seeing through a glass darkly now but then face to face; Jesus on preparing a place for me, etc. Having gone through some of the ten steps for "Understanding," I would then try to move toward the "Affections" in order to arouse my will to make true my imagined meeting with God. "For a full conclusion," Hall tells us to "lift up our heart and voice to God in singing some versicle of David's divine Psalms . . . answering to our disposition and matter" (chapter XXXVI). Perhaps Psalm 34—"I sought the Lord, and he heard me" or Psalm 27—"When thou saidst 'Seek ye my face' my heart said unto thee, 'Thy face; Lord, will I seek.'"

Since the next steps, for the "Affections," are largely based on those in the scale of Mauburnus, that is, that half which Hall did not "reject," they come more properly under:

Sources of The Art of Divine Meditation. The very first sentence of

the dedication of *The Art*, conceived in the Protestant setting of the
Low Countries, echoes the spirit of medieval Roesbrook and the
Augustinian pre-Reformation reformers of the monastery of
Deventer: "Sir, ever since I began to bestow myself upon the common good, studying wherein my labours might be most serviceable; I
still found they could be no way so well improved, as in that part
which concerneth devotion, and the practice of true piety." As openly critical of the Jesuits as he was, Hall would never admit that "devotion" and "the practice of true piety" would be found among them.
Throughout *The Art* he inveighs against the cloistered life, although
he recognized that some monks, obviously before the Counter Reformation, had given him valuable ideas. As late as 1643 in *The Devout
Soul*, again, he writes: "We shall not need to send you to the cells or
cloisters for this skill, although it will be hardly believed how far
some of their contemplative men have gone in the theory thereof"
(Wynter, 1:506). Given the Platonic-Augustinian ambience of his
thought, he has gained most from "the best directions of Origen,
Austen, Bernard, Hugo[,] Bonaventura, [and] Gerson" (chapter XVI).
Among these, Hall cites most often Augustine, Bernard, and
Bonaventura,[36] whose Platonic rather than Aristotelian world-view
Gilson has so passionately described.

To these three Platonic Christian saints, Hall adds Jean Charlier de
Gerson (1363–1429), Chancellor of the University of Paris.[37] Long
thought to have been the author of *The Imitation of Christ*, Gerson is
best known for his *De Monte Contemplationis*. Like the three ar-
ticulate saints before him, Gerson insisted that he could not write
down a system for meditation (which remained for St. Ignatius to
do). The reason for this refusal was his reiterated distinction between
scientific theology and the affections of the ordinary man. His *in-
dustriae*, or preparations for meditation, consist of knowing one's
own temperament, avoiding vain learning, and cultivating pious
affection. Hence Gerson has been hailed as an early "Protestant," and
as a "practical" Christian rather than merely a logician. "It was a just
answer, that John Gerson reports, given by a Frenchman," Hall
wrote, "who, being asked by one of his neighbours if the Sermon
were done; 'No,' saith he, 'it is said, but it is not done, neither will be,
I fear, in haste,'" (Wynter, 6:531). Within *The Art* Gerson appears
several times.[38] Although in chapter VIII, Hall deplored the part the

Chancellor had taken at the Council of Constance in condemning the doctrines of Wycliffe and Huss, he admired Gerson's appeal to the average mind, not to the unusually subtle or militarily disciplined. He depends upon Gerson as an early "Protestant" and uses him as an authority "because our adversaries [meaning the Jesuits] disclaim him for theirs" (chapter VIII).

This brings us, in a discussion of the possible sources of Hall's *The Art of Divine Meditation*, to the crucial question of his indebtedness to the work of Mauburnus (the Dutch Jean Mombaer), whose *Rosetum*, published anonymously in 1494, Hall quotes and rejects in chapter XVI, but whose second half of the *scala*, that having to do with the "Affections," he takes over in full (chapters XXVIII to XXXVI).

Professor Martz has gone into this source so thoroughly that there is no need to recapitulate here. Martz places his argument for Mauburnus in an Appendix that links the "steps" and Joseph Hall not to what we would call "Protestant" religious poetry of the seventeenth century but to Richard Crashaw's hymn "To the Name above every name, the Name of Jesus," which could hardly be called Augustinian meditation. Since, as Martz points out, the *Rosetum* of Mauburnus is a book "whose labyrinths of meditation easily lose the reader" and which "directly or indirectly, came to exert a strong influence upon the creation of the *Spiritual Exercises* of St. Ignatius,"[39] it is not likely that Hall's quotation and paraphrase of it is more important for Hall than "the directions of all other writers," including the five he mentions most often. Furthermore, Mauburnus occupies in Hall only nine short chapters out of a total of thirty-seven, and in the edition of 1606 only thirty-six pages out of one hundred and ninety-three.

"In this Art of mine," Hall writes in his dedication, "I confess to have received more light from one obscure nameless monk, which wrote some hundred and twelve years ago than from the directions of all other writers. I would his humility had not made him niggardly of his name, that we might have known whom to have thanked." So, Martz concludes that if Hall is writing in 1606, exactly "112 years ago" would bring us to the year 1494, the publication date of Mauburnus' *Rosetum*.

Trenchant though this is, I believe that Hall is acknowledging more

a spiritual influence than a verbal one, and that in his first inspira-
tional meeting with pre-Reformation meditation in the Lowlands in
1605, he is referring to *The Imitation of Christ* by Thomas à Kempis.
Some of its innumerable editions appeared under his own name,
others under the name of Charlier de Gerson, and, significantly, still
others were "nameless." In the year 1492, close enough to Hall's
"some 112 years ago," since he became aware of the art of meditation
in 1605, an edition of the *Imitatio* appeared, with no place of origin
on the title-page, combining (not unusually) two separate works. It
assigns the second piece, *Tractulo de meditatione cordis* to Gerson, but
gives no author for the first piece, *Tractatus de Ymitatione Christi.* [40]

Debongnie has shown that Mauburnus is quoting the "scale" from
Wessel Gansfort's *Opera*. [41] Mauburnus, moreover, introduces his
anonymous author as "doctor," and whether recognized or not by
Hall, Gansfort was known to the faculties of law, medicine, and
theology in the universities of Europe as *Lux Mundi*. Hall calls him
"an author ancient but nameless," not "an obscure nameless monk."
The author of the *Imitation* is a monk, obviously a member of a
monastery living under a rule which he gladly embraces. [42] The life of
a monk fills him with joy: "I have accepted it, and will bear it until
death," he cries (3, 56, p. 172). Hall envies this kind of commitment,
but his purpose is to bring meditation out of the monastery into ordinary life: "And however of old some hidden Cloysterers have ingrossed it to themselves and confined it within their Cells" (chapter I),
every Christian, he asserts, should practice it, particularly those
Christians who cannot devote their entire lives to religion.

The adjective "obscure," meaning "unknown to fame," that Hall applies to this nameless monk is expanded in the phrase, "I would his
humility had not made him niggardly of his name." If any one had
been "niggardly of his name" it was not the "monk" but Mauburnus
for failing to give the name of Wessel Gansfort to his quoted *scala*.
On the other hand, one of the rules of the Augustinian Canons
Regular required the monk "to learn the lesson of Humility, according to the most perfect pattern set forth in the life of Christ, and in
that of his nearest and most faithful followers; and especially in this,
that the greatest among them should be the younger, and he that is
chief as he that doth serve." [43] Christian humility is reflected on almost
every page of the *Imitation*.

Hall's emphasis upon the heart over the mind and upon instinctive simplicity over borrowed unintelligibility is more likely to have sprung from *The Imitation of Christ* than from Mauburnus. "Blessed is that simplicity," writes the author of the *Imitatio*, "which rejects obscure enquiry, and advances along the sure and open road of God's Commandments" (4, 18, p. 214). "Amo nescire," I love not to know, was the motto of the Augustinians.

Thomas à Kempis' constant divisions into pairs of contrary states, furthermore, like the "heart vs. the mind," would appeal to Hall's Ramistic bent. One of the most notable oppositions of the *Imitatio*, strikingly like Hall's favorite, is chapter 54 of Part 3, "On the Contrary Workings of Nature and Grace," which proceeds by dozens of disjunctives built on the adversative "but," like "Nature is quick to complain of want and hardship; but Grace bears poverty with courage" (p. 167). "A man is a man by his understanding part," writes Hall as he passes from one area of meditation to the other, "*but* he is a Christian by his will and affection" (chapter XXVIII).

Finally, in an epistle (no. 8 of Decade 3) to Mr. Robert Hay, the son of Lord Doncaster, registered for publication on October 17, 1608, Hall gives his young friend "a discourse of the continual exercise of a Christian." It is a shortened account of the whole meditative process. "Much of this good counsel" he confesses to "have learned from the table of an unknown author at Antwerp. It contented me, and therefore I have thus made it, by many alterations, my own for form, and yours for the use; our practice shall both commend it and make us happy" (Wynter 6, 210). The word "table" is important. In the front of the 1492 anonymous *Imitatio Christi* a "table" (*tabula capitulorum*), not a "scale," divides the work into two parts: the "Incipit," which recounts the specialities of God's grace, and the "Explicit" or confession and petition for mercy. The book describes the "outer" and "inner" life of the Christian. Hall admired the combination of the active and contemplative life, and in *The Art* praises "those ancient monks who intermeddled bodily labour with their contemplations" (chapter VIII), not, he adds, like "certain religious at this day" who "having mewed and mured themselves from the world, spend themselves wholly upon their beads and Crucifix, pretending no other work but meditation."

Could it be that from the *tabula capitulorum* of that book Hall read in Antwerp he got the idea for making, in the front of his *Art of Divine Meditation*, a "Sum of the Chapters" instead of an "analysis or resolution" as he had made for his *Heaven upon Earth* ? The method of division is identical; only the name and the form are different.

There have been many thousands of real life witnesses to the power of Thomas à Kempis' *Imitation of Christ*, but perhaps even more moving than these is the fictional witness that George Eliot places in the middle of *The Mill on the Floss*. There we read that during a spiritual crisis Maggie Tulliver finds in the attic an old copy of *The Imitation of Christ*, and becomes absorbed by several random passages. It was a "voice out of the far-off middle ages [Eliot writes], the direct communication of a human soul's belief and experience, and came to Maggie as an unquestioned message. It was written down [Eliot continues] by a hand that waited for the heart's prompting; it is the chronicle of a solitary, hidden anguish, struggle, trust and triumph. . . . And so it remains to all time a lasting record of human needs and human consolations: the voice of a brother who, ages ago, felt and suffered and renounced." The book marks a conversion in Maggie: "For the first time she saw the possibility of shifting the position from which she looked at the gratification of her own desires, of taking her stand out of herself, and looking at her own life as an insignificant part of a divinely guided whole."

Important though the seven "steps" for the "Affections" are which Hall takes from the book by Mauburnus, the inspired *heart* of Hall's theory, emerging especially in the two examples of meditation he affixed to it, is very likely to have come from a memorable reading in Antwerp in the year 1605 of *The Imitation of Christ*.

So much for Hall's theory of meditation and its probable sources. During the next fifty years he wrote and published hundreds of meditations for his brothers in the common life.

IV

Hall's Three Kinds of Meditations; their General Characteristics

Joseph Hall wrote three kinds of meditations, initially outlined in chapter XII of *The Art of Divine Meditation* and based on the "three books" in which one can "read" God. In chapter XII, speaking of "The Matter and Subject of our Meditation," Hall describes (1) God's "work in the creation, preservation, government of all things, according to the Psalmist, 'I will meditate of the beauty of Thy glorious Majesty, and Thy wonderful work.' "; (2) "meditations concerning Christ Jesus our Mediator, His incarnation, miracles, life, passion, burial, resurrection, ascension, intercession"; and (3) meditations on "those matters in divinity which can most of all work compunction in the heart and most stir us up to devotion." Again, in Book XV of the *Contemplations*, though Hall says there are "two books," there are really three: "There are but two books where we can read God: the one is his Word, his Works the other. . . . In [1] the works of God we see the shadow or footsteps of the Creator; in [2] his Word we see the face of God through a glass. [3] Happinesse [within one's own soul] consists in the vision of that Infinite Majesty" (Wynter, 1:437). The third book and category of meditation consists of psychological states. Though to each book and kind of meditation is assigned in major proportion the memory, understanding, and will, the three powers coalesce and act simultaneously. In the first, the matter is the beauty and wisdom of the Creator; in the second, God's remarkable providence in Christ's sacrifice; in the third, the sinner's view of his own imperfections, his inevitable death, and his irrepressible joy at the promise of salvation. He remembers the first, tries to understand the second, and vows to be worthy of the third.

Thus the "three books of God" and Hall's three kinds of meditation are not unrelated to the trinitarian bases of Christianity. They rest on the Trisagion, "Holy, Holy, Holy," and the ancient Tersanctus. They echo the Nicene Creed: (1) "I believe in one God the Father Almighty, Maker of heaven and earth"; (2) "And in one Lord Jesus Christ, the only-begotten Son of God"; (3) "And I believe in the Holy

Ghost, The Lord and Giver of Life." Finally, they follow the
"General Thanksgiving" in *The Book of Common Prayer*, in which the
worshipper expresses his gratitude for (1) his creation (the Book of
Creatures), (2) for his preservation (God's providence written in the
Scriptures), (3) "but above all for thine inestimable love in the
redemption of the world by our Lord Jesus Christ, for the means of
grace, and for the hope of glory" (the individual soul).

The first kind of meditation that Hall wrote, the one hundred and forty brief *Occasional Meditations*, includes not only the
birds, animals, stars, insects, and man-made objects such as a lute, but
also the varied "occasions" of ordinary life: a court trial, a wedding, or
a bout of the ague. The second kind are those based on "The Book of
the Scriptures," nine volumes in all, in which Hall vivifies and applies
the various "lessons" to be gained from "contemplating" (his term) the
principal stories in the Old and New Testaments. The third kind
comprises those meditations on "The Book of the Soul" in which Hall
searches for the ways and meaning of the individual's communion
alone with God. Since, along with *The Art of Divine Meditation*, I include here a text of Hall's *Occasional Meditations*, my present account
of them will be much more detailed; the description of the other two
kinds on the two far bulkier books will be briefer and each illustrated
with a single example.

The *Occasional Meditations* on God's Creatures rest on the *topos* of
deus artifex and attracted Hall as a creative artist himself. As God
created matter in an intelligently conceived and foreordained form,
so, Hall wrote, "that which we are wont to say of fine wits we may as
truly affirm of the Christian heart, that it can make use of anything"
(*The Art*, chapter IV). Again, "It is the praise of us men if when we
have matter, we can give fashion." But God gave being to matter
without form, and a form to that matter. "If," he concludes, "we can
but finish a slight and unperfect matter [say a poem or a meditation
or a book] according to a former pattern, it is the height of our skill;
but to begin that which never was, whereof there was no
example . . . is proper only to such power as Thine." "The Book of
Creatures," with Hall's meditations that proceed from it, is not that
zoological one of Aristotle the biologist. Since an idea has been placed
between the thing and God, it is, rather, the world of Plato and
Hermes Trismegistus, the world of poetry and imagination that

allowed Browne to wonder at the mystical mathematics of the city of heaven etched upon the back of a turtle.

The term "creatures" includes more than the animals, the flowers, and the rain; it embraces man. Also everything God has provided for man by allowing him to create it—such as wine, a whetstone, or music at night—becomes an "occasion" for meditating upon God. Those of us who may boggle at Hall's finding a ready sermon in every stone may be reminded of a sentence in C.S. Lewis' dedication of *A Preface to Paradise Lost* (1942) to Charles Williams: "Reviewers, who have not had time to re-read Milton, have failed for the most part to digest your criticism of him; but it is a reasonable hope that of those who heard you in Oxford many will understand that when the old poets made some virtue their theme they were not teaching but adoring, and what we take for the didactic is often the enchanted." "I desire not to comprehend, O Lord," wrote Hall; "teach me to do nothing but wonder" (*Oc. Med.* no. CXXI). We must come away impressed with the simplicity and charm of these "essays" that arise out of Hall's own experience and that of seventeenth-century England.

Certainly they are livelier and more personal than Francis Bacon's. Although a pacifist, Hall is a royalist in the politics of church and state; a well-tuned peal of church bells (LXXX) reminds him that domestic peace comes about only when every one keeps his due place of degree and order. At times Hall shows himself to be proud and independent: a crow can pull fleece off a sheep's back, but "whosoever will be tearing my fleece let him look to himself" (XXVIII). An acute and devout observer of nature, he shows an interest in the growing science of his day, for example in astronomy and magnetism. Still, he believes that since shellfish have no sex, they are born of corruption, hence a fair pearl of great price (CXI). Almost every page bears witness to his familiarity with the Bible, and this sometimes with humor as in his description of Elijah scanning the sky to see from what quarter his uncouth caterers, the ravens, will bring him breakfast (LXVIII). Hall shows himself to be a student and lover of books, as when he finds himself in a great library, probably the Bodleian (LXXI).

Apart from the personality of the author, we get in these "essays" of Joseph Hall an intimate view of the customs of the seventeenth century—in the city, on the farm, and within the home. He pauses, as

John Donne did, before a plague-stricken front door (LXXII). Ladies carry "sweet-bags" in which they place the root of the fleur-de-lys (CXXVIII). He listens to the cries of streetvendors in London (XXX). Through his pages parade a beggar, a lunatic, a dwarf, a blind man, and a felon sentenced to be hanged. A mob throw rotten eggs and insults at a whore being drawn in a cart, and mountebanks swallow dismembered frogs, drinking the juice for a fee (CXIX). He watches a cockfight (XXIV).

These are religious meditations, but they are also literary essays of such merit as to justify this first printing of them since 1863. Mild Calvinist though Hall was, no where else does his feeling for the synergistic principle more strongly emerge than from these essays: the double thrust of Creator and creature, of God and man, of the world of things and of spirit. "If any English writer was responsible for popularizing the contemplation of the creatures as a religious exercise," observed Kitty Scoular, "it was probably Joseph Hall, Bishop of Exeter."[44]

In *The Devout Soul* (1643) Hall defined at greater length meditation on "The Book of Creatures" in such a way as to allow us to see its relation to the literary traditions of the bestiary, the herbal, the fable, the emblem, the proverb, and the age-old habit of thinking in similitudes:

Every herb, flower, spire of grass, every twig and leaf, every worm and fly, every scale and feather, every billow and meteor speaks the power and wisdom of their infinite Creator. Solomon sends the sluggard to the ant; Isaiah sends the Jews to the ox and the ass; our Saviour sends his disciples to the ravens, and to the lilies of the field. There is no creature of whom we may not learn something. We shall have spent our time ill in this great school of the world, if, in such store of lessons, we be non-proficients in devotion. . . . And indeed, wherefore serve all the volumes of natural history but to be so many commentaries upon the several creatures wherein we may read God? and even those men who have not the skill or leisure to peruse them, may yet, out of their own thoughts and observation, raise, from the sight of all the works of God, sufficient matter to glorify him. Who can be so stupid as not to take notice of the industry of the bee, the providence of the ant, the cunning of the spider, the reviving of the fly, the worm's endeavour of revenge, the subtlety of the fox, the sagacity of the hedgehog, the innocence and profitableness of the sheep, the laboriousness of the ox, the obsequiousness of the dog, the timorous shifts of the hare, the nimbleness of the deer, the generosity of the lion, the courage of the horse, the fierceness of the tiger, the cheerful music of birds, the harmlessness of the dove, the true love of the turtle, the cock's observation of time, the swallow's architecture; shortly—for it were easy here to be endless—of the several qualities and dispositions of every one of those our fellow creatures with whom we converse on the face of the earth? and who that takes notice of them cannot fetch from every act and motion of theirs some monition of duty and occasion for devout thoughts? (6:509–10)

The literary flavor of Hall's *Occasional Meditations* lies not only in their concreteness but in their brevity, individuality, and freshness. At what period in his life did he compose them, and why did he never include them in collected editions of his *Works?*

The very idea of glorifying God's creation in literature may have come from Hall's meeting with Joshua Sylvester in the inner circle of Prince Henry's household. For Hall an object of admiration as well as a lifelong friend, Sylvester had published his translation of du Bartas' *Les Semaines* in 1605, and Hall's two favorite poets after David were the Protestant Spenser and the Englished Huguenot. After Prince Henry died, Hall contributed three poems to Sylvester's *Lachrymae Lachrymarum*, and was chosen to preach the sermon at the dissolution of the Prince's "family" of over five hundred persons. From his own proem to *Occasional Meditations* and from his son Robert's dedication of them in 1630 to James Hay Viscount Doncaster, it is safe to assume that they were written during the first dozen years or so on the Denny-Hay estate in Waltham when Hall was close to the royal court. "These papers," Robert tells us when Joseph Hall was the very busy Bishop of Exeter, were found "amongst others lying aside in my Father's study."

Only one of the *Occasional Meditations*, "Upon the Rumors of War" (XCVII) can be dated with some accuracy. Hall mentions the appearance of a comet, and comets were taken as portents of national dread, as Shakespeare witnessed in *Julius Caesar*: "When beggars die, there are no comets seen / The heavens themselves blaze forth the death of princes" (2.2.30–31). The "rumors" of Hall's title evidently refers to the beginnings of what came to be known as The Thirty Years War (1618–1648), notorious for its devastation. The comet believed to be its evil omen appeared over England in the early winter of 1618. Of the seven books describing it, the most famous was that of Dr. John Bainbridge of Ashby-de-la-Zouch, Hall's birthplace in Leicestershire: *Description of the late Comet from the 18. of Novemb. 1618 to the 16. of December following* (London, 1619), dedicated to King James.

If the *Occasional Meditations* are so good, why did not their author take more care for them? In his *Art* he gave them the smallest amount of space in order to concentrate on "deliberate meditation" that requires greater effort. To Hall meditations without "rule" may have seemed too easy to write. As Edmund Calamy, later in the century, was to say: "Deliberate and Solemn meditation is very hard and difficult; but this way of meditation is very easie, and the reaason is this, because there is no Creature of God but is a teacher of some good thing."[45] Calamy's example is a meditation on a spider, obviously copied from Hall's no. XV. The twentieth century, echoing the phrase "Protestant work ethic," might wish that Hall had not felt himself so constantly pressed to meet the greater challenge, and had given us, instead, more "occasional" meditations. To Joseph Hall, however, such meditations, springing from sense-data, may have represented the bottom of the Platonic scale. A man has more than an *eye* and a *ear*; he has a *mind* to contemplate God's Word and a *soul* to prepare to meet its maker.

Hall's Bible-Meditations. Between "the Book of the Creatures" and "the Book of the Soul," as David himself witnessed (Ps. 19), lies "the Book of the Scriptures." Not only had Joseph Hall read the whole Bible from his boyhood, but at Cambridge he had studied it in Hebrew, Greek, Latin, and English. Besides, he was an Anglican preacher in charge of a congregation. Provided the priest follows the lectionary in *The Book of Common Prayer* for both morning and evening services, his congregation will hear from God's "Word" the Psalms read through once a month, the rest of the Old Testament once a year, and the whole of the New Testament every four months. A glance at the two texts here included will show how often a biblical allusion appears in his writing. Though the figures may not be accurate (they depend upon my ability to recognize biblical sources), I count in both works 179 biblical allusions. Hall's three favorite authors are the Bible's most literary ones: Solomon is quoted 23 times; St. Paul, 27 times; and the Psalms, 45 times. In view of the

Calvinist's emphasis upon God's beginning and completing His good work in mankind, it is not surprising that in these two works of Joseph Hall the allusions to the Old Testament comprise 56 percent of the total, and those to the New Testament 44 percent.

Hall's meditations on the Bible are called *Contemplations upon the Principal Passages in the Holy Story*. In his dedication of their beginnings to Prince Henry, he refers to them as "these meditations" and "these holy speculations" (Wynter, 1:2). Their purpose is to "give light to the thoughts of any reader[;] let him with me give the praise to Him from whom that light shone forth to me" (1:3). May that Spirit, he adds, "which hath penned all these things for our learning . . . sanctify these my unworthy meditations to the good of his church" (1:25). They differ from his exegetical work, *A Paraphrase upon the Hard Texts in the Whole Divine Scriptures*, in that they contain very little citation of authority or etymological and historical explanation. Their signature as meditation rather than exegesis or sermon is the reiterated phrase "O my God" or "O my Saviour" or "O my soule." Their tone is exemplified by the meditation on Jacob's "sweet vision of angels climbing up and down that sacred ladder which God hath set between heaven and earth" (1:325). They are filled with joy: "What is this, other than the exaltation of Isaac's delight to walk forth into the pleasant fields of the Scriptures, and to meditate of nothing under heaven" (ibid.)? After a period of polemical writing, Hall returns to this healing work with the wish "that all the professors of the dear name of Christ might be taken up with nothing but holy and peaceable thoughts of devotion" (1:400).

The meditations on Scripture occupied a far longer period in Hall's life than those on God's creatures. He started them after he had become the rector in Lord Denny's benefice at Waltham, and continued them into the reign of Charles the First. "None can challenge so much right in these Meditations," Hall writes in dedicating Book XIX to Denny, "as your lordship, under whose happy shade they received their first conception." Offering the "7th and last volume" of meditations on the Old Testament to King Charles, Hall writes: "Now at last, thanks be to my good God, I have finished the long task of my meditations upon the historical part of the Old Testament" (2:141). And dedicating his initial meditation on the New Testament to the same king, he asserts: "More than twenty years are slipped

away since I entered upon this task of sacred Contemplations"
(2:291). Seven volumes on the Old Testament and two on the New
show, again, an emphasis quite different from that of the Roman
Catholic meditators.

Just as most of the *Occasional Meditations* begin with an emblem
and end in a little homily and an affectionate devotion to God, so
these meditations on the Bible usually begin with the story and end
with application to our lives and a heartfelt adoration. The whole
body of them, also, rises in emotion from the Old Testament to the
New. The last meditation is the longest and most fervent of them all,
hardly falling in attention and zeal throughout all of its two hundred
and eighty-eight pages.

My reader shall find the discourse in all these passages more large [warns
their author]; and in the latter, as the occasion gives, more fervent: and if he
shall miss some remarkable stories, let him be pleased to know, that I have
purposely omitted those pieces which consist rather of speech than of act,
and those that are in respect of the matter coincident to these I have
selected. I have so done my task as fearing, not affecting, length: and as
careful to avoid the cloying my reader with other men's thoughts (2:410).

In *The Devout Soul* of 1643, Hall expands his concept of a meditation based on "The Book of Scriptures" by citing the experience of
the poet David:

Before we put our hand to this sacred volume, it will be requisite to
elevate our hearts to that God whose it is, for both his leave and his blessing. *Open mine eyes*, saith the sweet singer of Israel, *that I may behold the won-
drous things of thy law*. Ps. cxix. 18. Lo, David's eyes were open before to
other objects; but when he comes to God's book, he can see nothing
without a new act of apertion: letters he might see, but wonders he could
not see, till God did unclose his eyes and enlighten them. It is not therefore
for us presumptuously to break in upon God, and to think by our natural
abilities to wrest open the precious caskets of the Almighty, and to fetch out
all his hidden treasure thence at pleasure: but we must come tremblingly
before him, and, in all humility, crave his gracious admission (6:226).

As an example of Hall's scriptural meditations I choose a passage
from his retelling of the story of Samson. With admiration, rage,
pity, and sorrow, we have gone through Samson's life, and are now
come to his last day when in mockery he is forced by the Philistines

to dedicate his strength in public to their fish-god Dagon. By such a sacrifice Samson becomes a type of Christ:

No Musitian would serve for this feast, but *Sampson*; hee must now bee their sport, which was once their terror; that hee might want no sorrow, scorne is added to his miserie: Every wit and hand playes upon him: Who is not ready to cast his bone and his jest at such a captive? So as doubtlesse hee wisht himselfe no lesse deafe, then blinde, and that his soule might have gone out with his eyes. Oppression is able to make a wise man madde: and the greater the courage is, the more painfull the insultation.

Now *Sampson* is punished, shall the Philistins escape? If the judgement of God beginne at his owne, what shall become of his enemies? This advantage shall *Sampson* make of their tyrannie, that now death is no punishment to him, his soule shall flie forth in this bitternesse, without paine; and that his dying revenge shall be no lesse sweet to him, then the libertie of his former life. Hee could not but feele God mockt through him; and therefore whilst they are scoffing, he prayes; his seriousnesse hopes to pay them for all those jests. If hee could have beene thus earnest with God in his prosperitie, the Philistins had wanted this laughing stocke. No devotion is so fervent, as that which arises from extremitie: *O Lord God, I pray thee thinke upon me; O God I beseech thee strengthen mee at this time only*. Though *Sampson's* haire were shorter, yet he knew Gods hand was not; as one therefore that had yet eyes enow to see him that was invisible, and whose faith was recovered before his strength, he sues to that God, which was a party in this indignitie, for power to revenge his wrongs, more then his owne: It is zeale that moves him, and not malice; his renued faith tels him, that he was destin'd to plague the Philistins; and reason tells him, that his blindness put him out of the hope of such another opportunitie. Knowing therefore, that this play of the Philistins must end in his death, hee recollects all the forces of his soul and body, that his death may be a punishment in stead of a disport; and that his soule may be more victorious in the parting, then in the animation: and to addresse himselfe both to die, and kill; as one, whose soule shall not feele his owne dissolution, whiles it shall carry so many thousand Philistins with it to the pit. All the acts of *Sampson* are for wonder, not for imitation: So didst thou, O blessed Saviour, our better *Sampson*, conquer in dying; and triumphing upon the chariot of the Crosse, didst leade captivitie captive: The law, sinne, death, hell, had never beene vanquisht, but by thy death: all our life, libertie, and glory, springs out of thy most precious bloud (*Contemplations, The First Booke* [1617]; pp. 247–48).

Soul-Meditations. Hall's meditations on the "Book of the Soul" rank highest in volume, time-span, and intensity. Problems of God's "incomprehensible justice and mercy" must be settled in the soul, the heart, the Protestant's conscience, that "paradise [or else hell] within" where the individual as a free agent alone confronts his God. Only two of these soul-meditations obey Hall's own rules set down in *The Art of Divine Meditation*, the two that illustrate that text. At the beginning of the century, through the Civil War, and up to his death, the art and practice of soul-devotion became for Hall the central Christian duty. Constantly he called attention to his own "often and serious meditation," to his daily practice of looking into his heart to know God, and his hope that by setting these meditations down and publishing them he could show the way to others—a life-time devotion to the "meditations of my heart" (David) that had a deeper origin than the "seven steps of the Affections" he found in 1605 in a book by Mauburnus. His soul-meditations bear some resemblance to the large number of seventeenth century books of devotion, of which the most popular was Bishop Bayly's *The Practice of Piety*. But they are less catechetical and more filled with what Hall termed "the sweet fruits of invisible comforts" (*The Art*, chapter 1). Hall's soul-meditations show the learning, reasonableness, and joy of the devout Anglican.

Many of them were collected in *The Devout Soul*, composed amid the Civil War's drums and tramplings, a time above all times when it was proper "to direct our address to the throne of God." "Blessed be my God," Hall adds, "who, in the midst of these woful tumults, hath vouchsafed to give me these calm and holy thoughts: which I justly suppose he meant not to suggest that they should be smothered in the breast wherein they were conceived, but with a purpose to have the benefit communicated to many. . . . I direct the way; God bring us to the end " (6:503).

As an example of a soul-meditation in which Hall wrestles with problems of his conscience and God's inexplicable justice, I quote from Section V of *The Souls Farewell to Earth* published in 1651:[46]

But with a trembling adoration, O my soule, must thou needs look upon the infinite Justice of thy God; whose inviolable rule is to render to every man according to his workes. Alas, the little good thou wert able to doe, hath beene allayed with so many, and great imperfections, that it can expect no retribution but displeasure; and for the many evills whereof thou art guilty, what canst thou look for but the wages of sinne, Death? not that temporary, and naturall onely, which is but a separation of thee, a while, from thy load of earth; but the spirituall and eternall separation from the presence of thy God, whose very want is the height of torments. Lo, whatever become of thee, God must be himself: In vaine shouldst thou hope that for thy sake hee will abate ought of his blessed Essence, of his sacred Attributes; That righteous doome must stand, The soule that sinnes shall die: Hell claimes his due; Justice must bee satisfied; where art thou now, O my soule? What canst thou now make account of but to despaire and die? surely, in thy selfe, thou art lost; there is no way with thee but utter perdition. But looke up, O soule, look up above the Hills whence commeth thy salvation; see the heavens opening upon thee; see what reviving, and comfortable raies of grace and mercy shine forth unto thee from that excellent glory; and out of that heavenly light heare the voice of thy blessed Saviour, saying to thee, O Israel, thou hast destroyed thy selfe, but in mee is thy help [margin: Hos. 13:9]. Even so, O Jesu, in thee, onely in thee is my help: wretched man that I am: in my self I stand utterly forfeited to death and hell: it is thou that hast redeemed mee with no lesse ransome than thy precious bloud. Death was owing by me; so as now my debt is fully discharged, & my soul clearly acquitted: Who shall lay any thing to the charge of God's Elect? It is God that justifieth; who is he that condemneth? It is Christ that dyed, yea rather that is risen againe [margin: Rom. 8:33,34]. Lo now the rigor of thine inviolable Justice is taken off by thine infinite mercy: The sum that I could never pay, is by the power of that faith which thou hast wrought in me, set off to my all-sufficient surety, & by thy divine goodnesse graciously accepted as mine; I have paid it in him, he hath paid it for me; Thy justice is satisfied, thy Debtor freed, & thy mercy magnified (1651, pp. 359–63).

General Characteristics. Some generalizations may be made concerning Hall's three kinds of meditations. For one thing, neither the kind nor the "book of God" from which it is drawn is ever discrete. Just as Vaughan, in "Regeneration," cannot notice a bush in Wales without remembering the voice that came to Moses when he stood on Sinai, so Hall, before him, while meditating on a pair of spectacles must end with St. Paul's hope to see as he is seen. Many of Hall's *Contemplations* on the Bible are illustrated from natural and psychological facts, and the meditations that arise from the "Book of the Soul" often begin with a text from the scriptures, or with one of God's creatures, thus deliberately melding the three categories. In any one he may repeat from the book of creatures such outward occasions as the heavens, a singing bird, a bee, or a worm. To these he may add such temporal occasions as the morning, or the evening, or Basil's lighting of the candles; and such inward occasions as affliction, remorse, doubt, gratitude, or elation. One literary genre flows into another as a "meditation" verges upon a "vow," or a "soliloquy," or a "devotion," or a "prayer,"

Mixed as the three kinds often are, it is even more difficult to descry the "steps." In contrast to the *Spiritual Exercises* of St. Ignatius, in Joseph Hall there is no single method, whether of three steps, or seven, or none, which can raise the soul of Everyman from earth to heaven. Hall believed that God's grace in man can be furthered by art, but method is not everything. Many books have been written on chemistry, he remarks, but few men have made gold (8:7). Nor does God work by miracle but "in such methods and by such means as may most conduce to his blessed ends." The methods are those only of "sweet conversation" or "self-conferences" or "heavenly soliloquies" or sometimes gentle and sometimes fierce "arguments with one's own soul" — all terms which Hall freely uses for what is technically called meditation. "Devotion is the life of religion," he wrote, "the very soul of piety, the highest employment of grace, and no other than the prepossession of heaven by the saints of God here on earth" (6:504). Though suspicious of too rigid a method, Hall, nevertheless, insists that there is an "art" of meditation which can be acquired by a mature person willing to practice. With no discipline at all, as he charmingly put it in another context, one's *cogitations* and *affections* (the two parts of a meditation asserted in the early *Art*) can go astray:

> In this case it fals out with thee, O my soule, as with some fond child, who eagerly following a Bee in hope of her bag, sees a gay Butterflie crosse his way; and thereupon leaues his first cause, and runs after those painted wings; but in that pursute seeing a Bird flie close by him, he leaues the flie in hope of a better purchase; but in the meane time is disappointed of all, and catcheth nothing. It mainely behoues thee therefore to keep up thy Cogitations and Affections close to these heauenly obiects; and to check them whensoeuer thou perceiuest an inclination to their wandering.[47]

Joseph Hall, as we have said, was a Calvinist who never left the Anglican church. As an Anglican he was devoted, of course, to the Bible, to the tradition of the Apostolic Church, to *The Book of Common Prayer*, and to reason. He was sufficiently free from Laudian restrictions to bring to all his Christian writings, especially those that include his theory and practice of meditation, the assumption that all men are not built the same, that strait-jackets impede the individual's free access to God. Protestant individualism and an Anglican capacity for adaptation, then, are two important notes in Hall's contribution to seventeenth-century meditation.

Along with these goes his insistence that any Christian, not merely the professional or the recluse or the man of leisure, can learn to meditate. There is hardly a book of his that does not take time out to appeal to the "unlearned," the beginner, whose heart can be taught to love God before his brain can understand Him. That is why Hall, in his *Art of Divine Meditation*, rejected as far too subtle the step-by-step ratiocination which he found in Mauburnus. "I doubt not," he wrote, "but an ordinary Reader will easily espie a double fault at the least, *Darkness* and *Coincidence*" (chapter XVI), that is, needless obscurity and an over-lapping in logic that makes the thing more difficult than it really is.

Hall's three kinds of meditation, based as they are on the "three books of God," may represent stages in his own growth, like the three books traditionally ascribed to Solomon: the sensuous Canticles written as a young man, the Proverbs when he was fully mature, and the Ecclesiastes towards the end of his life.[48] Hall wrote his brief ejaculatory meditations in his early manhood, the *Contemplations* on the Bible during twenty years of his full maturity; and he kept on writing soul-meditations even after he was driven from his cathedral in 1643 until his death in semi-exile in 1656. Faced with the political and religious necessity to resist the Jesuits, in theory and practice he was completely independent of the *Spiritual Exercises* of St. Ignatius of Loyola.

V

Hall's Use of the Senses and Imagination: His Style

Joan Webber nicely describes an angry Milton's view of Joseph Hall's prose style: "Just as good style is a sign of grace, so bad style characterizes the unregenerate. Bishops being bad men, it is impossible that Bishop Hall should be able to write well, but in case any

doubt should remain in the reader's mind, Milton proves Hall's in-
famy by describing his style, which he finds immodest, self- aggran-
dizing, full of three-inch sentences as if written to measure, and inade-
quate in grammar."⁴⁹ Similarly in the nineteenth century, Coleridge,
possibly soothed by the mellifluous periods of his favorite, Jeremy
Taylor, seemed to make Hall's "curt style" a reason for detesting the
whole person: "I have always considered [Bishop Hall] . . . a self-
conceited, coarse-minded, persecuting, vulgar Priest, and (by way of
anti-climax) one of the first corrupters and *epigrammatizers* of our
English Prose Style."⁵⁰ The brevity Milton and Coleridge object to
refers to an earlier Hall mode, the Senecan, which, with Hall's
Neostoicism, has been over-emphasized.⁵¹

More germane to the present discussion is that some critics have at-
tributed to Hall's style an almost total lack of concreteness stemming
from his Neoplatonism. They appear to think that Protestants and
Christian Platonists are so completely immersed in IDEAS that,
unlike Roman Catholics in their religious writings, they never taste,
feel, touch, hear, or smell. So U. Milo Kaufmann, whose book, *The
Pilgrim's Progress and Traditions in Puritan Meditation* (New Haven,
1966), helped me in the present study, distinguishes between "the line
of Joseph Hall, who elected not to use the imagination and senses"⁵²,
and those Puritan meditators like Baxter and Bunyan who wrote
"heavenly meditations" in which the senses and the imagination have
full scope. To my mind there are not "two divergent traditions," as I
shall argue further in the next section on Hall's influence.

And why should we limit ourselves, in Protestant meditation, to
"heavenly meditation?" With characteristic bifurcation the
seventeenth-century pilgrim was faced with this life and the next. In
the next life he was faced with eternal bliss or eternal punishment. In
both these latter contemplations he was able to use all his sensuous
imagination to its utmost.

Hall's "heavenly meditations" are filled with sense impressions,
many of them from the traditional interpretation of the Canticles, in-
viting an almost exotic reveling in the sweet odors of a garden and the
tastes of a rich banquet. And in heaven there is invariably music.
Hall, like the Puritan Milton, loved music and associated it with joy,
even mirth. Who of us has not watched the faces of choristers singing

Handel's *Messiah* or Beethoven's *Ninth* and not seen their look of pure joy? So Hall uses this experience in his "heavenly meditation": "No marvel, then, if from this glory proceed unspeakable joy, and from this joy the sweet songs of praise and thanksgiving. The spirit bids us when we are merry, sing. How much more, then, when we are merry without all mixture of sorrow, beyond all measure of our earthly afflictions, shall we sing joyful 'Hallelujahs' and 'Hosannahs' to him that dwelleth in the highest heavens" [Matt. 31:9] (*The Art*, chapter XXI).

And in the midst of *The Art*, Hall draws upon the following sense-impressions in a description of hell:

"Cast down thine eyes yet lower into that deep and bottomless pit full of horrour, full of torment, where there is nothing but flames and tears and shrieks and gnashing of teeth, nothing but fiends and tortures; where there is palpable darkness and yet perpetual fire; where the damned are ever boiling, never consumed; ever dying, never dead; ever complaining, never pitied; where the glutton that once would not give a crust of bread now begs for one drop of water [Luke 16:24]; and yet, alas, if whole rivers of water should fall into his mouth, how should they quench those rivers of brimstone that feed this flame?" (Chapter XXIV)

The *Occasional Meditations* are most filled with sense-impressions, as may be gleaned even by their titles: "Upon the Heavens Moving" (L), "Upon the Barking of a Dog" (XXIII), "Upon the quenching of Iron in Water" (XLVII), "Upon the Smell of a Rose" (XCIII). And yet such use of the creatures and of man's common experience as emblems of the multiple attributes of God, as well as Hall's strong anti-Jesuitical stand, differentiates this part of his matter from the Ignatian *compositio loci*, which uses the senses to bring more sharply into focus a scene from the passion of Christ. To the Protestant poetic imagination the "creatures," with all the sensuous imagery they evoke, offer themselves in thousands of different ways. But there is the inevitable hierarchy, even among the five senses: sight and hearing come near the top, and the other three—taste, touch, and smell—towards the bottom. Note how many of Hall's occasional meditations have in their title "Upon the sight of ": one hundred and three, to be exact. Seventeen use hearing, and for the other three

senses there are only seven or eight. Out of the one hundred and forty meditations, only fourteen are sensuously neutral. That the sense
of sight is the noblest is bound up with old theories about the reasons
God created man erect! The sense of smell, writes Hall in no. XCIII,
"is one of the meanest and least useful of the senses, yet there is none
of the five that receives or gives so exquisite a contentment to it." And
yet, he is sure that it has more affinity with the earth than with the
soul. This impression emerges strongly in his descriptions of death.
On the sight of a coffin he writes: "While here was nothing but mere
wood, no flower was to be seen here; now that this wood is lined
with an unsavory corpse, it is adorned with this sweet variety. The fir
whereof that coffin is made yields a natural redolence alone; now that
it is stuffed thus noisomely, all helps are too little to countervail that
scent of corruption" (*Oc. Med.* LXXXVI).

Sight, the noblest sense, Hall insists, belongs to the understanding;
taste, to the affections. Hence, theoretically, after we have
understood our subject of meditation by "looking" at it, we must experience the "sweet taste and relish of it" (*The Art*, chapter XXVIII).
And yet even the sense of sight can fool our understanding.. Wittily,
Hall suggests that a covetous man should keep his money at the bottom of a river, for looking at his coins through the medium of water
he may think every dime has become a quarter, every quarter a fifty-
cent piece (*Oc. Med.*, LIX).

Not unnaturally, many of the richest uses of the senses in Hall's
prose appear in those passages wherein he purposely mixes them.
One such example is his account of the common and often mean
ways in which death strikes at the human being. "One great conqueror finds it in a slate, another finds it in a fly; one finds it in the
kernel of a grape, another in the prick of a thorn; one in the taste of a
herb, another in the smell of a flower; one in a bit of meat, another in
a mouthful of air; one in the very sight of a danger, another in the
conceit of what might have been. Nothing in all our life is too little to
hide death under it. There need no cords, nor knives, nor swords,
nor pieces; we have made ourselves as many ways to death as there
are helps of living" (*The Art*, "On Death," Part IV, "Causes"). And all
of us who have felt like rejecting a doctor's prescription will recognize
Hall's reaction: "How loathsome a draught is this, how offensive both
to the eye and to the scent and to the taste! Yea, the very thought of

it is a kind of sickness; and when it is come once down, my very disease is not so painful for the time as my remedy. How doth it turn the stomach and wring the entrails and work a worse destemper than that whereof I formerly complained!" (*Oc. Med.*, CXXXIX).

Hall's use of the senses depends, finally, upon the hierarchy he perceived among the three kinds of meditations he wrote. The *Occasional Meditations* contain most sensory impressions, the *Contemplations* fewer, and the "soul-meditations" the least. But in all three kinds the Bible is alluded to extensively, particularly the Old Testament; and one could hardly say that biblical language is all abstract.

As for the imagination, in the latter two categories Hall plays upon stories in the Bible, as can be seen in the excerpt included here from the story of Samson, which Hall realizes both visually and dramatically. In *The Art* his familiarity with the Bible and his feeling for dramatic dialogue emerge in his allusion to the "chief of the Apostles," when, in putting words into Peter's mouth as the angels enter the prison cell to free him, he borrows the very human phrase "yet a litte sleep" not from the book of Acts, where the story is told, but from Proverbs 6:10, making Peter sound like a teen-age boy being awakened to go to school (*The Art*, "On Death," sect. IX). The Bible and Hall's prose, moreover, are filled with figurative imagery, in which the tenor is usually oriented towards the *logos* and the vehicle anchored in experience. To cite one simile, in choosing a subject for meditation Hall recommends "an inward inquisition made into our heart of what we both do and should think upon, rejecting what is unexpedient and unprofitable. In both which the soul, like unto some noble hawk, lets pass the crows, and larks and such other worthless birds that cross her way and stoopeth upon a fowl of price, worthy of her flight. . ." (*The Art*, chapter XV).

A person talking to himself or to God in the privacy of communion is really not conscious of style, yet Hall was always writing for others, like Browne, who studied books for the sake of those who did not (*Rel. Med.*, 2:3). Hall got his style partly from Seneca but mostly from the poetry of David, the pithy sentences ascribed to Solomon, and the persuasive prose of St. Paul. Hall's style cannot be characterized as Senecan, or Ciceronian, or Baroque, although M. W. Croll would call the following sentence, I think, Baroque for its shifts from iambs to spondees and its kinaesthetic images: "An empty cart runs lightly away, but if it be soundly laden, it goes sadly, sets hard, groans under the weight, and makes deep impressions; the wheels creak, and the axeltree bends, and all the frame of it is put to the utmost stress" (*Oc. Med.*, XCCCVI).

Particularly attractive are the emblematic impressions of the animals in God's creation. Of the owl Hall writes: "What a strange melancholic life doth this creature lead; to hide her head all day long in an ivy-bush, and at night, when all other birds are at rest, to fly abroad and vent her harsh notes" (LXV). He calls a spider "this little Arabian": "So soon as ever he hears the noise of a fly afar off, how he hastens to his door, and if that silly heedless traveler do but touch upon the verge of that unsuspected walk, how suddenly doth he seize upon the miserable booty and, after some strife, binding him fast with those subtle cords, drags the helpless captive after him into his cave" (XV). Hall pities the moth entering the candle flame: "How many bouts it fetched, every one nearer than other, ere it made this last venture; and now that merciless fire, taking no notice of the affection of an overfond client, hath suddenly consumed it" (XXXIV). While a worm is in its earthen house it is safe and secret, but "when it comes out into the light of the Sun, to the eye of passengers, how is it vexed with the scorching beams, and wrings up and down in an helpless perplexity, not finding where to shroud itself" (LXIX). I cannot understand why hundreds of observations like these are deprecated as "logos-oriented," leaving "no room for the imagination."

In much of Hall's meditative writing, divine wisdom speaks so directly to the hearts of men that it becomes proverbial, and most proverbs are memorable by their brevity and their appeal to the senses, experience, and imagination. In his *Art*, Hall asks why knock at the door of the heart if we depart before we have an answer (chapter VIII). Meditation, he says, is like medicine; an overdose does more harm than good (chapter IV). "The cloth that is white (which is wont to be the color of innocency) is capable of any dye; the black, of none other" (chapter V). "The mind of man is of a strange metal: if it be not used, it rusteth; if used hardly, it breaketh" (chapter VIII). Practice variety in your meditations, Hall counsels, "for even the strongest stomach doth not always delight in one dish" (chapter XII). Don't make the beginning too difficult: "If we break our teeth on the shell, we shall find small pleasure in the kernel" (chapter XXII). Hall addresses himself to the neophyte because "those that have but little stock had need to know the best rules of thrift" (chapter I). And of Christians, he asks quite simply, "how can they want water that have the spring?" (chapter XX).

No doubt a reader of the following two texts of Hall will mark (if he owns the book) passages that strike him as unusually good style. Some of these will be brief images; have not the saints and martyrs before us, Hall asks, "trod in these *red* steps?" (*The Art*, "On Death," sect. VI). And though you and I are used to "a sea of troubles," how often do we meet with a phrase like "a galley of servitude" (ibid., sect. VIII)? A longer passage, of tender and half-humorous innuendo, is Hall's description of iron being drawn to the lodestone and particles of dust and straw to the piece of jet: "With what a force do both these stones work upon their several subjects! Is there anything more heavy and unapt for motion than iron or steel? Yet these do so run to their beloved lode-stone as if they had the sense of desire and delight, and do so cling to the point of it as if they had forgotten their weight for this adherence. Is there anything more apt for dispersion than small straws and dust? Yet these gather to the jet and so sensibly leap up to it as if they had a kind of ambition to be so preferred" (*Oc. Med.*, No. XLIII). Finally, there are noble passages on death, not quite so grandiloquent as those of Browne, but nevertheless ringing in their images and rhythm. One such passage is Part XIII, "The Complaint" in his meditation on death that accompanies *The Art of Divine Meditation*, only the first part of which I shall quote: "But, O my soul, what ails thee to be thus suddenly backward and fearful? No heart hath more freely discoursed of death in speculation; no tongue hath more extolled it in absence. And now that it hath come to thy bed's side, and hath drawn thy curtains, and taken thee by the hand, and offers thee service, thou shrinkest inward and, by the paleness of thy face and wildnesss of thine eye, betrayest an amazement at the presence of such a guest."

Most of the sentences in *The Art of Divine Meditation* are non-art, like those in *De Meditatione Christi*; Hall's are simple, direct, lacking in copia, aphoristic, and mainly Anglo-Saxon. He writes in the English language of Cranmer that Anglicans had been using for over fifty years in *The Book of Common Prayer* and that at the very time Hall was publishing his own devotions, was being so gloriously enshrined in the King James version of the Bible. Rhetoric and logic, Hall insists several times, are "natural." All of us are born that way; hence one must resist the temptation to be, through their means, vain, subtle, and glozing. To be a Christian is beyond "nature." Hall's style is simple and profound, self-knowledgeable, and invariably to the point.

VI

Hall's Reputation and Influence

Although Joseph Hall helped initiate several literary genres associated with England's seventeenth century — satire, "character-writing," epistle, etc. — he became most famous for his meditations. Hall was proud of his contribution to the genre, constantly calling attention to the need for writing and publishing meditations in view of the large number of sermons, exegetical works, and controversy that kept pouring from the press. A volume of Hall's collected works published in 1617 (University of Michigan Library) has pasted on the spine a label in seventeenth-century hand that simply says "Hall's Meditations" as though the volume contained nothing else. The 1628 *Works of Joseph Hall Bishop of Exeter* has the portrait, engraved, probably by John Payne,[53] for Philemon Stevens and Christopher Meredith, of the bishop in his round cap, Elizabethan ruff, spade beard, and the Dort medal hanging on his breast. Under the portrait are lines by J. Sampson. After Hall had been publishing books of various kinds for over thirty years, that which the eulogist emphasizes is his meditations:

> How farre beyond a Picture is his worth
> Whom Pen, nor Pencill truly can set forth.
> Behold his Reverend FACE; his better PART
> Is left ungrav'd. This was beyond all Art.
> His holy Thoughts in sacred MEDITATIONS,
> His ravisht SOULE with heavenly CONTEMPLATIONS
> Could not be drawne. Here only are his Looks:
> The Pictures of the rest are in his Books.

John Owen singled out Hall's meditations to praise him by; clumsily translated by John Vicars and published in 1619, the epigram reads:

> Doctor Ios. Hals Vowes and Meditations
> Thou *Vowed'st Vowes*, fit to be *Vow'd*,
> Worth *Reading Workes* dost write:
> He's blest that *Reades* thy *Vowes*, if hee
> To doe them take delight.[54]

One of the Anglican clergymen in Hall's diocese of Exeter was the Reverend Robert Herrick. No record exists of the bishop admonishing him on the use of sack, but it is interesting that in a poem to Joseph Hall the Hesperidian should use a term that Hall himself often applied to a meditation, that is "a holy rapture":

> To Jos: Lo: Bishop of Exeter.
> Whom sho'd I feare to write to, if I can
> Stand before you, my learn'd *Diocesan?*
> And never shew blood-guiltinesse, or feare
> To see my Lines *Excathedrated* here.
> Since none so good are, but you may condemne;
> Or here so bad, but you may pardon them.
> If then, (my Lord) to sanctifie my Muse
> One onely Poem out of all you'l chuse;
> And mark it for a Rapture nobly writ,
> 'Tis Good Confirm'd; for you have Bishop't it.[55]

In his funeral sermon on Hall, the Reverend John Whitefoot takes pains to praise Joseph Hall's major contribution to the Christian life of his time: "He was one that conversed as much with God and drew as nigh to Him in divine meditation, which is the ordinary way of seeing God in the flesh, as any man of his time. . . . A great master he was, and one of the first that taught this church the art of divine meditation" (Wynter, 1:73).

In 1665 Robert Boyle, "the Christian virtuoso," wrote a secular "Discourse touching Occasional Meditations" to his "Dearest Sister Sophronia":

I know it is a new thing [he said in the preface] that I have ventured to put some Occasional Reflections into Dialogues. But the reader will be less startled at my deviating in this, and other things from *Bishop Hall's* way of writing *Occasional Meditations*, if I acknowledge, that not to Prepossess or

Byas my Fancy, I purposely (till of late) forbad myself, the perusing of that
Eloquent Praelates devout Reflections.[56]

   More than a century after Hall died, another Anglican parson, the
Reverend Lawrence Sterne, whimsically inventing his own
bibliographical citation in a masterpiece of humorous fiction, wrote:
"The learned Bishop Hall, I mean the famous Dr. Joseph Hall, who
was Bishop of Exeter in King James the First's reign, tells us in one of
his *Decads*, at the end of his divine art of meditation, . . . 'That it is an
abominable thing for a man to commend himself';—and I really
think it is so."[57]
   "The central tradition in formal Puritan meditation," writes Kaufmann, "may be said to begin with Joseph Hall. . . . In its categories
and emphases, his *Art of Divine Meditation* . . . proved the source of a
stream of influence that extended the length of the seventeenth century."[58] I depart radically from Mr. Kaufmann, however, as I have
already suggested, in his insistence that Hall represents a "line of
meditation" that has no room for the senses, so that most of the Protestant meditators who followed were "divergent." As if to deny the
statement just quoted, he finds only two who followed Hall's "steps":
Isaac Ambrose, whose *Prima, Media, Ultima* was published in 1654,
and Edmund Calamy, whose title *The Art of Divine Meditation* (1680)
was taken from Joseph Hall.
   In creating the "divergence" between Hall and the Puritan meditators, including Baxter and Bunyan, on the ground that they used experience in their "heavenly meditations," Kaufmann quotes[59] Thomas
Adams *The Sinners Passing Bell* (*The Workes*, 1629): "That a reverend
Preacher sitting among other Divines, and hearing a sweet consort of
Musicke as if his soule had been borne up to Heaven, tooke occasion
to thinke and speake thus; *What Musicke* may we thinke there is in
Heaven?" Unfortunately for the argument of "divergence" this is a
direct steal from the third chapter of Hall's *Art of Divine Meditation*:
"Thus that learned and heavenly soul of our late Estye, when we sat
together and heard a sweet consort of music, seemed upon this occasion carried up for the time before-hand to the place of his rest, saying, not without some passion, 'What music may we think there is in
heaven!'" Kaufmann's quotation from Thomas Adams continues: "*A
friend* of mine viewing attentively the great pompe and state of

Court, on a solemne day, spake not without some admiration: *What shall we thinke of the glory in the Court of God?*" Having taken one passage from Hall, Thomas Adams may have had in mind another passage by his "friend" such as this in chapter XXII of *The Art of Divine Meditation*: "Kings use not to dwell in cottages of clay but in royal courts fit for their estate. How much more shall the King of Heaven, who hath prepared so fair mansions on earth, make Himself an habitation suitable to His majesty! Even earthly princes have dwelt in cedar and ivory; but the great city, Holy Jerusalem, the palace of the Highest, hath her walls of jasper, her building of gold, her foundation of precious stones, her gates of pearl."

And so with most of the rest of Kaufmann's illustrations of the use of experience in "heavenly meditations." Thanks to the University Microfilm library of the STC, I have gone through many of them myself and find very little divergence from the line of Joseph Hall, particularly in his visions of the blessed habitation of the saints which forms his first example for the steps in *The Art of Divine Meditation*. There is, however, one difference and that not very significant: most of the others state on the title page or elsewhere that their meditations were afterwards written down from sermons which had been delivered. Thus in the preface to *A Godly and learned Treatise of Prayer* (1640) by George Downame, bishop of Derry, we learn that the bishop, who had died six years before, had written these meditations out from sermons which he had preached. I have no doubt that Hall used his sermon material in his meditations, but he purposely obscures their technical if not formal connection.

Is Baxter "divergent" from Hall? Part 4 of Richard Baxter's *The Saint's Everlasting Rest* is evidence of Hall's influence on seventeenth-century Protestant meditation. Like Hall, Baxter quotes liberally from Gerson, the early continental "Reformer": "As *Gerson* . . . saith, This Art or way of Meditation is not learned chiefly out of Books: but the spirit of God bestoweth it as he pleaseth: on some more plentifully, & on some more sparingly."[60] The art of meditation, says Baxter like Hall before him, is "the set and solemn acting of all the powers of the soul"; that is, not acting in separate stages as sensitive, intellectual, and rational, but acting conjunctively and simultaneously. "What powers of the soul must be acted?" he asks. "What affections excited? What considerations of their objects are necessary thereto? and in what order must we proceed? I joyn all these together, because though in themselves they are distinct things, yet in the practice they all concurre to the same action" (chapter 9, p. 724). As for the best time for meditation, Baxter prefers evening because Isaac and Bishop Hall did. In section 9 he practically paraphrases chapter 10 of *The Art of Divine Meditation*, as he freely acknowledges: "Doctor Hall in his excellent Treatise of Meditation."

Baxter's Herbertian metaphor for the proportion of thinking to feeling is "setting the instrument" and then playing the "music," like the tuning of the orchestra and then hearing the symphony. Part of that "music" as it affects the listener is the Protestant homiletic cast. The practitioner should argue with himself, plead, cajole, exemplify by every means of rhetoric he can muster. A godly soliloquy, therefore, should have the parts and the ordering of a little sermon preached to one's self, with the greatest and final emphasis on its application (chapter 10, section 2). A meditation is "nothing but a pleading of the case with our own souls," Baxter says; or as in a sermon there need be no more division than a clarification of the difficulties, a confirmation of faith through Scripture, and a powerful application according to the nature of the matter and the practitioner's need at the time — which allows and demands far greater variety than does the Ignatian scheme. With an unveiled thrust at *The Spiritual Exercises* of the Jesuits, Baxter writes: "This is it that hath deceived Christians in this business; They have thought that Meditation is nothing but the bare thinking on Truths, and the rolling of them in the Understanding and Memory" (p. 692). The treatise calls his Puritan flock to prayer at the time of England's Civil War, and like Hall's it too ends with "An Example of this Heavenly Contemplation, for the Help of the Unskillful."

Richard Baxter closes by quoting Protestant Christian poetry, not the kind of poetry written earlier by Southwell and later by Crashaw. He quotes two passages from Sylvester's translation of du Bartas,[61] and three poems by George Herbert. The first Herbert quotation (on p. 814) is the final stanza of "The Glance."[62] This is followed (on p. 835) by the fourth stanza of "Mans Medley":

> Not that we may not here
> Tast of the cheer:
> But as birds drink and then lift up the head:

> So we must sip and think
> Of better drink,
> We may attain to after we are dead[63]

—certainly a "relishing" of heaven upon earth made memorable by a simple emblem from God's "Book of Creatures." Finally, Baxter quotes in full for three pages (pp. 853–56) Herbert's poem "Home," which begins with "Come, Lord, my head doth burn, my heart is sick," and which ends each stanza with the refrain "O shew thy self to me, / Or take me up to thee"[64]—an appropriate colloquy to end a Protestant treatise on the art of meditation. We need not be surprised that Baxter the Puritan can visualize through Herbert's poetry the blood streaming down Christ's face (second stanza), nor need we assume that Herbert in this stanza was influenced by the *compositio loci* of St. Ignatius' *Spiritual Exercises*. Baxter quotes Herbert's poem as an example of "the poetry of meditation" at the end of a treatise on meditation which is largely based on Joseph Hall.

It is difficult to prove Hall's influence on the meditative poets of the seventeenth century because so many of the concepts they share are religious "commonplaces" (in the best sense of the word) and both they and Hall possessed the same religious sensitivity, knowledge of Scripture, and ejaculatory petitioning manner. There is a great affinity.

Hall and John Donne, for example, joined as members of Sir Robert Drury's family and were partners in literary exercise. They must have been well acquainted with each other's work. Throughout Hall's prose are numerous reminders of Donne's verse: the meditations on sickness and death; the red cross on the door; the passing-bell; the friends gathered around the bed of a dying person. For Hall, as for Donne, Death need not be proud since "he hath men, casualties, desires for his executioners," (*The Art*, "On Death," sect. III). Again, "Man is a little world," writes Hall; "my soul is heaven, my body is earth" (*Oc. Med.*, I, end). And of course there is the play on *Sun/Son*. "If the light of a poor candle be so comfortable," writes Hall, "what is the light of the glorious sun, the great lamp of heaven? But much more, what is the light of that infinitely resplendent Sun of righteousness who gave that light to the sun, that sun to the world?" (*Oc. Med.*, XX). Both poets are fond of the Psalmist's phrase "the issues of death," and Hall's architectural metaphor for building a

meditation reminds one of the opening of Donne's own funeral sermon, even in that wonderful word "contignations" (*Oc. Med.*, CX).

As for Herbert, we have seen how Baxter, building on Hall, closes
with quotations from the religious poetry of Sylvester's du Bartas and
the priest of Bemerton. Again, Hall's architectural metaphors remind
one of Herbert's building of *The Temple*: "A goodly building must
show some magnificence in the gate; and great personages have seemly ushers to go before them, who by their uncovered heads command
reverence and way." (*The Art*, chapter XIV), wherein the ushers are
like Herbert's "The Fore-runners" (Hutchinson, p. 196). The prayer
that opens a meditation, Hall says, should be brief, for it is "no otherwise than as a portal to this building of meditation" (ibid., end). Hall's
fondness for music, finally, would appeal to George Herbert.

Henry Vaughan and Hall are joined in their love of nature and
childhood, their deploring of the desecration of the British Church,
and their constant desire to "see beyond the veil." "Do but draw this
veil a little that I may see my glory," cries Hall (*The Art*, "On Death,"
sect. XVI); and "Couldst thou but (oh that Thou couldst) look within
that veil, how shouldst thou be ravished with that blissful sight" (*Oc.
Med.*, V). Hall's reiterated fascination with the cyclical effects of sun
and waters is a foretaste of Vaughan's "The Waterfall": "Many
vapours rising from the sea meet together in one cloud; that cloud
falls down divided into several drops; those drops run together and in
many rills of water meet in the same channels; those channels run into the brook, those brooks into the rivers, those rivers into the
sea. . . . Take back, O Lord, those few drops Thou hast rained upon
my soul, and return them into that great ocean of the glory of Thine
own bounty, from whence they had their beginning" (*Oc. Med.*,
XVIII).

Herrick and Marvell seem a little more removed, and yet for the
first the microcosm image is shared, for example, in Herrick's amber
bead and Hall's globe of the world accidentally broken (*Oc. Med.*,
VI). And Hall's meditation on the ruined abbey and the misguided
zealousness of both its former inhabitants and its demolishers reminds
one of Marvell's "Nunappleton" (*Oc. Med.*, LXXVI).

As with Donne so with Sir Thomas Browne, Hall was a friend, the
poet at the beginning of his career and the physician towards the end.
They must have had many a long conversation about their shared

love of their church, of friends, and of almost everything in nature, including some of its scientific aspects. In *The Art* Hall gives us a bit of seventeenth-century medical lore: physicians scoured their leeches with salt and nettles before applying them in order to make them thirstier for the blood of the patient (*The Art*, "On Death," sect. IV). Browne uses the same grand metaphor of death becoming merely another birth, of the urns that contained the incinerated bones being replicas of their mothers' wombs. Just as the mid-wife [Hall writes], "that receives us from the knees of our mother in our first entrance to the light washeth, cleanseth, dresseth us and presents us to the breast of our nurse or the arms of our mother . . . so death, . . . in our passage to the other life is the first that receives and presents our naked soul to the hands of those angels which carry us up to her glory" (*The Art*, "On Death," V).

Had not Hall died ten years before *Paradise Lost* was published, he might well have acclaimed the great poem by his former adversary to be above, in doctrine and poetic sublimity, the poems of his beloved Spenser and "divine du Bartas." That poets, even of different generations and centuries, see eye to eye impresses us once again when we look at Hall's descriptions of sin and death and compare them with Milton's "monstrous" figures that guard the gates of hell. Milton's picture of evil is one of sexual abnormality, self-generation, and circularity. Hall wrote, "It was not Thou, O God, that madest death; our hands are they that were guilty of this evil. Thou sawest all Thy work that it was good; we brought forth sin, and sin brought forth death. To the discharge of Thy justice and mercy we acknowledge this miserable conception, and needs must that child be ugly that hath such parents" (*The Art*, "On Death," IV, "Causes").

None of these semi-parallels can be defined as influences; they can only be reminders that Joseph Hall, one of England's most read religious writers, was a part of that devotion to God and good writing that characterizes so much of the seventeenth century.

The high place that Hall's meditations held among his contributions to English prose as well as to the religious writings of the seventeenth century was signaled by Thomas Fuller as he nominated Joseph Hall to be one of England's "Worthies": the bishop, he wrote, was "not unhappy at *Controversies*, more happy at *Comments*, very good in his *Characters*, better in his *Sermons*, best of all in his *Medita-*

tions."⁶⁵ Joseph Hall was seventeenth-century England's most eminent theorist and prose-artist in what he deftly called "the slow proficiency of Grace."⁶⁶

VII

Textual Matters

Joseph Hall was an unusually careful overseer of the first printings of his books. In the latest modern edition of two of them, *Heauen vpon Earth and Characters of Vertues and Vices* (New Brunswick, N.J.: Rutgers University Press, 1948), Rudolf Kirk, editor, had to make only sixteen corrections of words, many of them not of substantive significance, like *discontentment* for *discontent* (152.27) and *of want* for *of the want* (191.12). In the first edition of *Heaven upon Earth*, Hall had listed twenty-six errata, all but one of them being corrected in subsequent editions.

The Art of Divine Meditation, first published in 1606 a few months after *Heaven upon Earth* by the same printer and booksellers, contains no list of errata, as though Dr. Hall had taught them a lesson. Its titlepage was: *The | Arte of | Divine Me- | Ditation: | Profitable for all Christians | to know and practise: | Exemplified with a large Medi- | tation of eternal life.*|[rule] *By Ioseph Hall.* [rule] *Imprinted at London by Humfrey | Lownes, for Samuel Macham, and | Matthew Cooke: and are to bee | sold in Pauls Church-yard | at the signe of the Ti- | gers head, 1605.* Hall knew Samuel Macham, whose sign later became "The Bull-Head," through his father, Thomas Macham of Ashby-de-la-Zouch, Hall's birthplace. There were editions in 1607 and 1609, all three of these early editions being single duodecimo and offering very few changes.

In 1614, 1615, 1617, and 1621, *The Art of Divine Meditation* was included in a folio of Hall's collected works entitled *A Recollection of such Treatises as have been heretofore seuerally published, and are now re-uised, corrected, augmented by Jos: Hall Dr. of Diuinity. With addition of some others not hitherto extant. London. Printed for Henry Fetherstone in Paul's Churchyard at the signe of the rose.* The revisions and corrections in the *Art* are few, but in 1614 there was one important "addition" as shown by the separate titlepage (facing p. 123) indicating "two large Patternes of Meditation." The original *Art* had only the first ex-emplum, divided among the chapters (beginning at chapter XV). Thereafter the new exemplum was added without break at the end of the treatise. The edition of *A Recollection* of 1617 first bore a new honor to Hall's name, "Deane of Worcester," a title Hall proudly took with him to represent King James at the Synod of Dort.

After the four folio *Recollections*, Hall's *Art of Divine Meditation* appeared in *The Works* of 1625 and 1628, and finally of 1634, which becomes my basic text. This book is entitled THE | WORKS |OF | JOSEPH HALL | B. of | EXCETER. [rule] | *With a Table now* | *add-ed to the same.* [rule] LONDON. | *Printed for Ph. Stephens* | *and Ch. Meredith, at the* | *Golden Lion in* | *Pauls Church-yard. 1634.* The title is enclosed in a wide decorative border, and on the opposite page is the famous portrait and the twelve-line eulogy by J. Sampson. Facing page 88 of this folio is a separate titlepage: THE | *ART OF DIVINE* | *MEDITATION:* | *Exemplified* | WITH TWO LARGE PAT-TERNS | OF MEDITATION: | *The one of eternall life, as the end;* | *The other of Death, as the way.* | [rule] | *Revised and augmented.*|[rule] | *By IOS. Hall.* |[rule] | *Imprinted at* LONDON. *1633.* The printer's device is that of the serpent entwined around an anchor and the words *Sic elevabitur Filius Hominis.* Io. 3. ANCHORA FIDEI. The reference is John 3:14: "And as Moses lifted up the serpent in the wilderness even so must the Son of man be lifted up."

Previous to this, a French translation had appeared, *L'Art de la Divine Meditation . . . mis en langue Françoise par P. G. D. Genève.* 24°, Joseph Hall and King James being the first two English writers to be translated into French.[67] An Italian translation of the *Art* followed in 1668, combined with Bishop Bayly's *The Practice of Piety*, the book entitled *La Prattica di Pietate.* There were three English editions of *The Art of Divine Meditation* in the eighteenth century (1714, 1738, and 1788); and three in the nineteenth, included in the editions of Hall's *Works* by J. Pratt, 10 vols. (London, 1808); Peter Hall, 12 vols. (Oxford and London, 1837–39); and Philip Wynter, 10 vols. (Oxford, 1863), reissued by AMS in 1969. The present text is the first reprinting of the *Art* in one hundred and eighteen years, that is, since Philip Wynter's, which has no explanatory or textual notes.

In *The Art of Divine Meditation* of 1634 I make certain changes, to be explained shortly. The copy I used is in the Rare Book Room of The University of Michigan Graduate Library.

Occasional Meditations had only three editions during the life of Bishop Hall; evidently he thought so little of the work that, failing to edit it himself, he never included it in subsequent collections of his *Works*. The first edition, in 1630, set forth by his oldest son, Robert, had only ninety-one meditations. A second 12° edition appeared in 1631: *Occasional | Meditations | By | Ios. Exon. | Set forth by R.H. | The second Edition. | London. | Printed by W.S. for |Nath. Butter. | 1631.* Nathaniel Butter, whose first book was *King Lear* in 1604, published Dekker's *The Belman of London* (1609) and the 1611 folio of Chapman's *Iliad*. He and Bishop Hall had a long association as publisher and author, but in later years Butter turned journalist, becoming so famous for a weekly sheet of news from abroad that Ben Jonson ridiculed him as the character Cymbal in *Staple of News*. The "W.S.," printer of the 1631 *Occasional Meditations*, was William Stansby, with whom young Robert Hall, on his trips to London representing his father, must have had two associations: one was that Stansby was famous for music, having acquired the rights of Thomas East, a close composer-friend of the bishop; the other was that the sign of his shop was two crossed keys, the insignia of St. Peter that appears throughout Exeter Cathedral, over which the bishop presided.

This second edition contains forty-nine extra meditations. Nathaniel Butter evidently bound them onto unsold copies of the first edition, for appended to the title of No. XCI still appears the phrase "by way of conclusion," and there are two tables, the original one at the end of the ninety-first meditation and another at the end for the additional meditations. Despite the "1631" on the titlepage, the orthography, spacing, punctuation, and catchwords of the original ninety-one are exactly those of 1630 when they first appeared.

In 1633 a third edition, also 12° and completely reset, put the whole book together: *Occasional | Meditations | By | Jos. Exon. | Set forth by R.H. | The Third Edition: | with the Addition | of 49. Meditations | not heretofore published. | London. | Printed by M.F. for |Nathaniel Butter. | 1633* (STC 12689). "M.F.," the printer Butter hired for this book, was Miles Flesher (or Fletcher) in Little Britain, a prosperous tradesman, four times Master of the Company of Stationers, and ardent communicant of St. Botolph's-without-Aldergate. "By way of conclusion" is omitted from the heading of no. XCI, and a single table for all one hundred and forty meditations comes at the end.

Because there are actually only two editions of my basic text (1633), which are, apart from these changes, substantially identical, there is no necessity for any textual notes, only explanatory ones. It was probably Robert Hall, their first editor, who translated the *Occasional Meditations* into Latin and published them in 1635 as *Josephi Halli Exoniensis Episcopi* [Gk. *Autoschediasmata*] *vel Meditatiunculae Subitanae*. This was issued again the same year with a list of *errata*. Possibly for exercise, Robert Hall translated several of his father's English sermons into Latin.

Both texts. I call mine a modernized edition, and have chosen not to follow the editorial practice of Rudolf Kirk in *Heauen vpon Earth and Characters of Vertues and Vices*. Professor Kirk reproduces the 1634 text almost exactly, following the marginal headings, italics, capitals, all punctuation and spelling, even the *u* and *i* for *v* and *j*.

It would be difficult for anyone to match Professor Kirk's scholarship, but my aim is to make as authentic a text as I can and at the same time provide for the modern reader two of Hall's works with the same clarity and charm that they held in the earlier part of the seventeenth century. To accomplish this double end of making a book that Bishop Hall would be pleased with and that a twentieth-century undergraduate can read with understanding and delight, I have made the following changes in both my texts:

Headings: These have been removed from the margin and placed as we would place headings; some of them, occurring in the same chapter, I have combined, especially if they are grammatically congruent. Other marginalia, like the long quotation of Mauburnus' "Table" in chapter XVI, I put within the text.

Biblical references: Hall has none of these in either text. Many seventeenth-century works have biblical references in the margin; I have furnished them in square brackets within my text.

Spelling: I have modernized the spelling of both texts throughout, but have not thought it necessary to record in my textual notes the occasional interchange of "thinks" and "thinketh", or "unto him" and "to him." Words like these I retain as they exist in my basic text, on the assumption that they make an intentional difference in the rhythm. All possessives are indicated with an apostrophe, and the ampersand is consistently replaced with "and."

Capitalization: Throughout both texts I follow modern practice in the use of capital letters. Though the texts are inconsistent in the capitalization of "God," I have normalized the capitalization throughout, including such pronoun references to God as "He" and "Him."

Italics: Italics appear far more numerously than is the custom today. I omit, for example, the italics for proper nouns and for emphasis of particular words. The exempla of meditation in *The Art*, originally all in italics except for biblical quotations, I print in roman, with quotation marks.

Punctuation: Although Hall was meticulous in the wording of his first editions, he apparently paid little attention to the vagaries in pointing followed by various printers of subsequent editions. There are three or four times as many commas, for example, in the 1634 edition of *The Art* than there were in 1606. I have chosen to follow the modern practice of omitting a comma that separated a brief subject from the predicate (e.g. "some hidden Cloisterers, have ingrossed it"), and of distinguishing nonrestrictive from restrictive relative clauses by double commas or their omission. For colons and semicolons I follow modern practice; 1634 makes no distinction. The same holds true for question and exclamation marks. Today these are end-stops, whereas in 1634 they are often sprinkled throughout the sentence. Since the printer, moreover, used them interchangeably, I use one for an exclamatory sentence and the other for obvious interrogation. My modernized punctuation does not interfere with the rhythm of Hall's prose, even though I have shortened many of his sentences. Often, after struggling through a long period cluttered with "points," I was amazed how clearly Hall's meaning finally emerged. I hope my reader will agree.

References: In the following two texts of Joseph Hall, I have used three kinds of superscript: a number, as is usual, denotes an explanatory footnote; a † following an unfamiliar word refers to the glossary; and an * means that there is a textual note. All are to be found at the back of the book. At first I had placed both my biblical references and the meanings of unfamiliar words in the explanatory notes. The present scheme reduces their number by more than two hundred, simplifies the apparatus, and places less strain upon the reader.

THE

ART OF DIVINE

MEDITATION:

Exemplified

WITH TWO LARGE PATTERNS

OF MEDITATIONS:

The one of eternall life, as the end;

The other of Death, as the way.

Revised and agumented.

By IOS. Hall.

Imprinted at LONDON. 1633.

To the right worshipful Sir Richard Lea,
Knight, all increase of true honor
with God and men.[1]

Sir, ever since I began to bestow myself upon the common good,
studying wherein my labors might be most serviceable, I still found
they could be no way so well improved as in that part which concerneth devotion and the practice of true piety. For on the one side, I
perceived the number of polemical books rather to breed than end
strifes; and those which are doctrinal, by reason of their multitude
rather to oppress than satisfy the reader, wherein if we write the same
things, we are judged tedious; if different,* singular. On the other
part, respecting the reader, I saw the brains of men never more
stuffed, their tongues never more stirring, their hearts never more
empty, nor their hands idle. Wherefore, after those sudden meditations[2] which passed me without rule, I was easily induced by their
success (as a small thing moves the willing) to send forth this rule of
meditation; and after my *Heaven upon Earth*, to discourse (although
by way of example) of heaven above. In this *Art* of mine I confess to
have received more light from one obscure nameless monk, which
wrote some hundred and twelve years ago, than from the directions
of all other writers. I would his humility had not made him niggardly
of his name, that we might have known whom to have thanked. It
had been easy to have framed it with more curiosity;† but God and
my soul know that I made profit the scope of my labor, and not applause; and therefore (to choose) I wished rather to be rude than unprofitable. If now the simplicity of any reader shall bereave him of the
benefit of my precepts, I know he may make use of my examples.*
Why I have honored it with your name I need not give account to

the world, which already knoweth your worth and deserts; and shall see by this that I acknowledge them. Go you on happily (according to the heavenly advice of your Junius[3]) in your worthy and glorious profession, still bearing yourself as one that knoweth virtue the truest nobility, and religion the best virtue. The God you serve shall honor you with men and crown you in heaven. To His grace I humbly commend you, requesting you only to accept the work and continue your favor to the author.

Your Worship's humbly devoted,
JOS. HALL.

The Sum of the Chapters

The Art
of Divine Meditation

The benefit and uses of Meditation,
which are universal to all Christians
and not to be appropriated to some professions.

It is not, I suppose, a more bold than profitable labor, after the
endeavors of so many contemplative men, to teach the art of meditation, an heavenly business as any belongeth either to man or Christian, and such as whereby the soul doth unspeakably benefit itself.
For by this do we ransack our deep and false hearts, find out our
secret enemies, buckle with them, expel them, arm ourselves against
their re-entrance. By this we make use of all good means, fit ourselves
to all good duties; by this we descry our weakness, obtain redress,
prevent temptations, cheer up our solitariness, temper our occasions
of delight, get more light unto our knowledge, more heat to our
affections, more life to our devotion. By this we grow to be (as we
are) strangers upon earth, and out of a right estimation of all earthly
things into a sweet fruition of invisible comforts. By this we see our
Saviour with Steven [Acts 7:35], we talk with God as Moses [Exod.
24:12], and by this we are ravished with blessed Paul into Paradise [2
Cor. 12:2–4] and see that heaven which we are loath to leave, which
we cannot utter. This alone is the remedy of security and worldliness,
the pastime of saints, the ladder of heaven, and, in short, the best improvement of Christianity. Learn it who can and neglect it who list;
he shall never find joy neither in God nor in himself which doth not
both know and practice it. And however of old some hidden
cloisterers* have engrossed it to themselves and confined it within their cells, who, indeed, professing nothing but contemplation
through their immunity from those cares which accompany an active

life, might have the best leisure to this business; yet, seeing there is no man so taken up with action as not sometimes to have a free mind, and there is no reasonable mind so simple as not to be able both to discourse somewhat and to better itself by her secret thoughts, I deem it an envious wrong to conceal that from any whose benefit may be universal. Those that have but little stock had need to know the best rules of thrift.

CHAP. II

The description and kinds of Meditation.

The rather, for that whereas our divine meditation is nothing else but a bending of the mind upon some spiritual object, through divers forms of discourse, until our thoughts come to an issue; and this must needs be either extemporal and occasioned by outward occurrences offered to the mind; or deliberate and wrought out of our own heart; which again is either in matter of knowledge, for the finding out of some hidden truth and convincing of an heresy by profound traversing of reason, or in matter of affection for the enkindling of our love of God. The former of these two last we sending to the schools and masters of controversies search after the latter, which is both of larger use and such as no Christian can reject as either unnecessary or over-difficult; for, both every Christian had need of fire put to his affection, and weaker judgments are no less capable of this divine heat, which proceeds not so much from reason as from faith.

One saith (and I believe him) that God's school is more of affection than understanding; both lessons very needful, very profitable, but for this age especially the latter; for if there be some that have much zeal, little knowledge, there are more that have much knowledge without zeal. And he that hath much skill and no affection may do good to others by information of judgment, but shall never have thank either of his own heart or of God, who useth not to cast away His love on those of whom He is but known, not loved.

Chap. III

Concerning Meditation Extemporal.

Of extemporal meditation there may be much use, no rule;
forasmuch as our conceits herein vary according to the infinite
multitude of objects and their divers manner of proffering themselves
to the mind, as also for the suddenness of this act. Man is placed in
this stage of the world to view the several natures and actions of the
creatures; to view them, not idly, without his use, as they do him.
God made all these for man and man for His own sake; both these
purposes were lost if man should let the creatures pass carelessly by
him, only seen, not thought upon. He only can make benefit of what
he sees, which, if he do not, it is all one as if he were blind or brute.
Whence it is that wise Solomon putteth the sluggard to school unto
the ant [Prov. 6:6], and our Saviour sendeth the distrustful to the lily
of the field [Matt. 6:28; Luke 12:27].

In this kind was that meditation of the divine Psalmist, which,
upon the view of the glorious frame of the heavens, was led to
wonder at the merciful respect God hath to so poor a creature as man
[Ps. 103:11]. Thus our Saviour took occasion of the water fetched up
solemnly to the altar from the well of Shilo on the day of the great
Hosannah to meditate and discourse of the water of life [John
4:7–15]. Thus holy and sweet Augustine from occasion of the water-
course near to his lodging, running among the pebbles sometimes
more silently, sometimes in a baser murmur, and sometimes in a
shriller note, entered into the thought and discourse of that execellent
order which God hath settled in all these inferior things.[4] Thus that
learned and heavenly soul of our late Estye,[5] when we sat together
and heard a sweet consort of music, seemed upon this occasion carried up for the time beforehand to the place of his rest, saying, not
without some passion, "What music may we think there is in
heaven!" Thus lastly (for who knows not that examples of this kind
are infinite?) that faithful and reverend Deering,[6] when the sun shined
on his face, now lying on his deathbed, fell into a sweet meditation of
the glory of God and his approaching joy. The thoughts of this
nature are not only lawful but so behooveful that we cannot omit

them without neglect of God, his creatures, ourselves. The creatures are half lost if we only employ them, not learn something from them. God is wronged if His creatures be unregarded; ourselves most of all if we read this great volume of the creatures and take out no lesson for our instruction.

Chap. IV

Cautions of Extemporal Meditation.

Wherein yet caution is to be had that our meditations be not either too farfetched or savoring of superstition. Farfetched I call those which have not a fair and easy resemblance unto the matter from whence they are raised; in which case our thoughts prove loose and heartless, making no memorable impression in the mind. Superstitious, when we make choice of those grounds of meditation which are forbidden us as teachers of vanity, or employ our own devices (though well-grounded) to a use above their reach; making them, upon our own pleasures, not only furtherances but parts of God's worship; in both which our meditations degenerate and grow rather perilous to the soul. Whereto add that the mind be not too much cloyed with too frequent iteration of the same thought, which at last breeds a weariness in ourselves and an unpleasantness of that conceit which at first entertainment promised much delight. Our nature is too ready to abuse familiarity in any kind; and it is with meditations as with medicines, which, with over-ordinary use lose their sovereignty and fill instead of purging. God hath not straited† us for matter, having given us the scope of the whole world; so that there is no creature, event, action, speech which may not afford us new matter of meditation. And that which we are wont to say of fine wits we may as truly affirm of the Christian heart, that it can make use of anything. Wherefore, as travelers in a foreign country make every sight a lesson, so ought we in this our pilgrimage. Thou seest the heaven rolling above thine head in a constant and unmovable motion;[7] the stars so overlooking one another that the greatest show little, the least greatest, all glorious; the air full of the bottles of rain or fleeces of snow or divers forms of fiery exhalations; the sea under one

uniform face full of strange and monstrous shapes beneath; the earth
so adorned with variety of plants that thou canst not but tread on
many at once with every foot; besides the store of creatures that fly
about it, walk upon it, live in it. Thou idle truant, dost thou learn
nothing of so many masters? Hast thou so long read these capital letters of God's great book and canst thou not yet spell one word of
them? The brute creatures see the same things with as clear, perhaps
better, eyes. If thine inward eyes see not their use as well as thy bodily eyes their shape, I know not whether is more reasonable or less
brutish.

Chap. V

Of Meditation Deliberate. Wherein first, the qualities of the person. Of whom is required: First, that he be pure from his sins.

Deliberate meditation is that we chiefly inquire for, which both
may be well guided and shall be not a little furthered by precepts; part
whereof the labors of others shall yield us, and part the plainest
mistress, experience; wherein order requires of us, first, the qualities
of the person fit for meditation; then the circumstances, manner, and
proceedings of the work.

The hill of meditation may not be climbed with a profane foot; but
as in the delivery of the Law, so here no beast may touch God's hill
lest he die; only the pure of heart have promise to see God [Matt.
5:8]. Sin dimmeth and dazzleth the eye that it cannot behold spiritual
things. The guard of heavenly soldiers was about Elisha's servant
before [2 Kings 7:8–23]; he saw them not before, through the scales
of his infidelity. The soul must therefore be purged ere it can
profitably meditate. And as of old they were wont to search for and
thrust out malefactors from the presence ere they went to sacrifice, so
must we our sins ere we offer our thoughts to God. First, saith
David, "I will wash my hands in innocency, then I will compass
Thine altar" [Ps. 26:6]. Whereupon not unfitly did that worthy
Chancellor of Paris[8] make the first stair of his ladder of contemplation
humble repentance. The cloth that is white (which is wont to be the

color of innocency) is capable of any dye; the black, of none other. Not that we require an absolute perfection (which, as it is incident to none, so if it were would exclude all need and use of meditation), but rather an honest sincerity of the heart, not willingly sinning, willingly repenting when we have sinned; which whoso finds in himself let him not think any weakness a lawful bar to meditation. He that pleads this excuse is like some simple man which, being half starved with cold,† refuseth to come near the fire because he findeth not heat enough in· himself.

Chap. VI

Secondly, that he be free from worldly thoughts.

Neither may the soul that hopeth to profit by meditation suffer itself for the time entangled with the world, which is all one as to come to God's flaming bush on the hill of visions with our shoes on our feet [Exod. 3:2–5]. Thou seest the bird whose feathers are limed† unable to take her former flight; so are we when our thoughts are clinged together by the world [unable] to soar up to our heaven in meditation. The pair of brothers must leave their nets if they will follow Christ [Matt. 4:18–19]; Elisha his oxen if he will attend a prophet [2 Kings 4:38–41]. It must be a free and a light mind that can ascend this mount of contemplation, overcoming this height, this steepness. Cares are a heavy load and uneasy; these must be laid down at the bottom of this hill if we ever look to attain the top. Thou art loaded with household cares, perhaps public; I bid thee not cast them away. Even these have their season which thou canst not omit without impiety. I bid thee lay them down at thy closet door when thou attemptest this work. Let them in with thee, thou shalt find them troublesome companions, ever distracting thee from thy best errand. Thou wouldest think of heaven, thy barn comes in thy way or perhaps thy count-book, or thy coffers, or it may be thy mind is beforehand traveling upon the morrow's journey. So, while thou thinkest of many things, thou thinkest of nothing; while thou wouldest go many ways, thou standest still. And as in a crowd while many press forward at once through one door, none proceedeth; so when variety of thoughts tumultuously throng in upon the mind, each proveth a bar to the other, and all an hindrance to him that entertains them.

CHAP. VII

*Thirdly, that he be constant and that, First,
in time and matter.* *

And as our client of meditation must both be pure and free in undertaking this task, so also constant in continuing it; constant both in time and in matter, both in a set course and hour reserved for this work, and in an unwearied prosecution of it once begun. Those that meditate by snatches and uncertain fits when only all other employments forsake them, or when good motions are thrust upon them by necessity, let them never hope to reach to any perfection. For those feeble beginnings of lukewarm grace which are wrought in them by one fit of serious meditation are soon extinguished by inter-mission, and by mis-wonting perish. This day's meal (though large and liberal) strengthens thee not for tomorrow; the body languisheth if there be not a daily supply of repast. Thus feed thy soul by medita-tion. Set thine hours and keep them, and yield not to an easy distrac-tion. There is no hardness in this practice but in the beginning; use shall give it not ease only but delight. Thy companion enter-taineth thee this while in loving discourses, or some unexpected business offers to interrupt thee. Never any good work shall want some hindrance. Either break through thy lets,†* except it be with incivility or loss; or, if they be importunate, pay thyself the time that was unseasonably borrowed, and recompence thine omitted hours with the double labor of another day. For thou shalt find that deferring breeds (beside the loss) an indisposition to good; so that what was before pleasant to thee being omitted, tomorrow grows harsh, the next day unnecessary, afterwards odious. Today thou canst, but wilt not; tomorrow thou couldst, but listest not; the next day thou neither wilt nor canst bend thy mind on these thoughts. So I have seen friends that upon neglect or* duty grow overly;† upon overliness, strange; upon strangeness, to utter defiance. Those whose

very trade is Divinity (methinks) should omit no day without their*
line of meditation. Those which are secular men, not many,
remembering that they have a common calling of Christianity to attend as well as a special vocation in the world, and that other being
more noble and important, may justly challenge† both often and
diligent service.

CHAP. VIII

Secondly, that he be constant in the continuance.

And as this constancy requires thee to keep day with thyself unless
thou wilt prove bankrupt in good exercises, so also that thy mind
should dwell upon the same thought without flitting, without
weariness, until it have attained to some issue of spiritual profit;
otherwise it attempteth much, effecteth nothing. What availeth it to
knock at the door of the heart if we depart ere we have an answer?
What are we the warmer if we pass hastily along by the hearth* and
stay not at it? Those that do only travel through Africa become not
blackamoors, but those which are born there, those that inhabit
there. We account those damosels too light of their love which
betroth themselves upon the first sight, upon the first motion; and
those we deem of much price which require long and earnest
soliciting. He deceiveth himself that thinketh grace so easily won;
there must be much suit and importunity ere it will yield to our
desires. Not that we call for a perpetuity of this labor of meditation;
human frailty could never bear so great a toil. Nothing under heaven
is capable of a continual motion without complaint. It is enough for
the glorified spirits above to be ever thinking and never weary. The
mind of man is of a strange* metal: if it be not used, it rusteth; if used
hardly, it breaketh; briefly, is sooner dulled than satisfied with a continual meditation. Whence it came to pass that those ancient monks
who intermeddled bodily labor with their contemplations proved so
excellent in this divine business, when those at this day, which, having mewed and mured themselves from the world, spend themselves
wholly upon their beads and crucifix, pretending no other work but
meditation, have cold hearts to God, and to the world show nothing
but a dull shadow of devotion. For that, if the thoughts of these latter

were as divine as they are superstitious, yet, being without all inter-
changeableness bent upon the same discourse, the mind must needs
grow weary, the thoughts remiss and languishing, the objects tedious;
while the other refreshed themselves with this wise variety, employ-
ing the hands while they called off the mind, as good comedians so
mix their parts that the pleasantness of the one may temper the
austereness of the other; wherupon they gained both enough to the
body and to the soul more than if it had been all the while busied.

Besides, the excellency of the object letteth† this assiduity of
meditation, which is so glorious that like unto the sun it may abide to
have an eye cast up to it for a while, [but] will not be gazed upon.
Whoever ventureth so far loseth both his hope and his wits. If we
hold with that blessed Monica⁹ that such like cogitations are the food
of the mind, yet even the mind also hath her satiety and may surfeit
of too much. It shall be sufficient, therefore, that we persevere in our
meditation without any such affectation of perpetuity, and leave
without a light fickleness; making always not our hourglass but some
competent increase of our devotion the measure of our continuance;
knowing that, as for heaven so for our pursuit of grace, it shall avail
us little to have begun well without perseverance; and withal that the
soul of man is not always in the like disposition but sometimes longer
in* settling through some unquietness or more obstinate distraction,
sometimes heavier, and sometimes more active and nimble to
dispatch. Gerson [*margin:* Saving our just quarrel against him for the
Council of Constance¹⁰] whose authority I rather use because our
adversaries disclaim him for theirs professeth he hath been sometimes
four hours together working his heart ere he could frame it to purpose: a singular pattern of unwearied constancy, of an unconquerable
spirit, whom his present unfitness did not so much discourage as it
whetted him to strive with himself till he could overcome. And surely
other victories are hazardous, this certain, if we will persist to strive;
other fights are upon hope, this upon assurance while our success
dependeth upon the promise of God, which cannot disappoint us
[Josh. 23:5,10]. Persist, therefore, and prevail; persist till thou hast
prevailed, so that which thou began with difficulty shall end in comfort.

Chap. IX

*Of the Circumstances of Meditation. And therein
First, of the place.*

From the qualities of the person, we descend towards the action itself, where first we meet with those circumstances which are necessary for our predisposition to the work: place, time, site of the body.

Solitariness of place is fittest for meditation. Retire thyself from others if thou wouldst talk profitably with thyself. So Jesus meditates alone in the Mount, Isaac in the fields, John Baptist in the desert, David on his bed [Ps. 4:4], Chrysostom in his bath, each in several places but all solitary. There is no place free from God, none to which He is more tied. One finds his closet most convenient, where his eyes, being limited by the known walls, call in the mind* after a sort from wandering abroad. Another findeth his soul more free when it beholdeth his heaven above and about him. It matters not so we be solitary and silent. It was a witty and divine speech of Bernard,[11] that the spouse of the soul, Christ Jesus, is bashful, neither willingly cometh to his Bride in the presence of a multitude. And hence is that sweet invitation which we find of her: "Come, my well beloved, let us go forth into the fields; let us lodge in the villages; let us go up early to the vines; let us see if the vine flourish, whether it hath disclosed the first grape, or whether the pomegranates blossom; there will I give thee my love" [Cant. 7:11–12]. Abandon, therefore, all wordly society that thou mayest change it for the company of God and His angels; the society, I say, of the world not outward only, but inward also. There be many that sequester themselves from the visible company of men which yet carry a world within them; who, being alone in body, are haunted with a throng of fancies, as Jerome, in his wildest desert, found himself too oft in his thoughts amongst the dances of the Roman dames.[12] This company is worse than the other, for it is more possible for some thoughtful men to have a solitary mind in the midst of a market than for a man thus disposed to be alone in a wilderness. Both companies are enemies to meditation; whither tendeth that ancient counsel of a great master in this art of three things requisite to this business: secrecy, silence, rest, whereof the first excludeth company, the second noise, the third motion. It cannot be spoken how subject we are in this work to distraction, like Solomon's old man whom the noise of every bird wakeneth [Eccles. 12:4]. Sensual delights we are not drawn from with the three-fold cords of judgement [Eccles. 4:12], but our spiritual pleasures are easily hindered. Make choice, therefore, of that place which shall admit the fewest occasions of withdrawing thy soul from good thoughts, wherein also even change of places is somewhat prejudicial. And I know not how it falls out that we find God nearer us in the place where we have been accustomed familiarly to meet Him; not for that His presence is confined to one place above others, but that our thoughts are through custom more easily gathered to the place where we have ordinarily conversed with Him.

Chap. X

Secondly, of the time.

One time cannot be prescribed for all, for neither is God bound to hours, neither doth the contrary disposition of men agree in one choice of opportunities. The golden hours of the morning some find fittest for meditation, when the body newly raised is well calmed with his late rest, and the soul hath not as yet had from these outward things any motives of alienation. Others find it best to learn wisdom of their reins† in the night, hoping with Job that their bed will bring them comfort in their meditation [Job 7:13] when both all other things are still and themselves, wearied with these earthly cares, do out of a contempt of them grow into greater liking and love of heavenly things. I have ever found Isaac's time fittest, who went out in the evening to meditate [Gen. 24:63]. No precept, no practice of others can prescribe to us in this circumstance. It shall be enough that first we set ourselves a time; secondly, that we set apart that time wherein we are aptest for this service. And as no time is prejudiced with unfitness but every day is without difference seasonable for this work, so especially God's day. No day is barren of grace to the searcher of it, none alike fruitful to this; which, being by God sanctified to Himself and to be sanctified by us to God, is privileged with blessings above others; for the plentiful instruction of that day stirreth thee up to this action and fills thee with matter; and the zeal of thy public service warmeth thy heart to this other business of devotion. No manna fell to the Israelites on their Sabbath [Exod. 16:23]; our spiritual manna falleth on ours most frequent. If thou wouldst have a full soul, gather as it falls, gather it by hearing, reading, meditation; spiritual idleness is a fault this day, perhaps not less than bodily work.

Chap. XI

Of the site and gesture of the body.

Neither is there less variety in the site and gesture of the body, the due composedness whereof is no little advantage to this exercise. Even in our speech to God we observe not always one and the same position: sometimes we fall groveling on our faces; sometimes we bow our knees; sometimes stand on our feet; sometimes we lift up our hands, sometimes cast down our eyes. God is a Spirit who, therefore, being a severe observer of the disposition of the soul, is not scrupulous for the body, requiring not so much that the gesture thereof should be uniform as reverent; no marvel, therefore, though in this all our teachers of meditation have commended several positions of body according to their disposition and practice: one [*margin*: Gerson], sitting with the face turned heaven-wards according to the precept of the philosopher who taught him that, by sitting and resting, the mind gathereth wisdom; another [*margin*: Gugli.Paris][13] leaning to some rest towards the left side for the greater ing of the heart; a third [*margin*: Dionys. Carthus.][14] standing with the eyes lift up to heaven but shut for fear of distractions. But of all others (methinketh) Isaac's choice the best, who meditated walking [Gen. 24:63]. In this let every man be his own master, so be we use that frame of body that may both testify reverence and in some cases help to stir up further devotion, which also must needs be varied according to the matter of meditation. If we think of our sins, Ahab's soft pace [1 Kings 16:31], the publican's dejected eyes and his hand beating his breast [Luke 19: 2] are most seasonable. If of the joys of heaven, Steven's countenance fixed above [Acts 7:55] and David's hands lift up on high [Ps. 134:2] are most fitting. In all which, the body, as it is the instrument and vassal of the soul, so will easily follow the affections thereof; and in truth then is our devotion most kindly,[15] when the body is thus commanded his service by the Spirit, and not suffered to go before it and by his forwardness to provoke his master to emulation.

CHAP. XII

Of the matter and subject of our meditation. *

Now time and order call us from these circumstances to the matter and subject of meditation, which must be divine and spiritual, not evil and worldly. Oh the carnal and unprofitable thoughts of men! We all meditate: one, how to do ill to others; another, how to do some earthly good to himself; another, to hurt himself under a color of good, as how to accomplish his lewd desires the fulfilling whereof proveth the bane of the soul, how he may sin unseen and go to hell with the least noise of the world. Or perhaps some better minds bend their thoughts upon the search of natural things; the motions of every heaven and of every star, the reason and course of the ebbing and flowing of the sea, the manifold kinds of simples† that grow out of the earth and creatures that creep upon it, with all their strange qualities and operations. Or perhaps the several forms of government and rules of state take up their busy heads; so that while they would be acquainted with the whole world, they are strangers at home, and while they seek to know all other things, they remain unknown to themselves. The God that made them, the vileness of their nature, the danger of their sins, the multitude of their imperfections, the Saviour that bought them, the heaven that He bought for them are in the meantime as unknown, as unregarded, as if they were not.

Thus do foolish children spend their time and labor in turning over leaves to look for painted babes, not at all respecting the solid matter under their hands. We fools, when will we be wise, and turning our eyes from vanity, with that sweet singer of Israel, make God's statutes our song and meditation in the house of our pilgrimage [Ps. 119:54]? Earthly things proffer themselves with importunity; heavenly things must with importunity be sued to. Those, if they were not so little worth, would not be so forward, and being forward need not any meditation to solicit them. These, by how much more hard they are to entreat, by so much more precious they are being obtained, and therefore worthier our endeavors, as then they cannot go amiss so long as we keep ourselves in the track of divinity; while the soul is taken up with the thoughts either of the Deity in His essence and Persons (sparingly yet in this point and more in faith and admiration than inquiry), or of His attributes, His justice, power, wisdom, mercy, truth; or of His works in the creation, preservation, government of all things, according to the Psalmist, "I will meditate of the beauty of Thy glorious majesty, and Thy wonderful works" [Ps. 114:15]. So most directly in our way and best fitting our exercise of meditation are those matters in divinity which can most of all work compunction in the heart and most stir us up to devotion. Of which kind are the meditations concerning Christ Jesus our Mediator, His incarnation, miracles, life, passion, burial, resurrection, ascension, intercession, the benefit of our redemption, the certainty of our election, the graces and proceeding of our sanctification, our glorious estate in Paradise lost in our first parents, our present vileness, our inclination to sin, our several actual offences, the temptations and sleights of evil angels, the use of the sacraments, the nature and practice of faith and repentance, the miseries of life with the frailty of it, the certainty and uncertainty of our death, the glory of God's saints above, the awfulness of judgment, the terrors of hell; and the rest of this quality wherein both it is fit to have variety (for that even the strongest stomach doth not always delight in one dish) and yet so to change that our choice may be free from wildness and inconstancy.

Chap. XIII

Of the order of the work itself.

Now, after that we have thus orderly suited the person and his qualities with the circumstances of time, place, disposition of the body, and substance of the matter discussed, I know not what can remain besides the main business itself and the manner and degrees of our prosecution thereof; which above all other calleth for an intentive reader and resolute practice. Wherein, that we may avoid all niceness and obscurity (since we strive to profit) we will give direction for the entrance, proceeding, conclusion of this divine work.

CHAP. XIV

*The Entrance into the work. 1. The
common entrance, which is Prayer.*

A goodly building must show some magnificence in the gate; and great personages have seemly ushers to go before them, who by their uncovered heads command reverence and way. Even very poets of old had wont before their ballads to implore the aid of their gods; and the heathen Romans entered not upon any public civil business without a solemn appreciation of good success. How much less should a Christian dare to undertake a spiritual work of such importance not having craved the assistance of his God, which (methinks) is no less than to profess he could do well without God's leave. When we think evil, it is from ourselves; when good, from God. As prayer is our speech to God, so is each good meditation (according to Bernard) God's speech to the heart.[16] The heart must speak to God that God may speak to it. Prayer, therefore, and meditation are as those famous twins in the story, or as two loving turtles,† whereof separate one, the other languisheth.[17]

Prayer maketh way for meditation; meditation giveth matter, strength, and life to our prayers, by which, as all other things are sanctified to us, so we are sanctified to all holy things. This is as some royal eunuch to perfume and dress our souls, that they may be fit to converse with the King of Heaven [Matt. 19:12].

But the prayer that leadeth in meditation would not be long, requiring, rather, that the extension and length should be put into the vigor and fervency of it; for that is not here intended to be the principal business, but an introduction to another and no otherwise than as a portal to this building of meditation. The matter whereof shall be that the course of our meditation may be guided aright and blessed, that all distractions may be avoided, our judgments enlightened, our inventions quickened, our wills rectified, our affections whetted to heavenly things, our hearts enlarged to God-ward, our devotion enkindled; so that we may find our corruptions abated, our graces thriven, our souls and lives every way bettered by this exercise.

CHAP. XV

Particular and proper entrance into the
matter, which is our choice thereof.

Such is the common entrance into this work. There is another yet more particular and proper, wherein the mind, recollecting itself, maketh choice of that theme or matter whereupon it will bestow itself for the present, settling itself on that which it hath chosen; which is done by an inward inquisition made into our heart of what we both do and should think upon, rejecting what is unexpedient and unprofitable. In both which the soul, like unto some noble hawk, lets pass the crows and larks and such other worthless birds that cross her way and stoopeth upon a fowl of price, worthy of her flight, after this manner:

"What wilt thou muse upon, O my soul? Thou seest how little it availeth thee to wander and rove about in uncertainties; thou findest how little favor there is in these earthly things wherewith thou hast wearied thyself. Trouble not thyself any longer, with Martha, about the many and needless thoughts of the world [John 11:5–12]. None but heavenly things can afford thee comfort. Up then, my soul, and mind those things that are above, whence thyself art. Amongst all which wherein shouldest thou rather meditate than of the life and glory of God's saints? A worthier employment thou canst never find than to think upon that estate thou shalt once possess and now desirest."

Chap. XVI

The proceeding of our meditation, And therein a Method allowed by some authors, rejected by us.

Hitherto the entrance, after which our meditation must proceed in due order, not troubledly, not preposterously. It begins in the understanding, endeth in the affection; it begins in the brain, descends to the heart; begins on earth, ascends to heaven, not suddenly but by certain stairs and degrees till we come to the highest.

I have found a subtle scale of meditation, admired by some professors of this art above all other human devices, and far preferred by them to the best directions of Origen, Austen, Bernard, Hugo, Bonaventure, Gerson, and whosoever hath been reputed of greatest perfection in this skill. The several stairs whereof (lest I should seem to defraud my reader through envy) I would willingly describe were it not that I feared to scare him rather with the danger of obscurity from venturing further upon this so worthy a business. Yet, lest any man perhaps might complain of an unknown loss, my margin shall find room for that which I hold too knotty for my text.

[*Margin:* The Scale of Meditation of an Author, ancient but
nameless.
Degrees of Preparation
1. Question. What I { think.
should think.
2. Excussion. A repelling of what I should not think.
3. Choice or Election. { necessary.
Of what most { expedient.
comely.
Degrees of proceeding in the understanding.
4. Commemoration. An actual thinking upon the matter elected.
5. Consideration. A redoubled commemoration of the same till
it be fully known.
6. Attention. A fixed and earnest consideration whereby it is
fastened in the mind.
7. Explanation. A clearing of the thing considered by similitudes.
8. Tractation. An extending the thing considered to other points,

where all questions of doubts are discussed.
9. Dijudication. An estimation of the worth of the thing thus
   handled.
10. Causation. A confirmation of the estimation thus made.
11. Rumination. A sad and serious meditation of all the former
    till it may work upon the affections.
    From hence to the degrees of affection.]

   In all which, after the incredible commendations of some practi-
tioners, I doubt not but an ordinary reader will easily espie a double
fault at the least, darkness and coincidence: that they are both too
obscurely delivered, and that divers of them fall into other not
without some vain superfluity. For this part, therefore, which concerneth the understanding, I had rather to require only a deep and
firm consideration of the thing propounded, which shall be done if
we follow it in our discourse through all, or the principal, of those
"places" which natural reason doth afford us; wherein let no man
plead ignorance or fear difficulty. We are all thus far born logicians;
neither is there in this so much need of skill as of industry. In which
course, yet, we may not be too curious† in a precise search of every
"place" and argument, without omission of any (though to be fetched
in with racking the invention). For, as the mind, if it go loose and
without rule, roves to no purpose, so, if it be too much fettered with
the gyves† of strict regularity, moveth nothing at all.

CHAP. XVII

*Premonitions concerning our proceeding
in the first part of Meditation.*

   Ere I enter, therefore, into any particular tractation,† there are
three things whereof I would premonish my reader concerning this
first part, which is the understanding. First, that I desire not to bind
every man to the same uniform proceeding in this part. Practice and
custom may perhaps have taught other courses more familiar and not
less direct. If, then, we can by any other method work in our hearts
so deep an apprehension of the matter meditated as it may duly stir

the affections, it is that only we require.

Secondly, that whosoever applieth himself to this direction think him not necessarily tied to the prosecution of all these logical "places" which he findeth in the sequel of our treatise, so as his meditation should be lame and imperfect without the whole number; for there are some themes will not bear all these, as when we meditate of God, there is no room for "Causes" or "Comparisons"; and others yield them with such difficulty that their search interrupteth the chief work intended. It shall be sufficient if we take the most pregnant and most voluntary.

Thirdly, that when we stick in the disposition* of any of the "places" following (as if, meditating of sin, I cannot readily meet with the "Material and Formal Causes,"[18] or the "Appendances" of it), we rack not our minds too much with the inquiry thereof, which were to strive more for logic than devotion; but without too much disturbance of our thoughts, quietly pass over to the next. If we break our teeth with the shell, we shall find small pleasure in the kernel.

Now, then, for that my only fear is lest this part of my discourse shall seem over-perplexed unto the unlearned reader, I will in this whole process second my rule with his example, that so what might seem obscure in the one may by the other be explained, and the same steps he seeth me take in this he may accordingly tread in any other theme.

CHAP. XVIII

The practice of Meditation; wherein First, we begin with some "Description" of that we meditate of.

First, therefore, it shall be expedient to consider seriously what the thing is whereof we meditate, [thus]:

"What, then, O my soul, is the life of the saints whereof thou studiest? Who are the saints but those which, having been weakly holy upon earth, are perfectly holy above; which even on earth were perfectly holy in their Saviour, now are so in themselves; which, overcoming on earth, are truly canonized in heaven? What is their life but that blessed estate above wherein their glorified soul hath a full fruition of God?"

Chap. XIX

Secondly, follows an easy and voluntary "Division" of the matter meditated.

The nature whereof, after we have thus shadowed out to ourselves by a "Description," not curious always and exactly framed according to the rules of art but sufficient for our own conceit; the next is (if it shall seem needful or if the matter will bear or offer it) some easy and voluntary "Division" whereby our thoughts shall have more room for them, and our proceeding shall be more distinct:

"There is a life of nature when thou, my soul, dwellest in this body and informest thine earthly burthen. There is a life of grace when the spirit of God dwells in thee. There is a life of glory when thy body being united to thee, both shall be united to God, or when, in the meantime being separated from thy companion, thou enjoyest God alone. This life of thine, therefore, as the other, hath his ages, hath his statures; for it entereth upon his birth when thou passest out of thy body and changest this earthly house for an heavenly. It enters into his full vigor when, at the day of the common resurrection, thou resumest this thy companion, unlike to itself, like to thee, like to thy Saviour, immortal now and glorious. In this life there* may be degrees, there can be no imperfections. If some be like the sky, others like the stars, yet all shine. If some sit at their Saviour's right hand, others at His left, all are blessed. If some vessels hold more, all are full; none complaineth of want, none envieth* him that hath more."

Chap. XX

3. A consideration of the "Causes" thereof in all kinds of them.

Which done, it shall be requisite for our perfecter understanding and for the laying grounds of matter for our affection to carry it through those other principal "places" and heads of reason which nature hath taught every man both for knowledge and amplification;

the first whereof are the "Causes," of all sorts:

"Whence is this eternal life but from Him which only is eternal, which only is the fountain of life, yea, life itself? Who but the same God that gives our temporal life giveth also that eternal? The Father bestoweth it, the Son meriteth it, the Holy Ghost seals and applieth it. Expect it only from Him, O my soul, whose free election gave thee thy first title to it, to be purchased by the blood of thy Saviour. For thou shalt not therefore be happy because He said that Thou wouldst be good, but therefore art thou good because He hath ordained thou shalt be happy. He hath ordained thee to life; He hath given thee a Saviour to give this life unto thee; faith, whereby thou mightest attain to this Saviour; His word, by which thou mightest attain to this faith. What is there in this not His? And yet not His so simply as that it is without thee; without thy merit indeed, not without thine act. Thou livest here through His blessing but by bread; thou shalt live above through His mercy but by thy faith below apprehending the Author of thy life. And yet, as He will not save thee without thy faith, so thou canst never have faith without His gift. Look up to Him, therefore, O my soul, as the beginner and finisher of thy salvation; and while thou magnifiest the Author, be ravished with the glory of the work, which far passeth both the tongues of angels and the heart of man. It can be no good thing that is not there. How can they want water that have the spring? Where God is enjoyed, in Whom only all things are good, what good can be wanting? And what perfection of bliss is there where all goodness is met and united! 'In Thy presence is fullness* of joy, and at Thy right hand are pleasures for evermore' [Ps. 16:11]. O blessed reflection of glory! We see there as we are seen. In that we are seen, it is our glory; in that we see, it is God's glory. Therefore doth He glorify us that our glory should be to His. How worthy art Thou, O Lord, that through us Thou shouldest look at Thyself!"

Chap. XXI

4. The consideration of the "Fruits and Effects."

The next "place" shall be the "Fruits and Effects" following upon their several "Causes," which also affords very feeling and copious matter to our meditation; wherein it shall be ever best not so much to seek for all as to choose out the chiefest:

"No marvel, then, if from this glory proceed unspeakable joy, and from this joy the sweet songs of praise and thanksgiving. The Spirit bids us when we are merry, sing. How much more, then, when we are merry without all mixture of sorrow, beyond all measure of our earthly affections, shall we sing joyful 'Hallelujahs' and 'Hosannahs' to Him that dwelleth in the highest heavens [Matt. 21:9]! Our hearts shall be so full that we cannot choose but sing, and we cannot but sing melodiously. There is no jar in this music, no end of this song. O blessed change of the saints! They do nothing but weep below and now nothing but sing above. We sowed in tears, reap in joy. There was some comfort in those tears when they were at worst [Ps. 126:5–6], but there is no danger of complaint in this heavenly mirth. If we cannot sing here with angels 'On earth peace,' yet there we shall sing with them, 'Glory to God on high' [Luke 2:14]; and joining our voices to theirs*, shall make up that celestial consort which none can either hear or bear part in and not be happy."

Chap. XXII

5. Consideration of the "Subject," wherein or whereabout it is.

After which comes to be considered the "Subject," either wherein it is or whereabout that is employed which we meditate of; as:

"And, indeed, what less happiness doth the very place promise wherein this glory is exhibited, which is no other than the paradise of God? Here below we dwell, or rather wander in a continued wilderness; there we shall rest us in the true Eden. 'I am come into my garden, my Sister, my Spouse' [Cant. 4:12]. Kings use not to dwell in cottages of clay but in royal courts fit for their estate. How much more shall the King of Heaven, who hath prepared so fair mansions on earth, make Himself an habitation suitable to His majesty! Even earthly princes have dwelt in cedar and ivory; but the great city, Holy Jerusalem, the palace of the Highest, hath her walls of jasper, her building of gold, her foundation of precious stones, her gates of pearl. 'How glorious things are spoken of thee, O thou City of God' [Ps. 83:3]! We see but the pavement, and yet how goodly it is! The believing centurion thought himself unworthy that Christ should come under his roof [Matt. 8:5], yet wert* Thou, O Saviour, in Thine humbled estate in the form of a servant. How then shall I think myself worthy to come under this roof of Thine so shining and glorified? O, if this clay of mine may come to this honor above, let it be trampled upon and despised on earth."

CHAP. XXIII

6. Consid. of the "Appendances and Qualities" of it.

Sixthly, shall follow the "Appendances and Qualities" which cleave unto the subject whereof we meditate, as:

"But were the place less noble and majestical, yet the company which it affordeth hath enough to make the soul more blessed.* For, not the place giveth ornament to the guest so much as the guest to the place. How loath are we to leave this earth only for the society of some few friends in whom we delight, which yet are subject every day to mutual dislikes! What pleasure shall we then take in the enjoying of the saints when there is nothing in them not amiable, nothing in us that may cool the fervor of our love! There shalt thou, my soul, thyself glorified, meet with thy dear parents and friends, alike glorious, never to be severed. There shalt thou then see and converse with those ancient worthies of the former world, the blessed patriarchs and prophets, with the crowned martyrs and confessors, with the holy apostles and the fathers of that primitive and this present church, shining each one according to the measure of his blessed labors. There shalt thou live familiarly in sight of those angels whom now thou receivest good from but seest not. There (which is the head of all thy felicity) thine eyes shall see Him whom now thy heart longeth for, that Saviour of thine, in the only hope of whom now thou livest. Alas, how dimly and afar off dost thou now behold Him! How imperfectly dost thou enjoy Him while every temptation bereaves thee for the time of His presence! 'I sought him whom my soul loveth; I sought him but found him not' [Ps. 37:36]. His back is now towards thee [Jer. 2:21] many times, through thy sins, and therefore thou hardly discernest Him. Otherwhile and often thy back is turned unto Him through negligence, that when thou mightest obscurely see Him, thou dost not. Now thou shalt see Him, and thine eyes thus fixed shall not be removed. Yet neither could this glory make us happy if, being thus absolute, it were not perpetual. To be happy is not so sweet a state as it is miserable to have been happy.[19] Lest ought, therefore, should be wanting, behold, this felicity knoweth no end, feareth no intermission, and is as eternal for the continuance as He that had no beginning. O blessedness truly infinite! Our earthly joys do scarce ever begin, but when they begin their end bordereth upon their beginning. One hour seeth us oft-times joyful and miserable; here alone is nothing but eternity. If then the divine prophet thought here one day in God's earthly house better than a thousand other-where [Ps. 84:10], what shall I compare to thousands of millions of years in God's heavenly temple? Yes, millions of years are not so much as a minute to eternity, and that other house not a cottage to this."

Chap. XXIV

7. *Of that which is "Diverse" from it or "Contrary" to it.*

Seventhly, our thoughts, leaving a while the consideration of the thing as it is in itself, shall descend unto it as respectively with others; and therefore first shall meditate of what is "Diverse" from it or "Contrary" unto it:

"What dost thou here, then, O my soul? What dost thou here groveling upon earth, where the best things are vanity, the rest no better than vexation [Eccles. 1:14]? Look round about thee and see whether thine eyes can meet with anything but either sins or miseries. Those few and short pleasures thou seest end ever sorrowfully, and in the meantime are intermingled with many grievances. Here thou hearest one cry out of a sick body, whereof there is no part which affords not choice of diseases. This man layeth his hand upon his consuming lungs and complaineth of short wind; that other, upon his rising spleen; a third shaketh his painful head; another roars out for the torment of his reinst or bladder; another for the racking of his gouty joints. One is distempered with a watery dropsy, another with a windy colic, a third with a fiery ague, a fourth with an earthen melancholy. One grovels and foameth with the falling sickness; another lies bed-rid, half senseless with a dead palsy. There are but few bodies that complain not of some disease; and, that thou mayst not look far, it is a wonder if thyself feel not always one of these evils* within thee. There thou hearest another lament his loss, either his estate is impaired by surityshipt or stealth or shipwreck or oppression; or his child is unruly or miscarried, or his wife dead or disloyal; another tormented with passions. Each one is some way miserable. But that which is yet more irksome, thy one ear is beaten with cursings and blasphemies, thy other with scornful or wanton or murthering speeches; thine eyes see nothing but pride, filthiness, profaneness, blood, excess, and whatsoever else might vex a righteous soul. And if* all the world besides were innocent,t thou findest enough within thyself to make thyself weary and thy life loathsome. Thou needest not fetch cause of complaint from others; thy corruptions yield thee too much at home: ever sinning, ever presuming, sinning even when thou hast repented, yea, even while thou repentest, sinning. Go to now, my soul, and solace thyself here below and suffer thyself besotted with these goodly contentments, worthy of no better while thou fixest thyself on these. See if thou canst find any of these above; and if thou canst meet with any distemper, any loss, any sin, any complaint from thyself or any other above, despise thine heaven as much as now thou lovest the earth. Or if all this cannot enough commend unto thee the state of heavenly glory, cast down thine eyes yet lower into that deep and bottomless pit full of horror, full of torment, where there is nothing but flames and tears and shrieks and gnashing of teeth [Matt. 8:12 etc.], nothing but fiends and tortures; where there is palpable darkness and yet perpetual fire; where the damned are ever boiling, never consumed; ever dying, never dead; ever complaining, never pitied; where the glutton that once would not give a crust of bread now begs for one drop of water [Luke 16:24]; and yet, alas, if whole rivers of water should fall into his mouth, how should they quench those rivers of brimstone that feed this flame, where there is no intermission of complaints, no breathing from pain, and after millions of years, no possibility of comfort? And if the rod wherewith Thou chastisest Thy children, O Lord, even in this life, be so smart and galling that they have been brought down to the brim of despair, and in the bitterness of their soul have entreated death to release them, what shall I think of their plagues, in whose righteous confusion thou consultest* and sayest, 'Aha, I will avenge me of mine enemies' [Isa. 1:24]? Even that thou shalt not be thus miserable, O my soul, is some kind of happiness. But that thou shalt be as happy as the reprobate are miserable, how worthy is it of more* estimation than thyself is capable of!"

CHAP. XXV

8. Of "Comparisons and Similitudes" whereby it may be most fitly set forth.

After this opposition, the mind shall make "Comparison" of the matter meditated with what may nearest resemble it; and shall illustrate it with fittest "Similitudes," which give no small light to the understanding nor less force to the affection:

"Wonder then, O my soul, as much as thou canst at this glory; and in comparison thereof contemn this earth which now thou treadest upon, whose joys, if they were perfect, are but short, and if they were long, are imperfect. One day when thou art above looking down from the height of thy glory and seeing the sons of men creeping like so many ants on this molehill of earth, thou shalt think, 'Alas, how basely I once lived! Was yonder silly dungeon the place I so loved and was so loath to leave?' Think so now before-hand; and since of heaven thou canst not, yet account of the earth as it is worthy. How heartless and irksome are ye, O ye best earthly pleasures, if ye be matched with the least of those above! How vile are you, O ye sumptuous buildings of kings, even if all the entrails of the earth had agreed to enrich you, in comparison of this frame not made with hands! It is not so high above the earth in distance of place as in worth and majesty. We may see the face of heaven from the heart of the earth, but from the nearest part of the earth who can see the least glory of heaven? The three disciples on Mount Tabor saw but a glimpse of this glory shining upon the face of their Saviour; and yet, being ravished with the sight, cried out, 'Master, it is good being here'; and, thinking of building of three tabernacles (for Christ, Moses, Elias), could have been content themselves to have lain without shelter so they might always have enjoyed that sight [Matt. 17:4]. Alas, how could earthly tabernacles have fitted those heavenly bodies? They knew what they saw; what they said they knew not. Lo, these three disciples were not transfigured; yet how deeply they were affected* even with the glory of others! How happy shall we be when ourselves shall be changed into glorious, and shall have tabernacles not of our own making but prepared for us by God, and yet not tabernacles but eternal mansions! Moses saw God but a while and shined; how shall we shine that shall behold His face for ever! What greater honor is there than* in sovereignty? What greater pleasure than in feasting? This life is both a kingdom and a feast. A kingdom: 'He that overcomes shall rule the nations, and shall sit with me in my throne' [Rev. 3:21]. O blessed promotion! O large dominion and royal seat to which Solomon's throne of ivory was not worthy to become a foot-stool [1 Kings 10:13]! A feast: 'Blessed are they that are called to the marriage-supper of the Lamb' [Rev. 19: 9]. Feasts have more than necessity of provision, more than ordinary diet; but marriage-feasts yet more than abundance. But the marriage-feast of the Son of God to His blessed Spouse the Church must so far exceed in all heavenly magnificence and variety as the persons are of the greater state and majesty. There is new wine, pure manna, and all manner of spiritual dainties; and with the continual cheer a sweet and answerable welcome, while the Bridegroom lovingly cheereth us up: 'Eat, O friends, drink and make you merry, O well beloved' [Cant. 5:1]. Yea, there shalt thou be, my soul, not a guest but (how unworthy soever) the bride herself whom He hath everlastingly espoused to Himself in truth and righteousness. The contract is passed here below the marriage is consummate above and solemnized with a perpetual feast, so that now thou mayest safely say, 'My well beloved is mine, and I am his' [Cant. 2:16]. Wherefore hearken, O my soul, and consider and incline thine ear [Ps. 116:2]. Forget also thine own people and thy father's house (thy supposed home of this world), so shall the King have pleasure in thy beauty, for He is thy Lord and worship thou Him."

Chap. XXVI

9. The "Titles and Names" of the thing considered.

The very "Names and Titles" of the matter considered yield no small store to our meditation, which * being so commonly imposed that they secretly comprehend the nature of the thing which they represent, are not unworthy of our discourse:

"What need I seek those resemblances when the very name of 'life' implieth sweetness to men on earth, even to them which confess to live with some discontentment? Surely the light is a pleasant thing, and it is good to the eyes to see the sun; yet when 'temporal' is added to 'life,' I know not how this addition detracteth something and doth greatly abate the pleasure of 'life'; for those which joy to think of 'life' grieve to think it but 'temporal,' so vexing is the end of that whose continuance was delightful. But now when there is an addition (above time) of 'eternity,' it maketh 'life' so much more sweet as it is most lasting; and lasting infinitely, what can it give less than an infinite contentment? Oh dying and false life which we enjoy here and scarce a shadow and counterfeit of that other! What is more esteemed than glory, which is so precious to men of spirit that it makes them prodigal of their blood, proud of their wounds, careless of themselves? And yet, alas, how pent and how fading is this glory, effected with such dangers and death, hardly, after all trophies and monuments, either known to the next sea or surviving him that dieth for it! It is true glory to triumph in heaven, where is neither envy nor forgetfulness.

"What is more dear to us than our 'country,' which the worthy and faithful patriots of all times have respected above their parents, their children, their lives; counting it only happy to live in it and to die for it? The banished man pines for the want of it; the traveler digesteth all the tediousness of his way, all the sorrows of an ill journey, in the only hope of 'home'; forgetting all his foreign miseries when he feeleth his own smoke. Where is our 'country' but above? Thence thou camest, O my soul, thither thou art going in a short but weary pilgrimage. O miserable men, if we account ourselves at 'home' in our pilgrimage, if in our journey we long not for 'home'! Dost thou see men so in love with their native soil that even when it is all deformed with the desolations of war and turned into rude heaps, or while it is even now flaming with the fire of civil broils, they covet yet still to live in it, preferring it to all other places of more peace and pleasure? And shalt thou, seeing nothing but peace and blessedness at home, nothing but trouble abroad, content thyself with a faint wish of thy dissolution? If heaven were thy jail, thou couldst but think of it uncomfortably. Oh what affection can be worthy of such a 'home'!"

CHAP. XXVII

10. Consid. of fit "Testimonies of Scripture" concerning our Theme.

Lastly, if we can recall any pregnant "Testimonies of Scripture" concerning our theme, those shall fitly conclude this part of our meditation. Of Scripture, for that in these matters of God none but divine authority can command assent and settle the conscience. Witness* of holy men may serve for "colors,"† but the ground must be only from God:

"There it is (saith the Spirit of God which cannot deceive thee) that 'all tears shall be wiped from our eyes, there shall be no more death, nor sorrow, nor crying, neither shall there be any more pain' [Rom. 8:18]. Yea, there shall not only be an end of sorrow but an abundant recompense for the sorrows of our life; as he that was rapt up into the third heaven[20] and there saw what cannot be spoken speaketh yet thus of what he saw: 'I count that the afflictions of this present time are not worthy of the glory which shall be showed to us' [2 Cor. 12:2–4]. It was showed unto him what should hereafter be showed unto us; and he saw that if all the world full of miseries were laid in one balance and the least glory of heaven in another, those would be incomparably light; yea (as that divine father)[21] that one day's felicity above were worth a thousand years' torment below. What then can be matched with the eternity of such joys? Oh how great therefore is Thy goodness, O Lord, which Thou hast laid up for them that fear Thee and done to them that trust in Thee before the sons of men [Ps. 31:19]!"

Chap. XXVIII

Of our second part of Meditation, which is in the affections.
Wherein is required a Taste and Relish
of what we have thought upon.

The most difficult and knotty part of meditation thus finished, there remaineth that which is both more lively and more easy unto a good heart: to be wrought altogether by the affections, which if our discourse reach not unto, they prove vain and to no purpose. That which followeth, therefore, is the very soul of meditation, whereto all that is past serveth but as an instrument. A man is a man by his understanding part, but he is a Christian by his will and affections. Seeing, therefore, that all our former labor of the brain is only to affect the heart, after that the mind hath thus traversed the point proposed through all the heads of reason, it shall endeavor to find in the first place some feeling touch and sweet relish in that which it hath thus chewed; which fruit, through the blessings of God, will voluntarily follow upon a serious meditation. David saith, "Oh taste and see how sweet the Lord is" [Ps. 24:8]. In meditation we do both see and taste, but we see before we taste. Sight is of the understanding; taste, of the affections. Neither can we see but we must taste; we cannot know aright but we must needs be affected. Let the heart, therefore, first conceive and feel itself the sweetness or bitterness of the matter meditated, which is never done without some passion, nor expressed without some hearty exclamation:

"Oh blessed estate of the saints! Oh glory not to be expressed even by those who are glorified! Oh incomprehensible salvation! What favor hath this earth to thee? Who can regard the world that believeth thee? Who can think of thee and not be ravished with wonder and desire? Who can hope for thee and not rejoice? Who can know thee and not be swallowed up with admiration at the mercy of Him that bestoweth thee? Oh blessedness worthy of Christ's blood to purchase thee, worthy of the continual songs of saints and angels to celebrate thee! How should I magnify thee! How should I long for thee! How should I hate all this world for thee!"

Chap. XXIX

Secondly, a Complaint, bewailing our wants and untowardness.

After this taste shall follow a complaint, wherein the heart bewaileth to itself his own poverty, dullness, and imperfection; chiding and abasing itself in respect of his wants and indisposition, wherein humiliation truly goeth before glory. For the more we are cast down in our conceit,† the higher shall God lift us up at the end of this exercise in spiritual rejoicing:

"But alas, where is my love? Where is my longing? Where art thou, O my soul? What heaviness hath overtaken thee? How hath the world bewitched and possessed thee, that thou art become so careless of thine home, so senseless of spiritual delights, so fond upon these vanities? Dost thou doubt whether there be a heaven, or whether thou have a God and a Saviour there? O far be from thee this atheism; far be from thee the least thought of this desperate impiety. Woe were thee if thou believedst not. But, O thou of little faith, dost thou believe there is happiness and happiness for thee and desirest it not and delightest not in it? Alas, how weak and unbelieving is thy belief! How cold and faint are thy desires! Tell me, what such goodly entertainment hast thou met withal here on earth that was worthy to withdraw thee from these heavenly joys? What pleasure in it ever gave thee contentment, or what cause of dislike findest thou above? Oh no, my soul, it is only thy miserable drowsiness, only thy security. The world, the world hath besotted thee, hath undone thee with carelessness. Alas, if thy delight be so cold, what difference is there in thee from an ignorant heathen that doubts of another life; yea, from an Epicure that denies it? Art thou a Christian or art thou none? If thou be what thou professest, away with this dull and senseless

worldliness; away with this earthly uncheerfulness; shake off at last
this profane and godless security that hath thus long weighed thee
down from mounting up to thy joys. Look up to thy God and to thy
crown and say with confidence, 'O Lord, I have waited for thy salvation' [Gen. 49:18]."

Chap. XXX

Thirdly, an hearty Wish of the soul for what it complaineth to want.

After this complaint must succeed an hearty and passionate wish of
the soul, which ariseth clearly from the two former degrees; for that
which a man hath found sweet and comfortable and complains that
he still wanteth, he cannot but wish to enjoy:

"Oh Lord, that I could wait and long for Thy salvation! Oh that I
could mind the things above, that as I am a stranger in deed, so I
could be also in affection! Oh that mine eyes, like the eyes of the first
martyr [Acts 22:20], could by the light of faith see but a glimpse of
heaven! Oh that my heart could be rapt up thither in desire! How
should I trample upon these poor vanities of the earth! How willingly
should I endure all sorrows, all torments! How scornfully should I
pass by all pleasures! How should I be in travail of my dissolution!
Oh when shall that blessed day come when, all this wretched
worldliness removed, I shall solace myself in my God? Behold, 'As the
hart brayeth for the rivers of water, so panteth my soul after Thee, O
God. My soul thirsteth for God, even for the living God. Oh when
shall I come and appear before the presence of God?' [Ps. 42:1–2]."

Chap. XXXI

4. An humble Confession of our disability to effect what we wish.

After this wishing shall follow humble confession by just order of
nature, for, having bemoaned our want and wished supply, not finding this hope in ourselves, we must needs acknowledge it to Him

of whom only we may both seek and find; where it is to be duly observed how the mind is by turns depressed and lifted up. Being lifted up with our estate of joy, it is cast down with complaint; lift up with wishes, it is cast down with confession, which order doth best hold it in ure† and just temper and maketh it more feeling of the comfort which followeth in the conclusion. This confession, must derogate all from ourselves and ascribe all to God:

"Thus I desire, O Lord, to be aright affected towards Thee and Thy glory. I desire to come to Thee, but alas, how weakly, how heartlessly! Thou knowest that I can neither come to Thee nor desire to come but from Thee. It is nature that holds me from Thee; this treacherous nature favors itself, loveth the world, hateth to think of a dissolution, and chooseth rather to dwell in this dungeon with continual sorrow and complaint than to endure a parting although to liberty and joy. Alas, Lord, it is my misery that I love my pain. How long shall these vanities thus besot me? It is Thou only that canst turn away mine eyes from regarding these follies and my heart from affecting them. Thou only, who as Thou shalt one day receive my soul in heaven, so now before-hand canst fix my soul upon heaven and Thee."

CHAP. XXXII

5. An earnest Petition for that which we confess to want.

After confession naturally follows petition, earnestly requesting at His hands that* which we acknowledge ourselves unable, and none but God able, to perform:

"Oh carry it up, therefore, Thou that hast created and redeemed it, carry it up to Thy glory. Oh let me not always be thus dull and brutish; let not these scales of earthly affection always dim and blind mine eyes. Oh Thou that layedst clay upon the blind man's eyes [John 9:6], take away this clay from mine eyes, wherewith (alas) they are so daubed up that they cannot see heaven. Illuminate them from above, and in Thy light let me see light. Oh Thou that hast prepared a place for my soul [John 14:2], prepare my soul for that place; prepare it with holiness, prepare it with desire; and even while it sojourneth on earth let it dwell in heaven with Thee, beholding ever the beauty of Thy face, the glory of Thy saints and of itself."

Chap. XXXIII

6. A vehement Enforcement of our petition.

After petition shall follow the enforcement of our request, from argument and importunate obsecration, wherein we must take heed of complementing in terms with God, as knowing that He will not be mocked by any fashionable form of suit but requireth holy and feeling entreaty:

"How graciously hast Thou proclaimed to the world that whoever wants wisdom shall ask it of Thee [James 1:5], which neither deniest nor upbraidest! O Lord, I want heavenly wisdom to conceive aright of heaven; I want it and ask it of Thee. Give me to ask it instantly and give me, according to Thy promise [John 10:10], abundantly. Thou seest it is no strange favor I beg of Thee, no other than that which Thou hast richly bestowed upon all Thy valiant martyrs, confessors, servants from the beginning, who never could have so cheerfully embraced death and torment if through the midst of their flames and pain they had not seen their crown of glory. The poor thief on the cross had no sooner craved Thy remembrance when Thou camest to Thy kingdom, than Thou promisedst to take him with Thee into heaven [Luke 23:42–43]. Presence was better to him than remembrance. Behold, now Thou art in Thy kingdom, I am on earth, remember Thine unworthy servant and let my soul, in conceit, in affection, in conversation, be this day and forever with Thee in paradise. I see man walketh in a vain shadow and disquieteth himself in vain; they are pitiful pleasures he enjoyeth while he forgetteth Thee. I am as vain, make me more wise. Oh let me see heaven and I know I shall never envy nor follow them. My times are in Thine hands; I am no better than my fathers [1 Kings 19:4], a stranger on earth. As I speak of them, so the next, yea, this generation shall speak of me as one that was. My life is a bubble, a smoke, a shadow, a thought; I know it hath no abiding in this thoroughfare. Oh suffer me not so mad as while I pass on the way I should forget the end. It is that other life that I must trust to. With Thee it is that I shall continue. Oh let me not be so foolish as to settle myself on what I must leave and to neglect eternity. I have seen enough of this earth, and yet I love it too much. Oh let me see heaven another while and love it so much more than the earth by how much the things there are more worthy to be loved. Oh God, look down on Thy wretched pilgrim, and teach me to look up to Thee and to see Thy goodness in the land of the living. Thou that boughtest heaven for me, guide me thither; and for the price that it cost Thee, for Thy mercy's sake in spite of all temptations, enlighten my soul, direct it, crown it."

CHAP. XXXIV

7. *A cheerful Confidence of obtaining what we have requested and enforced.*

After this enforcement doth follow confidence, wherein the soul, after many doubtful and unquiet bickerings, gathereth up forces and cheerfully rouzeth up itself, and like one of David's worthies breaketh through a whole army of doubts and fetcheth comfort from the well of life [Prov. 10:11], which, though in some later yet in all, is a sure reward from God of sincere meditation:

"Yea, be thou bold, O my soul, and do not merely crave but challenge this favor of God as that which He oweth thee. He oweth it thee because He hath promised it, and by His mercy hath made His gift His debt: 'Faithful is he that hath promised, which will also do' [Heb. 10:23]. Hath He not given thee not only His hand in the sweet hopes of the Gospel but His seal also in the sacraments? Yet, besides promise, hand, seal, hath He not given thee a sure earnest† of thy salvation in some weak but true graces? Yet more, hath He not given thee, besides earnest, possession while He that is the Truth and Life saith, 'He that believeth hath everlasting life and hath passed from death to life' [John 5:24]? Canst thou not, then, be content to cast thyself upon this blessed issue: if God be merciful, I am glorious? I have thee already, O my life; God is faithful and I do believe. Who shall separate me from the love of Christ [Rom. 8:35], from my glory with Christ? Who shall pull me out of my heaven? Go to, then, and return to thy rest, O my soul, make use of that heaven wherein thou art and be happy."

Thus we have found that our meditation like the wind gathereth strength in proceeding; and as natural bodies, the nearer they come to their places, move with more celerity, so doth the soul in this course of meditation, to the unspeakable benefit of itself.

CHAP. XXXV

The Conclusion of our Meditation, in what order it must be.
First, with Thanksgiving.

The conclusion remaineth, wherein we must advise (like as physicians do in their sweats and exercise) that we cease not over-suddenly but leave off by little and little. The mind may not be suffered to fall headlong from this height, but must also descend by degrees.

The first whereof, after our confidence, shall be an hearty gratulation and thanksgiving. For, as man naturally cannot be miserable but he must complain and crave remedy, so the good heart cannot find itself happy and not be thankful; and this thankfulness which it feeleth and expresseth maketh it yet more good and affecteth it more:

"What shall I then do to Thee for this mercy, O Thou Saviour of men? What should I render to my Lord for all his benefits? Alas, what can I give Thee which is not Thine own before? Oh that I could give Thee but all Thine! Thou givest me to drink of this cup of salvation; I will therefore take the cup of salvation and call upon the name of the Lord [Ps. 116:12, 13]: 'Praise thou the Lord, O my soul, and all that is within me praise His holy name' [Ps. 103:1]. And since here thou beginnest thine heaven, begin here that joyful song of thanksgiving which there thou shalt sing more sweetly and never end."

CHAP. XXXVI

Secondly, with Recommendation of our souls and ways to God.

After this thanksgiving shall follow a faithful recommendation of ourselves to God, wherein the soul doth cheerfully give up itself and repose itself wholly upon her Maker and Redeemer, committing herself to Him in all her ways, submitting herself to Him in all His ways, desiring* in all things to glorify Him and to walk worthy of her high and glorious calling.

Both which latter shall be done (as I have ever found) with much life and comfort if, for the full conclusion, we shall lift up our heart and voice to God in singing some versicle of David's divine Psalms answerable to our disposition and matter, whereby the heart closes up itself with much sweetness and contentment.

This course of meditation thus heartily observed, let him that practiceth it tell me whether he find not that his soul, which at the beginning of this exercise did but creep and grovel upon earth, do not now in the conclusion soar aloft in heaven and, being before aloof off, do not now find itself near to God, yea, with Him and in Him.

CHAP. XXXVII

An Epilogue. Reproving the neglect of Meditation. Exhorting to the use of Meditation.

Thus have I endeavored (Right Worshipful Sir), according to my slender faculty, to prescribe a method of meditation, not upon so strict terms of necessity that whosoever goeth not my way erreth. Divers paths lead oft-times to the same end, and every man aboundeth in his own sense. If experience and custom hath made another form familiar to any man, I forbid it not; as that learned father said of his translation, 'Let him use his own, not contemn mine,'[22] If any man be to choose and begin, let him practice mine till he meet with a better master; if another course may be better, I am sure this is good. Neither is it to be suffered that, like as fantastical† men while they doubt what fashioned suit they should wear put on nothing, so we Christians* should neglect the matter of this worthy business while we nicely stand upon the form thereof. Wherein give me leave to complain with just sorrow and shame that if there be any Christian duty whose omission is notoriously shameful and prejudicial to the souls of professors,† it is this of meditation. This is the very end God hath given us our souls for; we misspend them if we use them not thus. How lamentable is it that we so employ them as if our faculty of discourse served for nothing but our earthly provision, as if our reasonable and Christian minds were appointed for the slaves and drudges of this body, only to be the caters† and cooks of our appetite!

The world filleth us, yea, cloyeth us. We find ourselves work enough to think, "What have I yet? How may I get more? What must I lay out? What shall I leave for posterity? How may I prevent the wrong of my adversary? How may I return it? What answers shall I make to such allegations? What entertainment shall I give to such friends? What courses shall I take in such suits? In what pastimes shall I spend this day? In what the next? What advantage shall I reap by this practice, what loss? What was said, answered, replied, done, followed?"

Goodly thoughts and fit for spiritual minds? Say there were no other world, how could we spend our cares otherwise? Unto this neglect let me ascribe the commonness of that Laodicean† temper of men, or (if that be worse) of the dead coldness which hath stricken the hearts of many, having left them nothing but the bodies of man and visors of Christians, to this only: THEY HAVE NOT MEDITATED. It is not more impossible to live without an heart than to be devout without meditation. Would God, therefore, my words would be in this, as the wise man saith the words of the wise are [Eccles. 13:11], like unto goads in the sides of every reader to quicken him up out of this full and lazy security to a cheerful practice of this divine meditation. Let him curse me upon his death-bed if, looking back from thence to the bestowing of his former times, he acknowledge not these hours placed the most happily in his whole life, if he then wish not he had worn out more days in so profitable and heavenly a work.*

*   *   *   *   *   *

A Meditation of Death:
According to the Former Rules.

[I.] The Entrance.

"And now, my soul, that thou hast thought of the end, what can fit thee better than to think of the way? And though the forepart of the way to heaven be a good life, the latter and more immediate is death. Shall I call it the way or the gate of life? Sure I am that by it only we pass into that blessedness whereof we have so thought that we have found it cannot be thought of enough.

[II.] The Description.

"What then is this death but the taking down of these sticks whereof this earthly tent is composed; the separation of two great and old friends till they meet again; the jail-delivery of a long prisoner; our journey into that other world for which we and this thoroughfare were made; our payment of our first debt to nature; the sleep of the body and the awaking of the soul?

[III.] The Division.

"But lest thou shouldest seem to flatter him whose name and face hath ever seemed terrible to others, remember that there are more deaths than one. If the first death be not so fearful as he is made (his horror lying more in the conceit† of the beholder than in his own aspect), surely the second is not made so fearful as he is. No living eye can behold the terrors thereof; it is as impossible to see them as to feel them and live. Nothing but a name is common to both. The first hath men, casualties, diseases for his executioners; the second, evils. The power of the first is the grave; the second, in hell. The worst of the first is senselessness, the easiest of the second is a perpetual sense of all the pain that can make a man exquisitely miserable.

[IV.] The Causes.

"Thou shalt have no business, O my soul, with the second death; thy first resurrection hath secured thee. Thank Him that hath redeemed thee for thy safety. And how can I thank Thee enough, O

my Saviour, which hast so mercifully bought off my torment with
Thy own, and hast drunk off that bitter potion of Thy Father's wrath
whereof the very taste had been our death? Yea, such is Thy mercy,
O thou Redeemer of men, that Thou hast not only subdued the second death but reconciled the first, so as Thy children taste not all of
the second and find the first so sweetened to them by Thee that they
complain not* of bitterness. It was not Thou, O God, that madest
death; our hands are they that were guilty of this evil. Thou sawest all
Thy work that it was good; we brought forth sin, and sin brought
forth death. To the discharge of Thy justice and mercy we
acknowledge this miserable conception, and needs must that child be
ugly that hath such parents. Certainly, if being and good be (as they
are) of an equal extent, then the dissolution of our being must needs
in itself be evil. How full of darkness and horror, then, is the privation of this vital light, especially since Thy wisdom intended it to the
revenge of sin, which is no less than the violation of an infinite justice.
It was Thy just pleasure to plague us with this brood of our own
begetting. Behold, that death which was not till then in the world is
now in everything: one great conqueror finds it in a slate, another
finds it in a fly; one finds it in the kernel of a grape, another in the
prick of a thorn; one in the taste of an herb, another in the smell of a
flower; one in a bit of meat, another in a mouthful of air; one in the
very sight of a danger, another in the conceit of what might have
been. Nothing in all our life is too little to hide death under it. There
need no cords, nor knives, nor swords, nor pieces†; we have made
ourselves as many ways to death as there are helps of living.

"But if we were the authors of our death, it was Thou that didst
alter it; our disobedience made it, and Thy mercy made it not to be
evil. It had been all one to Thee to have taken away the very being of
death from Thine own; but Thou thoughtest it best to take away the
sting of it only, as good physicians, when they would apply their
leeches, scour them with salt and nettles, and when their corrupt
blood is voided, employ them to the health of the patient. It is more
glory to Thee that Thou hast removed enmity from this Esau [Gen.
33:4] that now he meets us with kisses instead of frowns; and if we
receive a blow from this rough hand [Gen. 32:11], yet that very
stripe is healing. Oh how much more powerful is Thy death than our

sin! O my Saviour, how hast Thou perfumed and softened this bed of my grave by dying! How can it grieve me to tread in Thy steps to glory?

[V.] The Effects.

"Our sin made death our last enemy; Thy goodness hath made it the first friend that we meet with in our passage to another world. For, as she that receives us from the knees of our mother in our first entrance to the light washeth, cleanseth, dresseth us and presents us to the breast of our nurse or the arms of our mother challenges some interest in us when we come to our growth; so death (which in our passage to that other life is the first that receives and presents our naked soul to the hands of those angels which carry it up to her glory) cannot but think this office friendly and meritorious. What if this guide lead my carcass through corruption and rottenness, when my soul in the very instant of her separation know itself happy? What if my friends mourn about my bed and coffin, when my soul sees the smiling face and loving embracements of Him that was dead and is alive? What care I who shut these earthen eyes, when death opens the eyes of my soul to see as I am seen? What if my name be forgotten of men, when I live above with the God of Spirits?

[VI.] The Subject.

"If death would be still an enemy, it is the worst part of me that he hath anything to do withal; the best is above his reach and gains more than the other can lose. The worst piece of the horror of death is the grave, and set aside infidelity, what so great misery is this? That part which is corrupted feels it not; that part which is free from corruption feels an abundant recompense and foresees a joyful reparation. What is here but a just restitution? We carry heaven and earth wrapt up in our bosoms; each part returns homeward. And if the exceeding glory of heaven cannot countervail the dolesomeness of the grave, what do I believing? But if the beauty of that celestial sanctuary do more than equalize the horror of the bottomless pit, how can I shrink at earth like myself when I know my glory? And if examples can move thee any whit, look behind thee, O my soul, and see which of the worthies of that ancient latter world, which of the patriarchs, kings, prophets, apostles have not trod in these red steps. Where are those millions of generations which have hitherto peopled the earth? How many passing-bells hast thou heard for thy known friends? How many sick beds hast thou visited? How many eyes hast thou seen closed? How many vain men hast thou seen that have gone into the field to seek death in hope to find an honor as foolish as themselves? How many poor creatures hast thou mulcted† with death for thine own pleasure? And canst thou hope that God will make a byway and a postern for thee alone that thou mayst pass to the next world not by the gates of death, not by the bottom of the grave?

[VII.] The Adjunct.

"What then dost thou fear, O my soul? There are but two stages of death, the bed and the grave. This latter, if it have senselessness, yet it hath rest. The former, if it have pain, yet it hath speediness, and when it lights upon a faithful heart, meets with many and strong antidotes of comfort. The evil that is ever in motion is not fearful. That which both time and eternity find standing where it was is worthy of terror. Well may those tremble at death which find more distress within than without, whose consciences are more sick and nearer to death than their bodies. It was Thy Father's wrath that did so terrify Thy soul, O my Saviour, that it put Thy body into a bloody sweat. The mention and thought of Thy death ended in a Psalm [Matt. 27:46; Ps. 22:1], but this began in an agony. Then didst Thou sweat out my fears. The power of that agony doth more comfort all Thine than the angels could comfort Thee. That very voice deserved an eternal separation of horror from death where Thou saidst, 'My God, my God, why hast thou forsaken me?' Thou hadst not complained of being left if Thou wouldst have any of Thine left destitute of comfort in their parting. I know not whom I can fear while I know Whom I have believed. How can I be discouraged with the sight of my loss when I see so clear an advantage?

[VIII.] The Contrary.

"What discomfort is this, to leave a frail body to be joined unto a glorious head; to forsake vain pleasures, false honors, bootless hopes, unsatisfying wealth, stormy contentments, sinful men, perilous temptations, a sea of troubles, a galley of servitude, an evil world, and a consuming life, for freedom, rest, happiness, eternity? And if thou wert sentenced, O my soul, to live a thousand years in this body with these infirmities, how wouldst thou be weary, not of being only, but of complaining! Whiles, ere the first hundred, I should be a child; ere the second, a beast; a stone ere the third; and therefore should be so far from finding pleasure in my continuance that I should not have sense enough left to feel myself miserable. And when I am once gone, what difference is there betwixt the agedst of the first patriarchs and me, and the child that did but live to be born, save only in what was and that which was is not? And if this body had no weakness to make my life tedious, yet what a torment is it that while I live I must sin! Alas, my soul, every one of thy known sins is not a disease but a death. What an enemy art thou to thyself if thou canst not be content that one bodily death should excuse thee from many spiritual; to cast off thy body that thou mayest be stripped of the rags, yea, the fetters of thy sin, and clothed with the robes of glory! Yet these terms are too hard. Thou shalt not be cast off, O my body; rather, thou shalt be put to making. This change is no less happy for thee than for thy partner. This very skin of thine, which is now tawny and wrinkled, shall once more shine; this earth shall be heaven, this dust shall be glorious. These eyes, that are now weary of being witnesses of thy sins and miseries, shall then never be weary of seeing the beauty of the Saviour and thine own in His. These ears, that have been now tormented with the impious tongues of men, shall first hear the voice of the Son of God, and then the voices of saints and angels in their songs of 'Allelujah.' And this tongue, that now complains of miseries and fears, shall then bear a part in that divine harmony.

[IX.] The Comparisons.

"In the meantime thou shalt but sleep in this bed of earth; he that hath tried the worst of death hath called it no worse. Very heathens have termed them cousins, and it is no unusual thing for cousins of blood to carry both the same names and features. Hast thou wont, O my body, when the day hath wearied thee, to lie down unwillingly to thy rest? Behold in this sleep is more quietness, more pleasure of visions, more certainty of waking, more cheerfulness in rising. Why, then, are thou loath to think of laying off thy rags and reposing thyself? Why art thou like a child unwilling to go to bed? Hast thou ever seen any bird which, when the cage hath been opened, would rather sit still and sing within her grates than fly forth unto her freedom in the woods? Hast thou ever seen any prisoner in love with his bolts and fetters? Did the chief of the apostles, when the angel of God shined in his jail and struck him on the side and loosed his two chains and bade him arise quickly and opened both the wooden and iron gate, say, 'What? So soon? Yet a little sleep!' [Acts 12:6–7]? What madness had it been rather to slumber betwixt his two keepers than to follow the angel of God into liberty! Hast thou ever seen any mariner that hath saluted the sea with songs and the haven with tears? What shall I say to this diffidence, O my soul, that thou art unwilling to think of rest after thy toil, of freedom after thy durance, of thy haven after an unquiet and tempestuous passage? How many are there that seek death and cannot find it, merely out of the irksomeness of life? Hath it found thee and offered thee better conditions, not of immunity from evils but of possession of more good than thou canst think, and wouldest thou now fly from happiness to be rid of it?

[X.] The Names.

"What, is it a name that troubles thee? What if men would call sleep 'death,' wouldst thou be afraid to close thine eyes? What hurt is it, then, if He that sent the first sleep upon man while He made him an helper [Gen. 2:21], send this last and soundest sleep unto me, while he prepares my soul for a glorious spouse to Himself? It is but a parting which we call 'death,' as two friends, when they have led each other on the way, shake hands till they return from their journey. If either should miscarry, there were cause of sorrow; now they are more sure of a meeting than of a parture. What folly is it not to be content to redeem the unspeakable gain of so dear a friend with a little intermission of enjoying him? He will return laden with the riches of heaven and will fetch his old partner to the participation of this glorious wealth. Go, then, my soul, to this sure and gainful traffic, and leave my other half in an harbor as safe though not so blessed; yet so shalt thou be separated that my very dust shall be united to Thee still and to my Saviour in Thee.

[XI.] The Testimonies.

"Wert thou unwilling at the command of thy Creator to join thyself at the first with this body of mine? Why art thou then so loath to part with that which thou hast found, though entire, yet troublesome? Dost thou not hear Solomon say, 'The day of death is better than the day of thy birth' [Eccles. 7:1]? Dost thou not believe him, or art thou in love with the worse and displeased with the better? If any man could have found a life worthy to be preferred to death, so great a king must needs have done it; now, in his very throne, he commands his coffin. Yea, what wilt thou say to those heathens that have mourned at the birth and feasted at the death of their children? They knew the miseries of living as well as thou; the happiness of dying they could not know. And if they rejoiced out of a conceit of ceasing to be miserable, how shouldest thou cheer thyself in an expectation, yea, an assurance, of being happy! He that is the Lord of Life and tried what it was to die hath proclaimed them blessed that die in the Lord; those are blessed, I know, that live in Him, but they rest not from their labors [Rev. 14:13]. Toil and sorrow is between them and a perfect enjoying of that blessedness which they now possess only in hope and inchoation.† When death hath added rest, their happiness is finished.

[XII.] The Taste of our Meditation.

"O death, how sweet is that rest wherewith thou refreshest the weary pilgrims of this vale of mortality! How pleasant is thy face to those eyes that have acquainted themselves with the sight of it which to strangers is grim and ghastly! How worthy art thou to be welcome unto those that know whence thou art and whither thou tendest! Who that knows thee can fear thee? Who that is not all nature would rather hide himself amongst the baggage of this vile life than follow thee to a crown? What indifferent judge (that should see life painted over with vain semblances of pleasures, attended with troops of sorrows on the one side and on the other with uncertainty of continuance and certainty of dissolution, and then should turn his eyes unto death and see her black but comely [Cant. 1:5], attended on the one hand with a momentary pain, with eternity of glory on the other) would not say out of choice that which the prophet said out of passion, 'It is better for me to die than to live' [Jonah 4:3]?

[XIII.] The Complaint.

"But, O my soul, what ails thee to be thus suddenly backward and fearful? No heart hath more freely discoursed of death in speculation; no tongue hath more extolled it in absence. And now that it is come to thy bed's side, and hath drawn thy curtains, and takes thee by the hand, and offers thee service, thou shrinkest inward and, by the paleness of thy face and wildness of thine eye, betrayest an amazement at the presence of such a guest. That face which was so familiar to thy thoughts is now unwelcome to thine eyes. I am ashamed of this weak irresolution. Whitherto have tended all thy curious† meditations? What hath Christianity done to thee if thy fears be still heathenish? Is this thine imitation of so many worthy saints of God whom thou hast seen entertain the violentest deaths with smiles and songs? Is this the fruit of thy long and frequent instruction? Didst thou think death would have been content with words? Didst thou hope it would suffice thee to talk while all other suffer? Where is thy faith? Yea, where art thou thyself, O my soul? Is heaven worthy of no more thanks, no more joy? Shall heretics, shall pagans give death a better welcome than thou? Hath thy Maker, thy Redeemer sent for thee, and art thou loath to go? Hath He sent for thee to put thee in possession of that glorious inheritance which thy wardship hath cheerfully expected, and art thou loath to go? Hath God with this sergeant of His sent his angels to fetch thee, and art thou loath to go? Rouse up thyself, for shame, O my soul, and if ever thou hast truly believed, shake off this un-Christian diffidence and address thyself joyfully for thy glory.

[XIV.] The Wish.

"Yea, O my Lord, it is Thou that must raise up this faint and drooping heart of mine. Thou only canst rid me of this weak and cowardly distrust. Thou that sendest for my soul canst prepare it for Thyself; Thou only canst make Thy messenger welcome to me. Oh that I could but see Thy face through death! Oh that I could see death not as it was but as Thou hast made it! Oh that I could heartily pledge Thee, my Saviour, in this cup, that so I might drink new wine with Thee in Thy Father's kingdom!

[XV.] The Confession

"But alas, O my God, nature is strong and weak in me at once. I cannot wish to welcome death as it is worthy; when I look for most courage, I find strongest temptations. I see and confess that when I am myself, Thou hast no such coward as I. Let me alone and I shall shame that name of Thine which I have professed. Every secure worldling shall laugh at my feebleness. O God, were Thy martyrs thus hailed to their stakes? Might they not have been loosed from their racks but* chose to die in those torments? Let it be no shame for Thy servant to take up that complaint which Thou mad'st of Thy better attendants, 'The spirit is willing but the flesh is weak' [Matt. 26:41].

[XVI.] The Petition and Enforcement.

"O Thou God of spirits that hast coupled these two together, unite them in a desire of their dissolution; weaken this flesh to receive and encourage this spirit either to desire or to contemn death. And now as I grow nearer to my home, let me increase in the sense of my joys. I am Thine, save me, O Lord. It was Thou that didst put such courage into Thine ancient and late witnesses that they either invited or challenged death, and held their persecutors their best friends for letting them loose from these gyves of flesh. I know Thine hand is not shortened, neither any of them hath received more proofs of Thy former mercies. Oh let Thy goodness enable me to reach them in the comfortable steadiness of my passage. Do but draw this veil a little that I may see my glory, and I cannot but be inflamed with the desire of it. It was not I that either made this body for the earth or this soul for my body or this heaven for my soul or this glory of heaven or this entrance into glory. All is Thine own work. Oh perfect what Thou hast begun, that Thy praise and my happiness may be consummate at once.

[XVII.] The Assurance or Confidence.

"Yea, O my soul, what need'st thou wish the God of mercies to be tender of His own honor? Art thou not a member of that body whereof thy Saviour is the head? Canst thou drown when thy head is above? Was it not for thee that He triumphed over death? Is there any fear in a foiled adversary? Oh my Redeemer, I have already over-come in Thee, how can I miscarry in myself? Oh my soul, thou hast marched valiantly. Behold, the damosels of that heavenly Jerusalem come forth with timbrels and harps to meet thee [Ps. 68:25] and ap-plaud thy success. And now there remains nothing for thee but a crown of righteousness, which that righteous Judge shall give thee at that day. 'O death, where is thy sting? O grave, where is thy victory' [1 Cor. 15:55]?

[XVIII.] The Thanksgiving.

"Return now unto thy rest, O my soul, for the Lord hath been beneficial unto thee. O Lord God, the strength of my salvation, Thou hast covered my head in the day of battle [Ps. 140:7]. O my God and King, I will extol Thee and will bless Thy name for ever and ever [Ps. 165:1]. I will bless Thee daily and praise Thy name for ever and ever [Ps. 114:1]. Great is the Lord and most worthy to be praised, and His greatness is incomprehensible. I will meditate of the beauty of Thy glorious majesty and Thy wonderful works [Ps. 165:5]. Hosan-nah, Thou that dwellest in the highest heavens!"

Amen.

Occasional
Meditations

By
Jos. Exon.

Set forth by R. H.
The Third Edition:
with the Addition
of 49. Meditations not heretofore published.
Printed by M. F. for
Nathaniel Butter.
1633.

The Dedicatory Epistle

to

THE RIGHT HONORABLE

My very good Lord

JAMES

Lord Viscount

DONCASTER.

Right Hon:

Finding these papers amongst others lying aside in my Father's study, whereof I conceived good use might be made in regard of that spiritual advantage which they promised, I obtained of his good leave to send them abroad, whereto he professed himself the more easily induced for that continual and weighty employments in this large and and busy diocese will not yet afford him leisure to dispatch those his other fixed meditations on the story of the New Testament. In the meantime, the expressions of these voluntary and sudden thoughts of his shall testify how fruitfully he is wont to improve those short ends of time which are stolen from his more important avocations; and unless my hopes fail me the pattern of them may prove not a little beneficial to others. Holy minds have been ever wont to look through these bodily objects at spiritual and heavenly. So Sulpitius[1] reports of St. Martin that, seeing a sheep newly shorn, he could say, "Lo, here's one that hath performed that command in the Gospel: having two coats she hath given away one"; and, seeing an hog-herd freezing in a thin suit of skins, "Lo," said he, "there's Adam cast out of Paradise"; and seeing a meadow part rooted up, part whole but eaten down, and part flourishing, he said, "The first was the state of fornication, the second of marriage, the third virginity." But what do I seek any other author than the Lord of Life Himself, who, upon the drawing of water from the well of Shilo on the day of the great "Hosannah," took occasion to speak of those living waters which should flow from every believer, *John* 7. 37; and upon occasion of a bodily feast, *Luke* 14, entered into that divine discourse of God's gracious invitation of us to those spiritual viands of grace and glory? Thus, methinks, we should still be climbing up in our thoughts from earth to heaven, and suffer no object to cross us in our way without some spiritual use and application. Thus it pleased my Reverend Father sometimes to recreate himself, whose manner hath been, when any of these meditations have unsought offered themselves unto him, presently to set them down, a course which I wish had been also taken in many more which might no doubt have been very profitable.

These, as they are, I send forth under your honorable name out of those many respects which are in an hereditary right due to your Lordship, as being apparent heir to those two singular patrons of my justly reverenced Father, the eminent virtue of which your noble parents in a gracious succession yields to your Lordship an happy example, which to follow is the only way to true honor, for the daily increase whereof here and the everlasting crown of it hereafter his prayers to God shall not be wanting, who desires to be accounted

Your Lordship's devoted
in all humble observance
Ro. Hall.

Occasional Meditations

THE PROEM

I have heedlessly lost, I confess, many good thoughts. These few my paper hath preserved from vanishing, the example whereof may perhaps be more useful than the matter. Our active souls can no more forbear to think than the eye can choose but to see when it is open; would we but keep our wholesome notions together, mankind would be too rich. To do well, no object should pass us without use. Everything that we see reads us new lectures of wisdom and piety. It is a shame for a man to be ignorant or Godless under so many tutors. For me, I would not wish to live longer than I shall be better for my eyes, and have thought it thankworthy thus to teach weak minds how to improve their thoughts upon all like occasions. And if ever these lines shall come to the public view, I desire and charge my reader, whosoever he be, to make me and himself so happy as to take out my lesson and to learn how to read God's great book by mine.

I

Upon the Sight of the Heavens moving

I can see nothing stand still but the earth; all other things are in motion. Even the water which makes up one globe with the earth is ever stirring in ebbs and flowings; the clouds over my head, the heavens above the clouds, these, as they are most conspicuous, so are they the greatest patterns of perpetual action. What should we rather imitate than this glorious frame? O God, when we pray that Thy will may be done in earth as it is in heaven, though we mean chiefly the inhabitants of that place, yet we do not exclude the very place of those blessed inhabitants from being an example of our obedience. The motion of this Thy heaven is perpetual, so let me ever be acting somewhat of Thy will. The motion of Thine heaven is regular, never swerving from the due points; so let me ever walk steadily in the ways of Thy will, without all diversions or variations from the line of

Thy Law. In the motion of Thine heaven, though some stars have their own peculiar and contrary courses, yet all yield themselves to the sway of the main circumvolution of that First Mover. So, though I have a will of mine own, yet let me give myself over to be ruled and ordered by Thy spirit in all my ways.

Man is a little world: my soul is heaven, my body is earth. If this earth be dull and fixed, yet O God, let my heaven like unto Thine move perpetually, regularly, and in a constant subjection to Thine Holy Ghost.

II

Upon the Sight of a Dial

If the sun did not shine upon this dial, nobody would look at it; in a cloudy day it stnads like a useless post, unheeded, unregarded. But when one of those beams breaks forth, every passenger† Runs to it and gazes on it. O God, while Thou hidest Thy countenance from me, methinks all thy creatures pass by me with a willing neglect. Indeed, what am I without Thee? And if Thou have drawn in me some lines and notes of able endowments, yet, if I be not actuated by Thy grace, all is in respect of use no better than nothing. But when Thou renewest the light of Thy loving countenance upon me, I find a sensible† and happy change of condition: methinks all things look upon me with such cheer and observance as if they meant to make good that word of Thine, "Those that honor me I will honor" [Ps. 15:4]. Now every line and figure which it hath pleased Thee to work in me serve for useful and profitable direction. O Lord, all the glory is Thine. Give Thou me light, I shall give others information; both of us shall give Thee praise.

III

Upon the Sight of an Eclipse of the Sun

Light is an ordinary and familiar blessing, yet so dear to us that one hour's interception of it sets all the world in a wonder. The two great luminaries of heaven, as they impart light to us, so they withdraw light from each other. The sun darkens the full moon in casting the shadow of the earth upon her opposed face. The new moon repays this blemish to the sun in the interposing of her dark body betwixt our eyes and his glorious beams. The earth is troubled at both. O God, if we be so afflicted with the obscuring of some piece of one of Thy created lights for an hour or two, what a confusion shall it be that Thou who art the God of these lights (in comparision of whom they are mere darkness) shalt hide Thy face from Thy creatures forever! Oh Thou that art the Sun of righteousness, if every of my sins cloud Thy face, yet let not my grievous sins eclipse Thy light. Thou shinest always though I do not see Thee, but, oh, never suffer my sins so to darken Thy visage that I cannot see Thee.

IIII

Upon the Sight of a Gliding Star[2]

How easily is our sight deceived! How easily doth our sight deceive us! We saw no difference betwixt this star and the rest; the light seemed alike both while it stood and while it fell. Now we know it was no other than a base slimy meteor gilded with the sunbeams, and now our foot can tread upon that which ere-while our eye admired. Had it been a star, it had still and ever shined; now the very fall argues it a false and elementary apparition. Thus our charity doth and must mislead us in our spiritual judgments. If we see men exalted in their Christian profession, fixed in the upper region of the Church, shining with appearance of grace, we may not think them other than stars in this lower fimament. But if they fall from their holy station and embrace the present world, whether in judgment or practice, renouncing the truth and power of Godliness, now we may boldly say they had never any true light in them and were no other than a glittering composition of pride and hypocrisy. O God, if my charity make me apt to be deceived by others, let me be sure not to deceive myself. Perhaps some of these apostating stars have thought themselves true. Let their miscarriage make me heedful; let the inward light of Thy grace more convince my truth to myself than my outward profession can represent me glorious to others.

V

Upon a Fair Prospect

What a pleasing variety is here of towns, rivers, hills, dales, woods, meadows, each of them striving to set forth other and all of them to delight the eye! So as this is no other than a natural and real landscape drawn by the almighty and skillful hand in this table of the earth for the pleasure of our view, no other creature besides man is capable to apprehend this beauty. I shall do wrong to Him that brought me hither if I do not feed my eyes and praise my Maker. It is the inter-mixture and change of these objects that yields this contentment both to the sense and mind. But there is a sight, O my soul, that without all variety offers thee a truer and fuller delight, even this heaven above thee. All thy other prospects end in this. This glorious circumference bounds and circles and enlightens all that thine eye can see; whether thou look upward, or forward, or about thee, there thine eye alights, there let thy thoughts be fixed.

One inch of this lightsome firmament hath more beauty in it than the whole face of the earth. And yet, this is but the floor of that good-ly fabric, the outward curtain of that glorious tabernacle. Couldst thou but (oh that thou couldst) look within that veil, how shouldst thou be ravished with that blissful sight! There, in that incomprehen-sible light, thou shouldst see Him whom none can see and not be blessed. Thou shouldst see millions of pure and majestical angels, of holy and glorified souls; there, amongst Thy Father's many mansions [John 14:2] thou shouldst take happy notice of thine own. Oh the best of earth, now vile and contemptible! Come down no more, O my soul, after thou hast once pitched upon this heavenly glory; or, if this flesh force thy descent, be unquiet till thou art let loose to im-mortality.

VI

Upon the Frame of a Globe Casually Broken[3]

It is hard to say whether is the greater, man's art or impotence. He that cannot make one spire† of grass or corn† of sand will yet be framing of worlds; he can imitate all things who can make nothing.

Here is a great world in a little room by the skill of the workman, but in less room by mis-accident. Had he seen this who, upon the view of Plato's *Book of Commonwealth* eaten with mice,[4] presaged the fatal miscarriage of the public state, he would sure have construed this casualty as ominous. Whatever become of the material world, whose decay might seem no less to stand with divine providence than this microcosm of individual man, sure I am the frame of the moral world is and must be disjointed in the last times. Men do and will fall from evil to worse; He that hath made all times hath told us that the last shall be perilous [2 Tim. 3:1]. Happy is he that can stand upright when the world declines and can endeavor to repair the common ruin with a constancy in goodness.

VII

Upon a Cloud

Whether it were a natural cloud wherewith our ascending Saviour was intercepted from the eyes of His disciples upon Mount Olivet, I inquire not. This I am sure of, that the time now was when a cloud surpassed the sun in glory. How did the intentive eyes of those ravished beholders envy that happy meteor; and, since they could no more see that glorious body, fixed themselves upon that celestial chariot wherewith it was carried up [Act 1:9; Ps. 104:3]! The angels could tell the gazing disciples (to fetch them off from that astonishing prospect) that this Jesus should so come again as they had seen Him depart. He went up in a cloud and He shall come again in the clouds of heaven to His last judgment. O Saviour, I cannot look upward but I must see the sensible† monuments both of Thine ascension and return. Let no cloud of worldliness or infidelity hinder me from following Thee in Thine ascension or from expecting Thee in Thy return.

VIII

Upon the Sight of a Grave Digged up

The earth, as it is a great devourer, so also it is a great preserver too; liquors and fleshes are therein long kept from putrifying and are rather heightened in their spirits by being buried in it. But above all, how safely doth it keep our bodies for resurrection; we are here but laid up for custody. Balms and serecloths and leads cannot do so much as this lap of our common mother. When all these are dissolved into her dust (as being unable to keep themselves from corruption), she receives and restores her charge. I can no more withhold my body from the earth than the earth can withhold it from my Maker. O God, this is Thy cabinet or shrine wherein Thou pleasest to lay up the precious relics of Thy dear saints until the jubilee of glory. With what confidence should I commit myself to this sure reposition while I know Thy word just, Thy power infinite!

IX

Upon the Sight of Gold Melted

This gold is both the fairest and most solid of all metals, yet is the soonest melted with the fire. Others, as they are coarser, so more churlish and hard to be wrought upon by a dissolution. Thus a sound and good heart is most easily melted into sorrow and fear by the sense of God's judgments [Ps. 51:17], whereas the carnal mind is stubborn and remorseless. All metals are but earth, yet some are of finer temper than others; all hearts are of flesh, yet some are, through the power of grace, more capable of spiritual apprehensions. O God, we are such as Thou wilt be pleased to make us. Give me a heart that may be sound for the truth of grace and melting at the terrors of Thy Law. I can be for no other than Thy sanctuary on earth or Thy treasury of heaven.

X

Upon the Sight of a Pitcher Carried

Thus those that are great and weak are carried by the ears up and down of flatterers and parasites; thus ignorant and simple hearers are carried by false and miszealous teachers. Yet, to be carried by both ears is more safe than [to] be carried by one; it argues an empty pitcher to be carried by one alone. Such are they that, upon the hearing of one part, rashly pass their sentence, whether of acquittal or censure.

In all disquisitions of hidden truths, a wise man will be led by the ears, not carried; that implies a violence of passion overswaying judgment. But in the matter of civil occurrence and unconcerning rumor, it is good to use the ear, not to trust to it.

XI

Upon the Sight of a Tree Full Blossomed

Here is a tree overlaid with blossoms. It is not possible that all these should prosper; one of them must needs rob the other of moisture and growth. I do not love to see an infancy over-hopeful; in these pregnant beginnings one faculty starves another and at last leaves the mind sapless and barren. As therefore we are wont to pull off some of the too-frequent blossoms, that the rest may thrive, so it is good wisdom to moderate the early excess of the parts or progress of over-forward childhood. Neither is it otherwise in our Christian profession: a sudden and lavish ostentation of grace may fill the eye with wonder and the mouth with talk but will not at the last fill the lap with fruit.

Let me not promise too much nor raise too high expectations of my undertakings. I had rather men should complain of my small hopes than of my short performances.

XII

Upon the Report of a Man Suddenly Struck Dead in his Sin

I cannot but magnify the justice of God but withal I must praise His mercy. It were woe with any of us if God should take us at advantage. Alas, which of us hath not committed sins worthy of a present revenge? Had we been also surprised in those acts, where had we been? Oh God, it is more than Thou owest us that Thou hast waited for our repentance; it is no more than Thou owest us that Thou plaguest our offences. The wages of sin is death [Romans 6:23] and it is but justice to pay due wages. Blessed be Thy justice that hast made others examples to me. Blessed be Thy mercy that Thou hast not made me an example unto others.

XIII

Upon the View of the Heaven and the Earth

What a strange contrariety is here! The heaven is in continual motion, and yet there is the only place of rest; the earth ever stands still, and yet here is nothing but unrest and unquietness. Surely the end of that heavenly motion is for the benefit of the earth; and the end of all these earthly turmoils is our reposal in heaven. Those that have imagined the earth to turn about and the heavens to stand still have yet supposed that we may stand or sit still on that whirling globe of earth.⁵ How much more may we be persuaded of our perfect rest above those moving spheres! It matters not, O God, how I am vexed here below a while if, ere long, I may repose with Thee above forever.

XIIII

Upon Occasion of a Redbreast Coming into his Chamber

Pretty bird, how cheerfully dost thou sit and sing and yet knowest not where thou art, nor where thou shalt make thy next meal, and at night must shroud thyself in a bush for lodging! What a shame is it for me that see before me so liberal provisions of my God and find myself set warm under my own roof, yet am ready to droop under a distrustful and unthankful dullness! Had I so little certainty of my harbor and purveyance, how heartless should I be, how careful,† how little list should I have to make music to thee or myself! Surely thou camest not hither without a providence. God sent thee not so much to delight as to shame me, but all in a conviction of my sullen unbelief, who, under more apparent means, am less cheerful and confident. Reason and faith have not done so much in me as in thee mere instinct of nature; want of foresight makes thee more merry if not more happy here than the foresight of better things maketh me.

O God, Thy providence is not impaired by those powers Thou hast given me above these brute things. Let not my greater helps hinder me from an holy obscurity and comfortable reliance upon Thee.

XV

Upon Occasion of a Spider in his Window

There is no vice in man whereof there is not some analogy in the brute creatures. As amongst us men there are thieves by land and pirates by sea that live by spoil and blood, so is there in every kind amongst them variety of natural sharkers: the hawk in the air, the pike in the river, the whale in the sea, the lion and tiger and wolf in the desert, the wasp in the hive, the spider in our window. Amongst the rest, see how cunningly this little Arabian hath spread out his tent for a prey, how heedfully he watches for a passenger. So soon as ever he hears the noise of a fly afar off, how he hastens to his door, and if that silly† heedless traveler do but touch upon the verge of that unsuspected walk, how suddenly doth he seize upon the miserable booty and, after some strife, binding him fast with those subtle cords, drags the helpless captive after him into his cave! What is this but an emblem of those spiritual free-booters that lie in wait for our souls? They are the spiders, we the flies. They have spread their nets of sin; if we be once caught, they bind us fast and hail us into hell.

Oh Lord, deliver Thou my soul from their crafty ambushes. Their poison is greater, their webs both more strong and more insensibly† woven. Either teach me to avoid temptation or make me to break through it by repentance. Oh let me not be a prey to those fiends that lie in wait for my destruction.

XVI

Upon the Sight of a Rain in the Sunshine

Such is my best condition in this life: if the sun of God's countenance shine upon me, I may well be content to be wet with some rain of affliction. How oft have I seen the heaven overcast with clouds and tempest, no sun appearing to comfort me! Yet even those gloomy and stormy seasons have I rid out patiently; only with the help of the common light of day, at last those beams have broken forth happily and cheered my soul. It is well for my ordinary state if through the mists of my own dullness and Satan's temptations I can descry some glimpse of heavenly comfort. Let me never hope, while I am in this vale, to see the clear face of that sun without a shower.

Such happiness is reserved for above; that upper region of glory is free from these doubtful and miserable vicissitudes. There, O God, we shall see as we are seen [1 Cor. 13:12]. Light is sown for the righteous and joy for the upright in heart [Ps. 32:1].

XVII

Upon the Length of the Way

How far off is yonder great mountain! My very eye is weary with the foresight of so great a distance, yet time and patience shall overcome it. This night we shall hope to lodge beyond it. Some things are more tedious in their expectation than in their performance. The comfort is that every step I take sets me nearer to my end. When I once come there, I shall both forget how long it now seems and please myself to look back upon the way that I have measured.

It is thus in our passage to heaven. My weak nature is ready to faint under the very conceit† of the length and difficulty of this journey; my eye doth not more guide than discourage me. Many steps of grace and true obedience shall bring me insensibly thither; only, let me move and hope and God's good leisure shall perfect my salvation. O Lord, give me to possess my soul with patience and not so much to regard speed as certainty. When I come to the top of Thine holy hill [Ps. 43:3], all these weary paces and deep sloughs shall either be forgotten or contribute to my happiness in their remembrance.

XVIII

Upon the Rain and Waters

What a sensible† interchange there is in nature betwixt union and division! Many vapors rising from the sea meet together in one cloud; that cloud falls down divided into several drops; those drops run together and in many rills of water meet in the same channels; those channels run into the brook, those brooks into the rivers, those rivers into the sea. One receptacle is for all, though a large one, and all make back to their first and main original. So it either is or should be with spiritual gifts. O God, Thou distillest Thy graces upon us not for our reservation but conveyance. Those manifold faculties Thou lettest fall upon several men Thou wouldst not have drenched up where they light but wouldest have derived, through the channels of their special vocations, into the common streams of public use for Church or Commonwealth. Take back, O Lord, those few drops Thou hast rained upon my soul and return them into that great ocean of the glory of Thine own bounty, from whence they had their beginning.

XIX

Upon the Same Subject

Many drops fill the channels, and many channels swell up the brooks, and many brooks raise the rivers over the banks. The brooks are not out till the channels be empty; the rivers rise not while the small brooks are full. But when the little rivulets have once voided themselves into the main streams, then all is overflowed. Great matters arise from small beginnings; many littles make up a large bulk. Yea, what is the world but a composition of atoms? We have seen it thus in civil estates; the impairing of the commons† hath oft been the raising of the great; their streams have run low till they have been heightened by the confluence of many private inlets; many a mean channel hath been emptied to make up their inundation. Neither is it otherwise in my whether outward or spiritual condition. O God, Thou hast multiplied my drops into streams. As out of many minutes Thou hast made up my age, so out of many lessons Thou hast made up my competency of knowledge; Thou hast drained many beneficent friends to make me competently rich. By many holy motions Thou hast wrought me to some measure of grace.

Oh teach me wisely and moderately to enjoy Thy bounty and to reduce Thy streams into Thy drops and Thy drops into Thy clouds, humbly and thankfully acknowledging whence and how I have all that I have, all that I am.

XX

Upon Occasion of the Lights Brought In

What a change there is in the room since the light came in, yea, in ourselves! All things seem to have a new form, a new life; yea, we are not the same we were. How goodly a creature is light, how pleasing,

how agreeable to the spirits of man! No visible thing comes so near to
the resembling of the nature of the soul, yea, of the God that made it.
As contrarily, what an uncomfortable thing is darkness, insomuch as
we punish the greatest malefactors with obscurity of dungeons as
thinking they could not be miserable enough if they might have the
privilege of beholding the light. Yea, hell itself can be no more hor-
ribly described than by outward darkness [Ps. 88:6].

What is darkness but absence of light? The pleasure or the horror
of light or darkness is according to the quality and degree of the cause
whence it ariseth. And if the light of a poor candle be so comfortable,
which is nothing but a little inflamed air gathered about a moistened
snuff, what is the light of the glorious sun, the great lamp of heaven?
But much more, what is the light of that infinitely resplendent sun of
righteousness who gave that light to the sun, that sun to the world?
And if this partial and imperfect darkness be so doleful, which is the
privation of a natural or artificial light, how inconceivable, dolorous,
and miserable shall that be which is caused through the utter absence
of the all-glorious God who is the Father of lights [James 1:17]! Oh
Lord, how justly do we pity those wretched souls that sit in darkness
and the shadow of death [Ps. 107:10], shut up from the light of the
saving knowledge of Thee, the only true God! But how am I
swallowed up with horror to think of the fearful condition of those
damned souls that are forever shut out from the presence of God and
adjudged to exquisite and everlasting darkness! The Egyptians were
weary of themselves in their three days' darkness [Exod. 10:22], yet
we do not find any pain that accompanied their continuing night.
What shall we say to those woeful souls in whom the sensible†
presence of infinite torment shall meet with the torment of the
perpetual absence of God? O Thou who art the true light, shine ever
through all the blind corners of my soul; and from these weak glim-
merings of grace bring me to the perfect brightness of Thy glory.

XXI

Upon the Same Occasion

As well as we love the light, we are wont to salute it at the first
coming in with winking or closed eyes, as not abiding to see that
without which we cannot see. All sudden changes (though for the

better) have a kind of trouble attending them. By how much more excellent any object is, by so much more is our weak sense mis-affected in the first apprehending of it. Oh Lord, if Thou shouldest manifest Thy glorious presence to us here, we should be confounded in the sight of it. How wisely, how mercifully hast Thou reserved that for our glorified estate where no infirmity shall dazzle our eyes, where perfect righteousness shall give us perfect boldness, both of sight and fruition.

XXII

Upon the Blowing of the Fire

We beat back the flame not with a purpose to suppress it but to raise it higher and to diffuse it more. These afflictions and impulses which seem to be discouragements are indeed the merciful in-citements of grace. If God did mean judgment to my soul, He would either withdraw the fuel or pour water upon the fire, or suffer it to languish for want of new motions. But now that He continues to me the means and opportunities and desires of good, I shall misconstrue the intentions of my God if I shall think His crosses sent rather to damp than to quicken His spirit in me. O God, if Thy bellows did not sometimes thus breathe upon me in spiritual repercussions, I should have just cause to suspect my estate. These few weak gleedst of grace that are in me might soon go out if they were not thus refreshed. Still blow upon them till they kindle; still kindle them till they flame up to Thee.

XXIII

Upon the Barking of a Dog

What have I done to this dog that he follows me with this angry clamor? Had I rated him, or shaken my staff, or stooped down for a stone, I had justly drawn on this noise, this snarling importunity. But why do I wonder to find this unquiet disposition in a brute creature when it is no news with the reasonable?

Have I not seen innocence and merit bayed at by the quarrelsome and envious vulgar without any provocation save of good offices? Have I not felt (more than their tongue) their teeth upon my heels when I know I have deserved nothing but fawning on? Where is my grace or spirits if I have not learned to contemn both?

O God, let me rather die than willingly incur Thy displeasure, yea, than justly offend Thy Godly-wise, judicious, conscionable servants. But if humour† or faction or causeless prejudice fall upon me for my faithful service to Thee, let these bawling curs tire thmselves and tear their throats with loud and false censures. I go on in a silent constancy, and if my ear be beaten yet my heart shall be free.

XXIIII

Upon the Sight of a Cockfight

How fell these creatures out? Whence grew this so bloody combat? Here was neither old grudge nor present injury. What then is the quarrel? Surely nothing but that which should rather unite and reconcile them, one common nature; they are both of one feather. I do not see either of them fly upon creatures of different kind; but while they have peace with all others, they are at war with themselves. The very sight of each other was sufficient provocation. If this be the offence, why doth not each of them fall out with himself, since he hates and revenges in another the being of that same which himself is?

Since man's sin brought debate into the world, nature is become a great quarreler. The seeds of discord were scattered [Prov. 6:14] in every furrow of the creation⁶ and came up in a numberless variety of antipathies, whereof yet none is more odious and deplorable than those which are betwixt creatures of the same kind. What is this but an image of the woeful hostility which is exercised betwixt us reasonables, who are conjoined in one common humanity if not religion?

We fight with and destroy each other more than those creatures that want reason to temper their passions. No beast is so cruel to man as himself; where one man is slain by a beast, ten thousand are slain by man. What is that war which we study and practice but the art of killing? Whatever Turks and pagans may do, O Lord, how long shall this brutish fury arm Christians against each other? While even devils are not at enmity with themselves but accord in wickedness, why do we men so mortally oppose each other in good?

Oh Thou that are the God of peace, compose the unquiet hearts of men to an happy and universal concord, and at last refresh our souls with the multitude of peace.

XXV

Upon his Lying down to Rest

What a circle there is of human actions and events! We are never without change, and yet that change is without any great variety. We sleep and wake and wake and sleep, and eat and evacuate, labor in a continual interchange. Yet hath the infinite wisdom of God so ordered it that we are never weary of these perpetual iterations, but with no less appetite enter into our daily courses than if we should pass them but once in our life. When I am weary of my day's labor, how willingly I undress myself and betake myself to my bed; and ere morning, when I have wearied of my restless bed, how glad am I to rise and renew my labor!

Why am I not more desirous to be unclothed of this body that I may be clothed upon with immortality? What is this but my closest garment which, when it is once put off, my soul is at liberty and ease? Many a time have I lain down before in desire of rest, and after some tedious changing of sides have risen sleepless, disappointed, languishing. In my last uncasing, my body shall not fail of repose nor my soul of joy; and in my rising up neither of them shall fail of glory. What hinders me, O God, but my infidelity from longing for this happy dissolution? The world hath misery and toil enough, and heaven hath more than enough blessedness to perfect my desires of my last and glorious change. I believe, Lord, help my unbelief [Mark 10:24].

XXVI

Upon the Kindling of a Charcoal Fire

There are not many creatures but do naturally affect to diffuse and enlarge themselves. Fire and water will neither of them rest contented with their own bounds. Those little sparks that I see in those coals, how they spread and enkindle their next brands! It is thus morally both in good and evil; either of them dilates itself to their neighborhood, but especially this is so much more apparent in evil by how much we are more apt to take it. Let but some spark of heretical opinion be let fall upon some unstable, proud, busy spirit, it catcheth instantly and fires the next capable subject; they two have easily inflamed a third, and now the more society, the more speed and advantage of a public combustion. When we see the Church on a flame, it is too late to complain of the flint and steel. It is the holy wisdom of superiors to prevent the dangerous attritions of stubborn and wrangling spirits, or to quench their first sparks in the tinder.

But why should not peace and truth be as successful in dilating itself to the gaining of many hearts? Certainly these are in themselves more winning if our corruption had not made us indisposed to good. Oh God, out of an holy envy and emulation at the speed of evil, I shall labor to enkindle others with these heavenly flames. It shall not be my fault if they spread not.

XXVII

Upon the Sight of an Humble and Patient Beggar

See what need can do! This man, who in so lowly a fashion coucheth to that passenger, hath in all likelihood as good a stomach as he to whom he thus abaseth himself; and if their conditions were but altered, would look as high and speak as big to him whom he now answers with a plausible and dejected reverence.

It is thus betwixt God and us. He sees the way to tame us is to hold us short of these earthly contentments. Even the savagest beasts are made quiet and docible with want of food and rest. Oh God, Thou only knowest what I would do if I had health, ease, abundance. Do Thou in Thy wisdom and mercy so proportion Thy gifts and restraints as Thou knowest best for my soul. If I be not humbled enough, let me want; and so order all my estate that I may want anything save Thyself.[7]

XXVIII

Upon the Sight of a Crow Pulling off Wool from
the Back of a Sheep

How well these creatures know whom they may be bold with! That crow durst not do this to a wolf or a mastiff; the known simplicity of this innocent beast gives advantage to this presumption.

Meekness of spirit commonly draws on injuries; the cruelty of ill natures usually seeks out those, not who deserve the worst, but who will bear most.

Patience and mildness of spirit is ill bestowed where it exposes a man to wrong and insultation.† Sheepish dispositions are best to others, worst to themselves. I could be willing to take injuries, but I will not be guilty of provoking them by lenity. For harmlessness let me go for a sheep, but whosoever will be tearing my fleece let him look to himself!

XXIX

Upon the Sight of Two Snails

There is much variety even in creatures of the same kind. See there two snails: one hath an house, the other wants it, yet both are snails, and it is a question whether case is the better. That which hath a house hath more shelter, but that which wants it hath more freedom. The privilege of that cover is but a burden. You see if it have but a stone to climb over, with what stress it draws up that beneficial load and, if the passage prove strait, finds no entrance; whereas the empty snail makes no difference of way. Surely it is always an ease and sometimes an happiness to have nothing; no man is so worthy of envy as he that can be cheerful in want.

XXX

Upon the Hearing of the Street-cries in London

What a noise do these poor souls make in proclaiming their commodities! Each tells what he hath and would have all hearers take notice of it; and yet (God wot) it is but poor stuff that they set out with so much ostentation. I do not hear any of the rich merchants talk of what bags he hath in his chests or what treasures of rich wares in his store-house. Every man rather desires to hide his wealth and, when he is urged, is ready to dissemble his ability. No otherwise is it in the true spiritual riches. He that is full of grace and good work affects not to make show of it to the world but rests sweetly in the secret testimony of a good conscience and the silent applause of God's spirit witnessing with his own; while, contrarily, the venditation† of our own worth or parts or merits argues a miserable indigence in them all. Oh God, if the confessing of Thine own gifts may glorify Thee, my modesty shall not be guilty of a niggardly unthankfulness, but, for ought that concerns myself, I cannot be too secret. Let me so hide myself that I may not wrong Thee, and wisely distinguish betwixt Thy praise and my own.

XXXI

Upon the Flies Gathering to a Galled Horse

How those flies swarm to the galled part of this poor beast and there sit feeding upon that worst piece of his flesh, not meddling with the other sound parts of his skin! Even thus do malicious tongues of detractors. If a man have any infirmity in his person or actions, that they will be sure to gather unto and dwell upon; whereas his commendable parts and well-deservings are passed by without mention, without regard. It is an envious self-love and base cruelty that causeth this ill disposition in men. In the meantime this only they have gained: it must needs be a filthy creature that feeds upon nothing but corruption.

XXXII

Upon the Sight of a Dark Lantern

There is light indeed but so shut up as if it were not; and when the side is most open, there is light enough to give direction to him that bears it, none to others. He can discern another man by that light which is cast before him, but another man cannot discern him. Right such is reserved knowledge; no man is the better for it but the owner. There is no outward difference betwixt concealed skill and ignorance; and when such hidden knowledge will look forth, it casts so sparing a light as may only argue it to have an unprofitable being, to have ability without will to good; power to censure, none to benefit. The suppression or engrossing of these helps which God would have us to impart is but a thief's lantern in a true man's hand. Oh God, as all our light is from Thee, the Father of lights [James 1:17], so make me no niggard of that poor rush-candle† Thou hast lighted in my soul; make me more happy in giving light to others than in receiving it into myself.

XXXIII

Upon the Hearing of a Swallow in the Chimney

Here is music, such as it is, but how long will it hold? When but a cold morning comes in, my guest is gone without either warning or thanks. This pleasant season hath the least need of cheerful notes; the dead of winter shall want and wish them in vain. Thus doth an ungrateful parasite: no man is more ready to applaud and enjoy our prosperity, but when with the times our condition begins to alter, he is a stranger at least. Give me that bird which will sing in winter and seek to my window in the hardest frost. There is no trial of friendship but adversity. He that is not ashamed of my bonds, not daunted with my checks, not aliened† with my disgrace is a friend to me. One dram of that man's love is worth a world of false and inconstant formality.

XXXIV

Upon the Sight of a Fly† Burning Itself in the Candle

Wise Solomon says the light is a pleasant thing [Eccles. 11:7] and so certainly it is, but there is no true outward light which proceeds not from fire. The light of that fire, then, is not more pleasing than the fire of that light is dangerous; and that pleasure doth not more draw on our sight than that danger forbids our approach. How foolish is this fly that in a love and admiration of this light will know no distance but puts itself heedlessly into that flame wherein it perishes! How many bouts it fetched, every one nearer than other, ere it made this last venture; and now that merciless fire, taking no notice of the affection of an overfond client, hath suddenly consumed it. Thus do those bold and busy spirits who will needs draw too near unto that inaccessible light and look into things too wonderful for them. So long do they hover about the secret counsels of the Almighty till the wings of their presumptuous conceits be scorched, and their daring curiosity hath paid them with everlasting destruction. Oh Lord, let me be blessed with the knowledge of what Thou hast revealed; let me content myself to adore Thy divine wisdom in what Thou hast not revealed. So let me enjoy Thy light that I may avoid Thy fire.

XXXV

Upon the Sight of a Lark Flying Up

How nimbly doth that little lark mount up singing towards heaven in a right line, whereas the hawk, which is stronger of body and swifter of wing, towers up by many gradual compasses to his highest pitch. That bulk of body and length of wing hinders a direct ascent and requires the help both of air and scope to advance his flight; while that small bird cuts the air without resistance and needs no outward furtherance of her motion. It is no otherwise with the soul of men in flying up to their heaven. Some are hindered by those powers which would seem helps to their soaring thither. Great wit, deep judgment, quick apprehension sends men about with no small labor for the recovery of their own encumbrance; while the good affections of plain simple souls raise them up immediately to the fruition of God. Why should we be proud of that which may slacken our way to glory? Why should we be disheartened with the small measure of that the very want whereof (as the heart may be affected) facilitates our way to happiness?

XXXVI

Upon the Singing of the Birds in a Spring Morning

How cheerfully do these little birds chirp and sing out of the natural joy they conceive at the approach of the sun and entrance of Spring, as if their life had departed and returned with those glorious and comfortable beams! No otherwise is the penitent and faithful soul affected to the true Sun of righteousness, the Father of lights [James 1:17]. When He hides His face, it is troubled and silently mourns away that sad Winter of affliction. When He returns, in His presence is the fullness of joy; no song is cheerful enough to welcome Him. Oh Thou who art the God of all consolation[Rom. 15:5], make my heart sensible of the sweet comforts of Thy gracious presence, and let my mouth ever show forth Thy praise [Ps. 51:15].

XXXVII

Upon a Coal Covered with Ashes

Nothing appears in this heap but dead ashes. Here is neither light, nor smoke, nor heat, and yet, when I stir up these embers to the bottom, there are found some living gleeds† which do both contain fire and are apt to propagate it. Many a Christian's breast is like this hearth. No life of grace appears there for the time, either to his own sense or to the apprehension of others; while the season of temptation lasteth, all seems cold and dead. Yet still at the worst there is a secret coal from the altar of heaven [Isa. 6:6] raked up in their bosom, which, upon the gracious motions of the Almighty, doth both betray some reminders of that divine fire and is easily raised to a perfect flame. Nothing is more dangerous than to judge by appearances. Why should I deject myself or censure others for the utter extinction of that spirit which doth but hide itself in the soul for a glorious advantage?

XXXVIII

Upon the Sight of a Blackamoor

Lo, there is a man whose hue shows him to be far from home. His very skin betrays his climate; it is night in his face while it is day in ours. What a difference there is in men, both in their fashion and color, and yet all children of one Father! Neither is there less variety in their insides; their dispositions, judgments, opinions differ as much as their shapes and complexions. That which is beauty to one is deformity to another. We should be looked upon in this man's country with no less wonder and strange coyness than he is here; our whiteness would pass there for an unpleasing indigestion of form. Outward beauty is more in the eye of the beholder than in the face that is seen; in every color, that is fair which pleaseth. The very Spouse of Christ can say, "I am black but comely" [Cant. 1:5]. This is our color spiritually, yet the eye of our gracious God and Saviour can see that beauty in us wherewith He is delighted. The true Moses marries a blackamoor, Christ His Church.[8] It is not for us to regard the skin but the soul; if that be innocent, pure, holy, the blots of an outside cannot set us off from the love of Him who hath said, "Behold, thou art fair, my Sister, my Spouse" [Cant. 4:10]. If that be foul and black, it is not in the power of the angelical brightness of our hide to make us other than a loathsome eyesore to the Almighty. O God, make my inside lovely to Thee; I know that beauty will hold while weather, casualty, age, disease may deform the outer man and mar both color and features.

XXXIX

Upon the Small Stars in the Galaxy, or Milky Circle in the Firmament

What a clear lightsomeness there is in yonder circle of the heaven above the rest! What can we suppose is united there and causes that brightness? And yet those small stars are not discerned while the splendor which ariseth from them is so notably remarkable. In this lower heaven of ours many a man is made conspicuous by his good qualities and deserts; but I most admire the humility and grace of those whose virtues and merits are usually visible while their persons are obscure; it is secretly glorious for a man to shine unseen. Doubtless it is the height that makes those stars so small and insensible;† were they lower they would be seen more. There is no true greatness without a self-humiliation; we shall have made an ill use of our advancement if, by how much higher we are, we do not appear less. If our light be seen, it matters not for our hiding.

XL

Upon the Sight of Boys Playing

Every age hath some peculiar contentment; thus we did when we were of those years. Methinks I still remember the old fervor of my young pastimes. With what eagerness and passion do they pursue those childish sports! Now that there is a whole handful of cherrystones at the stake, how near is that boy's heart to his mouth for fear of his play-fellow's next cast, and how exalted with desire and hope for his own speed!⁹ Those great unthrifts who hazard whole manors upon the dice cannot expect their chance with more earnestness or entertain it with more joy or grief. We cannot but now smile to think of these poor and foolish pleasures of our childhood. There is no less disdain that the degenerate man conceives of the dearest delights of his natural condition. He was once jolly and jocund in the fruition of the world. Feasts and revels and games and dalliance were his life, and no man could be happy without these, and scarce any man but himself. But when once grace hath made him both good and wise, how scornfully doth he look back at these fond felicities of his carnal estate! Now he finds more manly, more divine contentments and wonders he could be so transported with his former vanity. Pleasures are much according as they are esteemed; one man's delight is another man's pain. Only spiritual and heavenly things can settle and satiate the heart with a full and firm contentation.† Oh God, Thou art not capable either of bettering or of change. Let me enjoy Thee, and I shall pity the miserable fickleness of those that want† Thee and shall be sure to be constantly happy.

XLI

Upon the Sight of a Spider and her Web

How justly do we admire the curious† work of this creature! What a thread doth it spin forth, what a web doth it weave, yet it is full of deadly poison! There may be much venom where is much art. Just like to this is a learned and witty heretic; fine conceits and elegant expressions fall from him, but his opinions and secretly couched doctrines are dangerous and mortal. Were not that man strangely foolish who, because he likes the artificial drawing out of that web, would therefore desire to handle or eat the spider that made it? Such would be our madness if our wonder at the skill of a false teacher should cast us into love with his person or familiarity with his writings. There can be no safety in our judgment or affection without a wise distinction, in the want whereof we must needs wrong God or ourselves: God, if we acknowledge not what excellent parts He gives to any creature; ourselves if upon the allowance of those excellencies we swallow their most dangerous enormities.

XLII

Upon the Sight of a Natural†

Oh God, why am not I thus? What hath this man done that Thou hast denied wit to him? Or what have I done that Thou shouldst give a competency to me? What difference is there betwixt us but Thy bounty which hath bestowed upon me what I could not merit and hath withheld from him what he could not challenge? All is, oh God, in Thy good pleasure, whether to give or deny. Neither is it otherwise in matter of grace. The unregenerate man is a spiritual fool; no man is truly wise but the renewed. How is it that while I see another man besotted with the vanity and corruption of his nature, I have attained to know God and the great mystery of salvation, to abhor those sins which are pleasing to a wicked appetite? Who hath discerned me? Nothing but Thy free mercy, oh my God. Why else was I a man, not a brute beast? Why right-shaped, not a monster?† Why perfectly limbed, not a cripple? Why well-sensed, not a fool? Why well affected, not graceless? Why a vessel of honor, not of wrath [Rom. 9:20–24]? If ought be not ill in me, oh Lord, it is Thine. Oh let Thine be the praise and mine the thankfulness.

XLIII

Upon the Lodestone† and the Jet[10]

If there is a natural commerce amongst men for the preservation of human society, so there is a natural commerce which God hath set amongst the other creatures for the maintenance of their common being. There is scarce anything, therefore, in nature which hath not a power of attracting some other. The fire draws vapors to it, the sun draws the fire, plants draw moisture, the moon draws the sea. All purgative things draw their proper humors,† a natural instinct draws all sensitive creatures to affect their own kind, and even in those things which are of imperfect mixture we see this experimented. So as the senseless stones and metals are not void of this active virtue, the lodestone draws iron, and the jet, rather than nothing, draws up straws and dust. With what a force do both these stones work upon their several subjects! Is there anything more heavy and unapt for motion than iron or steel? Yet these do so run to their beloved lodestone as if they had the sense of desire and delight, and do so cling to the point of it as if they had forgotten their weight for this adherence. Is there anything more apt for dispersion than small straws and dust? Yet these gather to the jet and so sensibly leap up to it as if they had a kind of ambition to be so preferred.

Methinks I see in these two a mere emblem of the hearts of men and their spiritual attractives. The grace of God's spirit, like the true lodestone or adamant, draws up the iron heart of man to it and holds it in a constant fixedness of holy purposes and good actions. The world, like the jet, draws up the sensual hearts of light and vain men and holds them fast in the pleasures of sin. I am Thine iron, oh Lord, be Thou my lodestone. Draw Thou me and I shall run after Thee; knit my heart unto Thee that I may fear Thy name [1 Chron. 12:17].

XLIIII

Upon Hearing of Music by Night

How sweetly doth this music sound in this dead season! In the daytime it would not, it could not, so much affect the ear; all harmonious sounds are advanced by a silent darkness. Thus it is with the glad tidings of salvation. The Gospel never sounds so sweet as in the night of persecution or of our private affliction. It is ever the same; the difference is in our disposition to receive it. Oh God, whose praise it is to give songs in the night, make my prosperity conscionable and my crosses cheerful.

XLV

Upon the Fanning of Corn

See how in the fanning of this wheat the fullest and greatest grains lie ever the lowest, and the lightest take up the highest place, It is no otherwise in mortality: those which are most humble are fullest of grace, and oft times those have most conspicuity which have the least substance. To affect obscurity or submission is base and suspicious, but that man whose modesty presents him mean to his own eyes and lowly to others is commonly secretly rich in virtue. Give me rather a low fullness than an empty advancement.

XLVI

Upon Herbs Dried

They say those herbs will keep best and will longer retain both their hue and verdure which are dried thus in the shade than those which are suddenly scorched with fire or sun.

Those wits are like to be most durable which are closely tutored with a leisurely education; time and gentle constancy ripens better than a sudden violence. Neither is it otherwise in our spiritual condition; a willful slackness is not more dangerous than an over-hastening of our perfection. If I may be every moment drawing nearer to the end of my hope, I shall not wish to precipitate.

XLVII

Upon the Quenching of Iron in Water

Mark how that iron quenched in the water hisseth and makes that noise, which while it was cold or dry it would never make. We cannot quench hot and unruly desires in youth without some mutiny and rebellious opposition.

Corruptions cannot be subdued without some reluctation,† and that reluctation cannot be without some tumult. After some short noise and smoke and bubbling, the metal is quiet and holds to the form whereinto it is beaten. Oh God, why should it trouble me to find my good endeavors resisted for the little brunt of a change while I am sure this insurrection shall end in an happy peace?

XLVIII

Upon a Fair-colored Fly†

What a pleasant mixture of colors there is in this fly! And yet, they say, no fly is so venomous as this, which by the outward touch of the hand corrodes the inmost passages of the body. It is no trusting to colors and shapes; we may wonder at their excellency without dotage upon their beauty. Homeliness makes less show and hath less danger. Give me inward virtues and usefulness; let others care for outward glory.

XLIX

Upon a Glowworm

What a cold candle is lighted up in the body of this sorry worm! There needs no other disproof of those that say there is no light at all without some heat, yet sure an outward heat helps on this cool light.

Never did I see any of these bright worms but in the hot months of summer; in cold seasons, either they are not or appear not when the nights are both darkest and longest and most uncomfortable. Thus do false-hearted Christians in the warm and lightsome times of free and encouraged profession; none shine more than they. In hard and gloomy seasons of restraint and persecution, all their formal light is either lost or hid; whereas true professors† either like the sunshine ever alike or like the stars shine fairest in the frostiest nights. The light of this worm is for some show but for no use. Any light that is attended with heat can impart itself to others, though with the expence of that subject wherein it is; this doth neither waste itself nor help others. I had rather never to have light than not to have it always; I had rather not to have light than not to communicate it.

L

Upon the Shutting of One Eye

When we would take aim or see most exquisitely, we shut one eye. Thus must we do with the eyes of the soul. When we would look most accurately with the eye of faith, we must shut the eye of reason, else the visual beams of these two apprehensions will be crossing each other and hinder our clear discerning. Yea, rather let me pull out this right eye [Matt. 18:9] of reason than it shall offend me in the interruptions of mine happy visions of God.

LI

Upon a Spring-water

How this spring smoketh while other greater channels are frozen up! This water is living while they are dead. All experience teacheth us that well-waters arising from deep springs are hotter in winter than in summer; the outward cold doth keep in and double their inward heat. Such is a true Christian in the evil day; his life of grace gets more vigor by opposition; he had not been so gracious† if the times had been better. I will not say he may thank his enemies but I must say he may thank God for his enemies. Oh God, what can put out that heat which is increased with cold? How happy shall I be if I grow so much more in grace as the world in malice!

LII

Upon Gnats in the Sun

What a cloud of gnats is here! Mark their motion; they do nothing but play up and down in the warm sun and sing, and when they have done sit down and sting the next hand or face they can seize upon. See here a perfect emblem of idleness and detraction. How many do thus miserably misspend their good hours who, after they have wasted the succeeding day in vain and merely unprofitable pastime, sit down and backbite their neighbors? The bee sings too sometimes, but she works also and her work is not more admirable than useful; but these foolish flies† do nothing but play and sing to no purpose. Even the busiest and most active spirits must recreate, but to make a trade of sport is for none but lazy wantons.

The bee stings too but it is when she is provoked; these draw blood unoffended and sting for their own pleasure. I would be glad of some recreation but to enable and sweeten my work. I would not but sting sometimes where is just cause of offence. But God bless me from those men which will ever be either doing nothing or ill.

LIII

Upon the Sight of Grapes

Mark the difference of these grapes. There you see a cluster whose grapes touch one another, well ripened; here you see some stragglers which grow almost solitarily, green and hard. It is thus with us: Christian society helpeth our progress and woe to him that is alone. He is well that is the better for others, but he is happy by whom others are better.

LIIII

Upon a Cornfield Overgrown with Weeds

Here were a goodly field of corn if it were not overlaid with weeds. I do not like these reds and blues and yellows amongst these plain stalks and ears; this beauty would do well elsewhere. I had rather see a plot less fair and more yielding. In this field I see a true picture of the world wherein there is more glory than true substance, wherein the greater part carries it from the better, wherein the native sons of the earth outstrip the adventitious brood of grace, wherein parasites and unprofitable hangbys† do both rob and over-top their masters. Both field and world grow alike, look alike, and shall end alike. Both are for the fire while the homely and solid ears of despised virtue shall be for the garners of immortality.

LV

Upon the Sight of Tulips and Marigolds, etc.
in His Garden

These flowers are true clients of the sun. How observant they are of his action and influence! At even they shut up as mourning for his departure, without whom they neither can nor would flourish; in the morning they welcome his rising with a cheerful openness; and at noon are fully displayed in a free acknowledgement of his bounty. Thus doth the good heart unto God. "When thou turnedst away thy face I was troubled," saith the man after God's own heart [Ps. 102:2]. "In thy presence is life, yea, the fullness of joy" [Ps. 16:11]. Thus doth the carnal heart to the world; when that withdraws his favor he is dejected and revives with a smile. All is in our choice; whatsoever is our sun will thus carry us. Oh God, be Thou to me such as Thou art in Thyself. Thou shalt be merciful in drawing me, I shall be happy in following Thee.

LVI

Upon the Sound of a Cracked Bell

What an harsh sound doth this bell make in every ear! The metal is good enough; it is the rift that makes it so unpleasantly jarring. How too like is this bell to a scandalous and ill-lived teacher. His calling is honorable, his noise is heard far enough, but the flaw which is noted in his life mars his doctrine and offends those ears which else would take pleasure in his teaching. It is possible that such a one, even by that discordant noise, may ring in others into the triumphant Church of Heaven, but there is no remedy for himself but the fire, whether for his reforming or judgment.

LVII

Upon the Sight of a Blind Man

How much am I bound to God that hath given me eyes to see this man's want of eyes! With what suspicion and fear he walks, how doth his hand and staff examine his way! With what jealousy doth he receive every morsel, every draught, and yet meets with many a post and stumbles at many a stone and swallows many a fly! To him the world is as if it were not, or as if it were all rubs and snares and downfalls; and if any man will lend him an hand, he must trust to his (however faithless) guide without all comfort save this, that he cannot see himself miscarry. Many a one is thus spiritually blind, and because he is so, discerns it not, and, not discerning, complains not of so woeful a condition. The God of this world hath blinded the eyes of the children of disobedience; they walk on in the way of death and yield themselves over to the guidance of him who seeks for nothing but their precipitation into hell. It is an addition to the misery of this inward occaecation† that it is ever joined with a secure confidence in them whose trade and ambition is to betray their souls.

Whatever become of these outward senses which are common to me with the meanest and most despicable creatures, Oh Lord, give me not over to that spiritual darkness which is incident to none but those that live without Thee and must perish eternally because they want Thee.†

LVIII

Upon a Beechtree Full of Nuts

How is this tree overladen with mast† this year! It was not so the last, neither will it (I warrant you) be so the next. It is the nature of these free trees so to pour out themselves into fruit at once that they seem afterwards either sterile or niggardly. So have I seen pregnant wits (not discreetly governed) overspend themselves in some one masterpiece so lavishly that they have proved either barren or poor and flat in all other subjects. True wisdom, as it serves to gather due sap for nourishment and fructification, so it guides the seasonable and moderate bestowing of it in such manner as that one season may not be a glutton while others famish. I would be glad to attain to that measure and temper that upon all occasions I might always have enough, never too much.

LIX

Upon the Sight of a Piece of Money under the Water

I should not wish ill to a covetous man if I should wish all his coin in the bottom of the river. No pavement could so well become that stream; no sight could better fit his greedy desires, for there every piece would seem double; every teston† would appear a shilling, every crown an angel.† It is the nature of that element to greaten appearing quantities; while we look through the air upon that solid body, it can make no other representations. Neither is it otherwise in spiritual eyes and objects. If we look with carnal eyes through the interposed mean of sensuality, every base and worthless pleasure will seem a large contentment. If with weak eyes we shall look at small and immaterial truths aloof off, in another element of apprehension every parcel thereof shall seem main and essential. Hence every knack of heraldry in the sacred genealogies and every scholastical quirk in disquisitions of divinity are made matters of no less than life and death to the soul. It is a great improvement of true wisdom to be able to see things as they are and to value them as they are seen. Let me labor for that power and staidness of judgment that neither my senses may deceive my mind nor the object may delude my sense.

LX

Upon the First Rumor of the Earthquake at Lyme, wherein
a Wood was Swallowed up with the Fall of Two Hills[11]

Good Lord, how do we know when we are sure? If there were man or beast in that wood, they seemed as safe as we now are; they had nothing but heaven above them, nothing but firm earth below them. And yet in what a dreadful pitfall were they instantly taken! There is no fence for God's hand; a man would as soon have feared that heaven would fall upon him as those hills. It is no pleasing ourselves with the unlikelihood of divine judgments. We have oft heard of hills covered with woods but of woods covered with hills I think never till now. Those that planted or sowed those woods intended they should be spent with fire, but, God meant they would be devoured with earth.

We are wont to describe impossibilities by the meeting of mountains, and behold here two mountains are met to swallow up a valley. What a good God it is whose providence overrules and disposes of all these events!

Towns or cities might as well have been thus buried as a solitary dale or a shrubby wood. Certainly the God that did this would have the use of it reach further than the noise: this He did to show us what He could, what He might do. If our hearts do not quake and rend at the acknowledgement of His infinite power and fear of His terrible judgments as well as that earth did, we must expect to be made warnings that would take none.

LXI

Upon the Sight of a Dormouse

At how easy a rate do these creatures live that are fed with rest! So the bear and the hedgehog (they say) spend their whole winter in sleep and rise up fatter than they lay down. How oft have I envied the thriving drowsiness of these beasts when the toil of thoughts hath bereaved me of but one hour's sleep and left me languishing to a new task! And yet, when I have well digested the comparison of these two conditions, I must needs say I had rather waste with work than batten with ease, and would rather choose a life profitably painful than uselessly dull and delicate. I cannot tell whether I should say those creatures live which do nothing, since we are wont ever to notify life by motion. Sure I am their life is not vital. For me, let me rather complain of a mind that will not let me be idle than of a body that will not let me work.

LXII

Upon Bees Fighting

What a pity it is to see these profitable, industrious creatures fall so furiously upon each other and thus sting and kill each other in the very mouth of the hive! I could like well to see the bees do this execution upon wasps and drones, enemies to their common stock; this savors but of justice. But to see them fall foul upon those of their own wing, it cannot but trouble their owner, who must needs be an equal loser by the victory of either. There is no more perfect resemblance of a commonwealth, whether civil or sacred, than in an hive. The bees are painful† and honest compatriots, laboring to bring wax and honey to the maintenance of the public state; the wasps and drones are unprofitable and harmful hangbys† which live upon the spoil of others' labors. Whether as common barattors† or strong thieves or bold parasites, they do nothing but rob their neighbors. It is an happy sight when these feel the dint of justice and are cut off from doing further mischief. But to see well-affected and beneficial subjects undo themselves with duels, whether of law or sword, to see good Christians of the same profession shedding each others' blood upon quarrels of religion, is no other than a sad and hateful spectacle; and so much the more by how much we have more means of reason and grace to compose our differences and correct our offensive contentiousness. Oh God who are at once the Lord of Hosts and Prince of Peace [Gen. 32: 2; Isa. 8:6], give us war with spiritual wickedness and peace with our brethren.

LXIII

Upon Wasps Falling into a Glass

See you that narrow-mouthed glass which is set near to the hive? Mark how busily the wasps resort to it, being drawn thither by the smell of that sweet liquor wherewith it is baited. See how mannerly they creep into the mouth of it and fall down suddenly from that slippery steepness into that watery trap from which they can never rise; there, after some vain labor and weariness, they drown and die. You do not see any of the bees look that way; they pass directly to their hive without any notice taken of such a pleasing bait. Idle and ill-disposed persons are drawn away with every temptation; they have both leisure and will to entertain every sweet allurement to sin and wantonly prosecute their own wicked lusts till they fall into irrecoverable damnation; whereas the diligent and laborious Christian that follows hard and conscionably work of an honest calling is free from the danger of these deadly enticements, and lays up honey of comfort [Rev. 10:9] against the winter of evil. Happy is that man who can see and enjoy the success of his labor; but, however, this we are sure of, if our labor cannot purchase the good we would have, it shall prevent the evil we would avoid.

LXIIII

Upon a Spring in a Wild Forest

Lo, here the true pattern of bounty! What clear crystal streams are here and how liberally do they gush forth and hasten down with a pleasing murmur into the valley! Yet you see neither man nor beast that takes part of that wholesome and pure water. It is enough that those may dip who will; the refusal of others doth no whit abate of this proffered plenty. Thus bountiful housekeepers hold on their set ordinary provisions whether they have guests or no. Thus conscionable preachers pour out the living waters of wholesome doctrine whether their hearers partake of those blessed means of salvation or neglect their holy endeavors. Let it be our comfort that we have been no niggards of these celestial streams; let the world give an account of the improvement.

LXV

Upon the Sight of an Owl in the Twilight

What a strange melancholic life doth this creature lead, to hide her head all day long in an ivy-bush and at night, when all other birds are at rest, to fly abroad and vent her harsh notes! I know not why the ancients have sacred† this bird to wisdom, except it be for her safe closeness and singular perspicacity; that when other domestical and airy creatures are blind, she only hath inward light to discern the least objects for her own advantage. Surely thus much wit they have taught us in her, that he is the wisest man that would have least to do with the multitude; that no life is so safe as the obscure; that retiredness, if it have less comfort, yet less danger and vexation; lastly, that he is truly wise who sees by a light of his own when the rest of the world sit in an ignorant and confused darkness, unable to apprehend any truth save by the helps of an outward illumination.

Had this owl come forth in the daytime, how had all the little birds flocked wondering about her, to see her uncouth visage, to hear her untuned notes! She likes her estate never the worse, but pleaseth herself in her own quiet reservedness. It is not for a wise man to be much affected with the censures of the rude and unskillful vulgar, but to hold fast unto his own well chosen and well fixed resolutions. Every fool knows what is wont to be done, but what is best to be done is known only to the wise.

LXVI

Upon an Arm Benumbed

How benumbed and (for the time) senseless is this arm of mine become only with the too long leaning upon it! While I used it to other services, it failed me not. Now that I have rested upon it I find cause to complain. It is no trusting to an arm of flesh; on whatsoever occasion we put our confidence, therein this reliance will be sure to end in pain and disapointment. Oh God, Thine arm is strong and mighty [Ps. 89:13]; all Thy creatures rest themselves upon that and are comfortably maintained. Oh that we were not more capable of distrust than Thine omnipotent hand is of weariness and subduction!†

LXVII

Upon the Sparks Flying Upward

It is a feeling comparison (that of Job) of man born to labor as the sparks fly upward [Job 5:7]; that motion of theirs is no other than natural. Neither is it otherwise wise for man to labor. His mind is created active and apt to some or other ratiocination: his joints all stirring, his nerves made for helps of moving, and his occasions of living call him forth to action; so as an idle man doth not more want grace than degenerate from nature. Indeed, at the first kindling of the fire, some sparks are wont, by the impulse of the bellows, to fly forward or sideward; and even so in our first age youthly vanity may move us to irregular courses. But when those first violences are overcome and we have attained to a settledness of disposition, our sparks fly up, our life is labor, and why should we not do that which we are made for? Why should not God rather grudge us our being than we grudge

Him our work? It is no thank to us that we labor out of necessity. Out of my obedience to Thee, oh God, I desire ever to be employed. I shall never have comfort in my toil if it be rather a purveyance for myself than a sacrifice to Thee.

LXVIII

Upon the Sight of a Raven

I cannot see that bird but I must needs think of Elijah and wonder less at the miracle of his faith than of his provision [1 Kings 17:2–7]. It was a strong belief that carried him into a desolate retiredness to expect food from ravens. This fowl, we know is ravenous; all is too little that he can forage for himself; and the prophet's reason must needs suggest to him that in a dry barren desert bread and flesh must be great dainties, yet he goes aside to expect victuals from that purveyance. He knew this fowl to be no less greedy than unclean, unclean as in Law and in the nature of his feed. What is his ordinary prey but loathsome carrion? Yet since God had appointed him this cater,† he stands not upon the nice points of a fastidious squeamishness but confidently depends upon that uncouth provision; and accordingly these unlikely purveyers bring him bread and flesh in the morning and bread and flesh in the evening.

Not one of those hungry ravens could swallow one morsel of those viands which were sent by them to a better mouth. The River of Cherith sooner failed him than the tender of their services. No doubt Elijah's stomach was often up before his incurious† diet came, when expecting from the mouth of his cave out of what coast of heaven these his servitors might be descried. Upon the sight of them he magnified with a thankful heart the wonderful goodness and truth of his God and was nourished more with his faith than with his food. Oh God, how infinite is Thy providence, wisdom, power! We creatures are not what we are but what Thou wilt have us; when Thy turn is to be served, we have none of our own. Give me but faith and do what Thou wilt.

LXIX

Upon a Worm

It was an homely expression which God makes of the state of His Church, "Fear not, thou worm of Jacob" [Isa, 41:14]. Every foot is ready to tread on this despised creature. While it keeps itself in that cold obscure cell of the earth (wherein it was hidden), it lay safe because it was secret; but now that it hath put itself forth of that close cave and hath presented itself to the light of the sun, to the eye of passengers,† how is it vexed with the scorching beams, and wrings up and down in an helpless perplexity, not finding where to shroud itself! How obnoxious is it to the fowls of the air, to the feet of men and beasts! He that made this creature such and calls His Church so well knew the answerableness of their condition. How doth the world overlook and contemn that little flock whose best guard hath ever been secrecy! And if ever that despicable number have dared to show itself, how hath it been scorched and trampled upon and entertained with all variety of persecutions! Oh Saviour, Thy Spouse fares no otherwise than Thyself. To match her fully Thou hast said of Thyself, "I am a worm and no man" [Ps. 22: 6]. Such thou wert in Thine humbled estate here on earth; such Thou wouldst be. But as it is a true word that He who made the angels in heaven made also the worm on earth, so it is no less true that He who made Himself and His Church worms upon earth hath raised our nature in His Person above the angels, and our person in His Church to little less than angels. It matters not how we fare in this valley of tears while we are sure of that infinite amends of glory above.

LXX

Upon the Putting on of his Clothes

What a poor thing were man if he were not beholden to other creatures! The earth affords him flax for his linen, bread for his belly; the beasts, his ordinary clothes; the silkworm, his bravery;† the back and bowels of the earth, his metals and fuel; the fishes, fowls, beasts, his nourishment. His wit indeed works upon all these to improve them to his own advantage, but they must yield him materials else he

subsists not. And yet we fools are proud of ourselves, yea, proud of
the cast suits of the very basest creatures. There is not one of them
that have so much need of us. They would enjoy themselves the
more if man were not. Oh God, the more we are sensible of our own
indigence, the more let us wonder at this all-sufficiency in Thyself and
long for that happy condition wherein Thou (which art all-
perfection) shalt be all in all to us.

LXXI

Upon the Sight of a Great Library[12]

What a world of wit is here packed up together! I know not
whether this sight doth more dismay or comfort me. It dismays me
to think that here is so much that I cannot know; it comforts me to
think that this variety yields so good helps to know what I should.
There is no truer word than that of Solomon, "There is no end of
making many books" [Eccles. 12:12] ; this sight verifies it. There is no
end; indeed, it were pity there should. God hath given to man a busy
soul, the agitation whereof cannot but through time and experience
work out many hidden truths. To suppress these would be no other
than injurious to mankind, whose minds, like unto so many candles,
should be kindled by each other. The thoughts of our deliberation are
most accurate; these we vent into our papers. What an happiness is it
that, without all offence of necromancy, I may call up any of the ancient worthies of learning, whether humane or divine, and confer
with them of all my doubts, that I can at pleasure summon whole
synods of reverend fathers and acute doctors from all the coasts of the
earth to give their well-studied judgments in all points of question
which I propose! Neither can I cast my eye casually upon any of
these silent masters but I must learn somewhat; it is a wantonness to
complain of choice.

No law binds us to read all, but the more we can take in and digest
the better-liking must the mind's needs be. Blessed be God that hath
set up so many clear lamps in his Church!

Now none but the willfully blind can plead darkness. And blessed
be the memory of those His faithful servants that have left their
blood, their spirits, their lives in these precious papers and have willingly wasted themselves into these during† monuments to give light
to others.

LXXII

Upon the Red Cross on a Door

Oh sight fearfully significant! This sickness is a cross indeed and that a bloody one; both the form and the color import death. The Israelites' doors whose lintels were besprinkled with blood were passed over by the destroying angel [Exod. 12:22–23]; here the destroying angel hath smitten and hath left this mark of his deadly blow. We are wont to fight cheerfully under this ensign abroad and be victorious. Why should we tremble at it at home? Oh God, there Thou fightest for us, here against us; under that we have fought for Thee, but under this (because our sins have fought against Thee) we are fought against by Thy judgments.

Yet, Lord, it is Thy cross, though an heavy one. It is ours by merit, Thine by imposition. Oh Lord, sanctify Thine affliction and remove Thy vengeance.

LXXIII

Upon the Change of Weather

I know not whether it be worse that the heaven look upon us always with one face or ever varying, for as continual change of weather causes uncertainty of health, so a permanent settledness of one season causeth a certainty of distemper. Perpetual moisture dissolves us, perpetual heat evaporates or inflames us, cold stupifies us, drought obstructs and withers us. Neither is it otherwise in the state of the mind. If our thoughts should be always volatile, changing, inconstant, we should never attain to any good habit of the soul, whether in matter of judgment or disposition; but if they should be always fixed, we should run into the danger of some desperate extremity. To be ever thinking would make us mad; to be ever thinking of our crosses or sins would make us heartlessly dejected; to be ever thinking of pleasures and contentments would melt us into a loose wantonness; to be ever doubting and fearing were an hellish servitude; to be ever bold and confident were a dangerous presumption; but the interchanges of these in a due moderation keep the soul in health. Oh God, howsoever these variations be necessary for my spiritual condition, let me have no weather but sunshine from Thee. Do Thou lift up the light of Thy countenance upon me [Ps. 4:6] and stablish† me ever with Thy free spirit.

LXXIIII

Upon the Sight of a Marriage

What a comfortable and feeling resemblance is here of Christ and His Church! I regard not the persons; I regard the institution. Neither the husband nor the wife are now any more their own; they have either of them given over themselves to other. Not only the wife, which is the weaker vessel, hath yielded over herself to the stronger protection and participation of an abler head, but the husband hath resigned his right in himself over to his feebler consort; so as now her weakness is his, his strength is hers. Yea, their very soul and spirit may no more be severed in respect of mutual affection than from their own several bodies. It is thus, Oh Saviour, with Thee and Thy Church. We are not our own but Thine, who has married us to Thyself in truth and righteousness [Rev. 19:7–8]. What powers, what endowments have we but from and in Thee? And as our holy boldness dares interest ourselves in Thy graces, so Thy wonderfully compassionate mercy vouchsafes to interest Thyself in our infirmities. Thy poor Church suffers on earth; Thou feelest in heaven and, as complaining of our stripes, canst say, "Why persecutest thou me" [Acts 26:14].

Thou again art not so Thine own as that Thou art not also ours. Thy sufferings, Thy merits, Thy obedience, Thy life, death, resurrection, ascension, intercession, glory, yea, Thy blessed humanity, yea, Thy glorious deity, by virtue of our right, of our union are so ours as that we would not give our part in Thee for ten thousand worlds.

Oh gracious Saviour, as Thou canst not but love and cherish this poor and unworthy soul of mine, which Thou hast mercifully espoused to Thyself, so give me grace to honor and obey Thee and, forsaking all the base and sinful rivality† of the world, to hold me only unto Thee while I live here, that I may perfectly enjoy Thee hereafter.

LXXV

Upon the Sight of a Snake

I know not what horror we find in ourselves at the sight of a serpent. Other creatures are more loathsome and some no less deadly than it, yet there is none at which our blood riseth so much as at this. Whence should this be but out of an instinct of our old enmity? We were stung in Paradise and cannot but feel it. But here is our weakness: it was not the body of the serpent that could have hurt us without the suggestion of sin, and yet we love the sin while we hate the serpent. Every day are we wounded with the sting of that old serpent and complain not, and so much more deadly is that sting by how much it is less felt. There is a sting of guilt and there is a sting of remorse; there is mortal venom in the first, whereof we are the least sensible;† there is less danger in the second. The Israelites found themselves stung by those fiery serpents in the desert [Num. 21:6], and the sense of their pain sent them to seek for cure. The world is our desert, and as the sting of death is sin so the sting of sin is death. I do not more wish to find ease than pain; if I complain enough I cannot fail of cure. Oh Thou, which art the true brazen serpent lifted up in this wilderness [Num. 21:9; John 3:14], raise up mine eyes to Thee and fasten them upon thee.[13] Thy mercy shall make my soul whole, my wound sovereign.

LXXVI

Upon the Ruins of an Abbey

It is not so easy to say what it was that built up these walls as what it was that pulled them down, even the wickedness of the possessors.[14] Every stone hath a tongue to accuse the superstition, hypocrisy, idleness, luxury of the late owners.

Methinks I see it written all along in capital letters upon these heaps: "A FRUITFUL LAND MAKETH HE BARREN FOR THE INIQUITY OF THEM THAT DWELL THEREIN" [Ps. 107:34]. Perhaps there wanted not some sacrilege in the demolishers; in all the carriage of these businesses there was a just hand that knew how to make a wholesome and profitable use of mutual sins. Full little did the builders or the indwellers think that this costly and warm fabric should so soon end violently in a desolate rubbish. It is not for us to be high-minded but to fear. No roof is so high, no wall so strong as that sin cannot level it with the dust. Were any pile so close that it could keep out air, yet it could not keep out judgment where sin hath been fore-admitted.

In vain shall we promise stability to those houses which we have made witnesses of and accessories to our shameful uncleannesses. The firmness of any building is not so much in the matter as in the owner. Happy is that cottage that hath an honest master and woe be to that palace that is viciously inhabited.

LXXVII

Upon the Discharging of a Piece†

Good Lord, how witty men are to kill one another! What fine devices they have found to murder afar off, to slay many at once, and so to fetch off lives that while a whole lane is made of carcasses with one blow, nobody knows who hurt him! And what honor do we place in slaughter! Those arms wherein we pride ourselves are such as which we or our ancestors have purchased with blood. The monuments of our glory are the spoils of a subdued and slain enemy, where, contrarily, all the titles of God sound of mercy and gracious respects to man. God the Father is the "Maker and Preserver" of man; God the son is the "Saviour" of mankind; God the Holy Ghost styles Himself the "Comforter" [John 14:26]. Alas, whose image do we bear in this disposition but his whose true title is the "Destroyer" [Ps. 17:4]? It is easy to take away the life. It is not easy to give it. Give me the man that can devise how to save troops of men from killing, his name shall have room in my calendar. There is more true honor in a civic garland for the preserving of one subject than in a laurel for the victory of many enemies. Oh God, there are enough that bend their thoughts to undo what Thou hast made; enable Thou me to bestow my endeavors in reprieving or rescuing that which might otherwise perish. Oh Thou who art our common Saviour, make Thou me both ambitious and able to save some other besides myself.

LXXVIII

Upon the Tolling of a Passing-bell†

How doleful and heavy is this summons of death! This sound is not for our ears but for our hearts. It calls us not only to our prayers but to our preparation; to our prayers for the departing soul, to our preparation for our own departing. We have never so much need of prayers as in our last combat. Then is our great adversary most eager, then are we the weakest, then nature is so overlabored that it gives us not leisure to make use of gracious motions. There is no preparation so necessary as for this conflict; all our life is little enough to make ready for our last hour.[15] What, am I better than my neighbors? How oft hath this bell reported to me the farewell of many more strong and vigorous bodies than my own, of many more cheerful and lively spirits! And now what doth it but call me to the thought of my parting? Here is no abiding for me; I must away too. Oh Thou that art the God of comfort, help Thy poor servant that is now struggling with his last enemy. His sad friends stand gazing upon him and weeping over him, but they cannot succor him; needs must they leave him to do this great work alone. None but Thou to whom belong the "issues of death" [Ps. 68:20] canst relieve his distressed and over-matched soul. And for me, let no man die without me. As I die daily so teach me to die once; acquaint me beforehand with that messenger which I must trust to. Oh teach me so to number my days that I may apply my heart to true wisdom [Ps. 90:12].

LXXIX

Upon a Defamation Dispersed

Were I the first or the best that ever was slandered perhaps it would be somewhat difficult to command myself patience. Grief is wont to be abated either by partners or precedents; the want whereof dejects us beyond measure as men singled out for patterns of misery. Now while I find this the common condition of all that ever have been reputed virtuous, why am I troubled with the whisperings of false tongues? Oh God [margin: —*Si Christus Judam passus est, cur non ego patior Birrhichionem? —Dial. de S. Martino. Sever. Sulpit.*][16], the Devil slandered Thee in Paradise. Oh Saviour, men slandered Thee on earth more than men or devils can reproach me. Thou art the best as Thou art the best that ever was smitten by a lying and venomous tongue. It is too much favor that is done me by malicious lips that they conform me to Thy sufferings. I could not be so happy if they were not so spiteful. Oh Thou glorious pattern of reproached innocence, if I may not die for Thee yet let me thus bleed for Thee.

LXXX

Upon a Ring of Bells

While eveiy bell keeps due time and order what a sweet and harmonious sound they make! All the neighbor villages are cheered with that common music. But when once they jar and check each other, either jangling together or striking preposterously, how harsh and unpleasing is that noise! So that as we testify our public rejoicing by an orderly and well-tuned peal, so when we would signify that the town is on fire we ring confusedly.

It is thus in church and commonwealth. When everyone knows and keeps their due ranks, there is a melodious consort of peace and contentment; but when distances and proportions of respects are not mutually observed, when either states or persons will be clashing with each other, the discord is grievous and extremely prejudicial. Such confusion either notifieth a fire already kindled or portendeth it. Popular states may ring the changes with safety, but the monarchical government requires a constant and regular course of the set degrees of rule and inferiority, which cannot be violated without a sensible† discontentment and danger. For me, I do so love the peace of the church and state that I cannot but with [Paul], the charitable apostle, say, "Would to God they were cut off that trouble them" [Gal. 5:12] and shall ever wish either no jar or no clappers.

LXXXI

Upon the Sight of a Full Table at a Feast

What a great variety is here of flesh, of fish, of both, of neither, as if both nature and art did strive to pamper us! Yet, methinks, enough is better than all this. Excess is but a burden, as to the provider so to the guest. It pities and grieves me to think what toil, what charge hath gone to the gathering of all these dainties together, what pain so many creatures have been put to in dying for a needless sacrifice to the belly. What a penance must be done by every accumbent† in sitting out the passage through all those dishes! What a task the stomach must be put to in the concoction of so many mixtures! I am not so austerely scrupulous as to deny the lawfulness of these abundant provisions upon just occasions. I find my Saviour Himself more than once at a feast; this is recorded as well as His one long fast. Doubtless our bountiful God hath given us His creatures not for necessity only but for pleasure. But these exceedings would be both rare and moderate, and when they must be require no less patience than temperance.

Might I have my opinion, oh God, give me rather a little with peace and love. He whose provision for every day was thirty measures of fine flour, and threescore measures of meal, thirty oxen, an hundred sheep, besides venison and fowl[17] yet can pray, "Give me the bread of sufficiency." Let me have no perpetual feast but a good conscience, and from these great preparations, for the health of soul and body, let me rise rather hungry than surcharged.

LXXXII

Upon the Hearing of a Lute Well Played On

There may be (for ought we know) infinite inventions of art the possibility whereof we should hardly ever believe if they were fore-reported to us. Had we lived in some rude and remote part of the world and should have been told that it is possible, only by an hollow piece of wood and the guts of beasts stirred by the fingers of men, to make so sweet and melodious a noise, we should have thought it utterly incredible; yet now that we see and hear it ordinarily done we make it no wonder. It is no marvel if we cannot fore-imagine what kind and means of harmony God will have used by his saints and angels in heaven, when these poor matters seem so strange to our conceits which yet our very senses are convinced of. Oh God, Thou knowest infinite ways to glorify Thyself by the creatures which do far transcend our weak and finite capacities. Let me wonder at Thy wisdom and power and be more aweful in my adorations than curious in my inquiries.

LXXXIII

Upon the Sight and Noise of a Peacock

I see there are many kinds of hypocrites. Of all birds this makes the fairest show and the worst noise, so as this is an hypocrite to the eye.

There are others, as the blackbird, that looks foul and sooty but sings well; this is an hypocrite to the ear. There are others that please as well both in their show and voice but are cross in their carriage and condition, as the popinjay, whose colors are beautiful and noise delightful yet is apt to do mischief in scratching and biting any hand that comes near it. These are hypocrites both to the eye and ear. Yet there is a degree further (beyond the example of all brute creatures) of them whose show, whose words, whose actions are fair but their hearts are foul and abominable.

No outward beauty can make the hypocrite other than odious. For me, let my profession agree with my words, my words with my actions, my actions with my heart; and let all of them be approved of the God of truth.

LXXXIIII

Upon a Penitent Malefactor

I know not whether I should more admire the wisdom or the mercy of God in His proceedings with men. Had not this man sinned thus notoriously he had never been happy. While his courses were fair and civil, yet he was graceless. Now his miscarriage hath drawn him into a just affliction; his affliction hath humbled him. God hath taken this advantage of his humiliation for his conversion; had not one foot slipped into the mouth of hell, he had never been in this forwardness to heaven.

There is no man so weak or foolish as that he hath not strength or wit enough to sin or to make use of his sins. It is only the goodness of an infinite God that can make our sin good to us though evil in itself. Oh God, it is no thank to ourselves or to our sins that we are bettered with evil. The work is Thine, let Thine be the glory.

LXXXV

Upon the Vision of a Lily

This must needs be a goodly flower that our Saviour hath singled out to compare with Solomon, and that not in his ordinary dress but in all his royalty [Matt. 6:28]. Surely the earth had never so glorious a king as he; nature yielded nothing that might not set forth royal magnificence that he wanted. Yet He that made both Solomon and this flower says that Solomon in all his royalty was not clad like it. What a poor thing is this earthly bravery† that is so easily over-matched! How ill judges are we of outward beauties that contemn these goodly plants which their Creator thus magnifies and admire those base metals which He (in comparison hereof) contemns! If it be their transitoriness that embaseth them, what are we? "All flesh is grass, and all the glory of man as the flower of grass" [Isa. 11:6; 2 Pet. 1:24]. As we cannot be so brave† so we cannot be more permanent. Oh God, let it be my ambition to walk with Thee hereafter in white. Could I put on a robe of stars here with proud Herod [Acts 12:23], that glittering garment could not keep me from lice and worms. Might I sit on a throne of gold within an house of ivory, I see I should not compare with this flower. I might be as transitory, I should not be so beautiful. What matters it whether I go for a flower or a weed here? Whethersoever, I must wither. Oh Thou which art greater than Solomon, do Thou clothe me with Thy perfect righteousness, so shall I flourish forever in the courts of the house of my God [Ps. 65:4].

LXXXVI

Upon the Sight of a Coffin Stuck with Flowers

Too fair appearance is never free from just suspicion. While here was nothing but mere wood, no flower was to be seen here; now that this wood is lined with an unsavory corpse, it is adorned with this sweet variety. The fir whereof that coffin is made yields a natural redolence alone; now that it is stuffed thus noisomely, all helps are too little to countervail that scent of corruption.

Neither is it otherwise in living. Perpetual use of strong perfumes argues a guiltiness of some unpleasing savor. The case is the same spiritually; an over-glorious outside of profession implies some inward filthiness that would fain escape notice. Our uncomely parts have more comeliness put on; too much ornament imports extreme deformity. For me, let my show be moderate, so shall I neither deceive applause nor merit too deep censure.

LXXXVII

Upon the View of the World

It is a good thing to see this material world, but it is a better thing to think of the intelligible world. This thought is the sight of the soul whereby it discerneth things like itself, spiritual and immortal, which are so much beyond the worth of these sensible objects as a spirit is beyond a body, a pure substance beyond a corruptible, and infinite God above a finite creature. Oh God, how great a word is that which the Psalmist saith of Thee that Thou abasest Thyself to behold the things both in heaven and earth [Ps. 113:6]!

It is our glory to look up even to the meanest piece of heaven. It is an abasement to Thine incomprehensible majesty to look down upon the best of heaven. Oh what a transcendent glory must that needs be that is abased to behold the things of heaven! What an happiness shall it be to me that mine eyes shall be exalted to see Thee who art humbled to see the place and state of my blessedness! Yea, those very angels that see Thy face are so resplendently glorious that we could not over-live the sight of one of their faces who are fain to hide their faces from the sight of Thine. How many millions of them attend Thy throne above and Thy footstool below [Isa. 66:1; Matt. 5:35; Acts 7:49] in the ministration to Thy saints? It is that, Thine invisible world, the communion wherewith can make me truly blessed. Oh God, if my body have fellowship here amongst beasts of whose earthly substance it participates, let my soul be united to Thee, the God of spirits, and be raised up to enjoy the insensible† society of Thy blessed angels. Acquaint me beforehand with those citizens and affairs of Thine heaven and make me no stranger to my Father's glory.

LXXXVIII

Upon the Stinging of a Wasp

How small things may annoy the greatest! Even a mouse troubles an elephant; a gnat, a lion; a very flea may disquiet a giant. What weapon can be nearer to nothing than the sting of this wasp, yet what a painful wound hath it given me! That scarce-visible point, how it envenoms and rankles and swells up the flesh! The tenderness of the part adds much to the grief.

And if I be thus vexed with the touch of an angry fly,† Lord, how shall I be able to endure the sting of a tormenting conscience? As that part is both most active and most sensible, so that wound which it receives from itself is most intolerably grievous. There were more ease in a nest of hornets than under this one torture. Oh God, howsoever I speed abroad, give me peace at home; and whatever my flesh may suffer, keep my soul free.

Thus pained, wherein do I find ease but in laying honey to the part infected? That medicine only abates the anguish. How near hath nature placed the remedy to the offence! Whensoever my heart is stung with the remorse for sins, only Thy sweet and precious merits, oh blessed Saviour, can mitigate and heal the wound; they have virtue to cure me, give me grace to apply them. That sovereign receipt† shall make my pain happy; I shall thus applaud my grief. It is good for me that I was thus afflicted.

LXXXIX

Upon the Arraignment of a Felon

With what terror doth this malefactor stand at that bar! His hand trembles while it is lift up for his trial; his very lips quake while he saith, "Not guilty"; his countenance condemns him before the judge; and his fear is ready to execute him before the hangman. Yet this judge is but a weak man that must, soon after, die himself; that sentence of death which he can pronounce is already passed by nature upon the most innocent; that act of death which the law inflicteth by him is but momentary. Who knows whether himself shall not die more painfully? Oh God, with what horror shall the guilty soul stand before Thy dreadful tribunal in the day of the great assizes of the world while there is the presence of an infinite Majesty to daunt him, a fierce and clamorous conscience to give evidence against him, legions of ugly and terrible devils waiting to seize upon him, a gulf of unquenchable fire ready to receive him; while the glory of the judge is no less confounding than the cruelty of the tormenters, where the sentence is unavoidable and the execution everlasting! Why do not these terrors of Thee, my God, make me wise to hold a privy session upon my soul and actions, that being acquitted by my own heart, I may not be condemned by Thee; and being judged by myself, I may not be condemned by the world?

XC

Upon the Crowing of a Cock

How harshly did this note sound in the ear of Peter, yea, pierced his very heart [Mark 14:66–72]! Many a time had he heard this bird and was no whit moved with the noise. Now there was a bird in his bosom that crowed louder than this, whose shrill accent, conjoined with this, astonished the guilty disciple.

The weary laborer, when he is awakened from his sweet sleep by this natural clock of the household, is not so angry at this troublesome bird nor so vexed at the hearing of that unseasonable sound as Peter was when this fowl awakened his sleeping conscience and called him to a timely repentance. This cock did but crow like others, neither made or knew any difference of this tone and the rest. There was a divine hand that ordered this morning's note to be a summons of penitence; He that foretold it had fore-appointed it. That bird could not but crow then, and all the noise in the high priests' hall could not keep that sound from Peter's ear. But oh Saviour, couldst Thou find leisure, when thou stoodst at the bar of that unjust and cruel judgment amidst all that bloody rabble of enemies, in the sense of all their fury and the expectation of Thine own death, to listen unto this monitor of Peter's repentance and upon the hearing of it to cast back Thine eyes upon Thy denying, cursing, abjuring disciple? Oh mercy without measure and beyond all possibility of our admiration, to neglect Thyself for a sinner, to attend the repentance of one when Thou wert about to lay down thy life for all!

Oh God, Thou art still equally merciful. Every elect soul is no less dear unto thee. Let the sound of Thy faithful monitors smite my ear and let the beams of thy merciful eyes wound my heart so as I may go forth and weep bitterly [Matt. 26:75].

XCI

Upon the Variety of Thoughts[18]

When I bethink myself how eternity depends upon this moment of life, I wonder how I can think of anything but heaven; but when I see the distractions of my thoughts and the aberations of my life, I wonder how I can be so bewitched as (while I believe in heaven) so to forget it. All that I can do is to be angry at my own vanity. My thoughts would not be so many if they were all right; there are ten thousand byways for one direct. As there is but one heaven so there is but one way to it, that living way wherein I walk by faith, by obedience. All things, the more perfect they are, the more do they reduce themselves towards that unity which is the center of all perfection. Oh Thou that art one and infinite, draw in my heart from all these straggling and unprofitable cogitations and confine it to Thine heaven and to Thyself, who art the Heaven of that heaven. Let me have no life but in Thee, no care but to enjoy Thee, no ambition but Thy glory. Oh make me thus imperfectly happy before my time that when my time shall be no more I may be perfectly happy with Thee to all eternity.

XCII

Upon the Sight of a Harlot Carted

With what noise and tumult and zeal of solemn justice is this sin punished! The streets are not more full of beholders than clamors. Every one strives to express his detestation of the fact by some token of revenge: one casts mire, another water, another rotten eggs upon the miserable offender; neither indeed is she worthy of less. But in the meantime no man looks home to himself; it is no uncharity to say that too many insult in this just punishment who have deserved more. Alas, we men value sins by the outward scandal, but the wise and holy God (against whom only our sins are done) esteems them according to the intrinsical iniquity of them and according to the secret violation of His will and justice. Thus those sins which are slight to us are to Him heinous. We ignorants would have rung David's adultery [2 Sam. 11: 2–5] with basins, but as for his numbering of the people [2 Sam. 24:10] we should have passed over as venial.† The wise justice of the Almighty found more wickedness in this which we should scarce have accused. Doubtless there is more mischief in a secret infidelity which the world either cannot know or cares not to censure than in the foulest adultery. Public sins have more shame, private may have more guilt. If the world cannot charge me of those, it is enough that I can charge my soul of worse. Let others rejoice in these public executions; let me pity the sins of others and be humbled under the sense of my own.

XCIII

Upon the Smell of a Rose

Smelling is one of the meanest and least useful of the senses, yet there is none of the five that receives or gives so exquisite a contentment as it. Methinks there is no earthly thing that yields so perfect a pleasure to any sense as the odor of the first rose doth to the scent. It is the wisdom and bounty of the Creator so to order it that those senses which have more affinity with the body and with the earth whereof it is made should receive their delight and contentation† by these things which are bred of the earth, but those which are more spiritual and have more affinity with the soul should be reserved for the perfection of their pleasure to another world. There and then only shall my sight make my soul eternally blessed.

XCIIII

Upon a Cancelled Bond

While this obligation was in force, I was in servitude to my parchment. My bond was double: to a payment, to a penalty. Now that is discharged, what is it better than a waste scroll, regarded for nothing but the witness of its own voidance and nullity? No otherwise is it with the severe law of my Creator. Out of Christ it stands in full force and binds me over either to perfect obedience, which I cannot possibly perform, or to exquisite torment and eternal death, which I am never able to endure. But now that my Saviour hath fastened it cancelled to His cross (in respect of the rigor and malediction of it), I look upon it as the monument of my past danger and bondage. I know by it how much was owed by me, how much is paid for me. The direction of it is everlasting, the obligation by it unto death is frustrate. I am free from curse who never can be from obedience. O Saviour, take Thou glory and give me peace.

XCV

Upon the Report of a Great Loss by Sea

The earth and the water are both of them great givers and both great takers. As they give matter and sustentation† to all sublunary creatures, so they take all back again, insatiably devouring at last the fruits of their own wombs. Yet of the two, earth is both more beneficial and less cruel, for as that yields us the most general maintenance and wealth and supportation, so it doth not lightly take aught from us but that which we resign over to it and which naturally falls back unto it. Whereas the water, as it affords but a small part of our live-load and some few knacks of ornament, so it is apt violently to snatch away both us and ours and to bereave that which it never gave. It yields us no precious metals and yet in an instant fetches away millions. And yet, notwithstanding all the hard measure we receive from it, how many do we daily see that might have firm ground under them who yet will be trusting to the mercy of the sea! Yea, how many that have hardly crawled out from a desperate ship-wreck will yet be trying the fidelity of that unsure and untrusty element! Oh God, how venturous we are where we have reason to distrust, how incredulously fearful where we have cause to be confident! Whoever relied upon Thy gracious providence and sure promises, oh Lord, and hath miscarried? Yet here we pull in our faith and make excuses for our diffidence; and if Peter have tried those waves to be no other than solid pavement under his feet while his soul trod confidently, yet when a billow and a wind agree to threaten him, his faith flags and he begins to sink [Matt. 14:28–31]. Oh Lord, teach me to doubt where I am sure to find nothing but uncertainty and to be assuredly confident where there can be no possibility of any cause of doubting.

XCVI

Upon Sight of a Bright Sky Full of Stars

I cannot blame Empedocles if he professed a desire to live upon earth only that he might behold the face of the heavens.[19] Surely (if there were no other) this were a sufficient errand for a man's being here below, to see and observe these goodly spangles of light above our heads, their places, their quantities, their motions. But the employment of a Christian is far more noble and excellent: heaven is open to him and he can look beyond the veil and see further above those stars than it is thither, and there discern those glories that may answer so rich a pavement. Upon the clear sight whereof, I cannot wonder if the chosen vessel desired to leave the earth in so happy an exchange [Acts 9:15]. Oh God, I bless Thine infiniteness for what I see with these bodily eyes, but if Thou shalt but draw the curtain and let me by the eye of faith see the inside of that Thy glorious frame, I shall need no other happiness here, My soul cannot be capable of more favor than sight here and fruition hereafter.

XCVII

Upon the Rumors of Wars

Good Lord, what a shambles is Christendom become of late! How are men killed like flies and blood poured out like water! Surely, the cruelty and ambition of the great have an heavy reckoning to make for so many thousand souls. I condemn not just arms; those are necessary as the unjust are hateful. Even Michael and his angels fight [Rev. 12:7], and the style of God is "the Lord of Hosts"† [Ps. 103:21]. But woe be to the man by whom the offence cometh. Usurpation of others' rights, violations of oaths and contracts, and lastly erroneous zeals are guilty of all these public murders. Private men's injuries are washed off with tears, but wrongs done to princes and public states are hardly wiped off but with blood. Doubtless that fearful comet did not more certainly portend these wars than these wars presage the approach of the end of the world.[20] The earth was never without some broils since it was peopled but with three men, but so universal a combustion was never in the Christian world since it was. Oh Saviour, what can I think of this but that, as Thou wouldst have a general peace upon Thy first coming into the world, so upon Thy second coming Thou meanest there shall be a less general war upon each? That peace made way for Thy meek appearance, this war for Thy dreadful and terrible.

XCVIII

Upon a Child Crying

It was upon great reason that the apostle charges us to be children in understanding [1 Cor. 14:20]. What fools we all once are! Even at first we cry and smile we know not wherefore; we have not wit enough to make sign what hurts us or where we complain; we can wry the mouth but not seek the breast; and if we want help we can only lament and sprawl and cry.²¹ After, when some months have taught us to distinguish a little betwixt things and persons, we cry for every toy, even that which may hurt us; and when there is no other cause, we cry only to hear our own noise and are straight stilled with a greater. And if it be but upon the breeding of a tooth, we are so wayward that nothing will please us; and if some formerly-liked knack be given to quiet us, we cast away that which we have if we have not what we would seem to like. We fear neither fire nor water; nothing scares us but either a rod or a feigned bugbear; we mis-know our parents, not acknowledging any friend but the tailor that brings us fine coats or the nurse that dresses us gay. The more that our riper years resemble these dispositions the more childish we are and more worthy both of our own and others' censure.

But again, it was upon no less reason that the apostle charges us to be children in maliciousness. Those little innocents bear no grudge; they are sooner pleased than angry. And if any man have wronged them, let them but have given a stroke unto the nurse to beat the offender, it is enough. At the same instant they put forth their hand for reconcilement and offer themselves unto those arms that trespassed. And when they are most froward, they are stilled with a pleasant song. The old word is that an old man is twice a child, but I say happy is he that is thus a child always. It is a great imperfection to want knowledge, but of the two it is better to be a child in understanding than a man in maliciousness.

XCIX

Upon the Beginning of a Sickness

It was my own fault if I looked not for this. All things must undergo their changes. I have enjoyed many fair days; there was no reason I should not at last make account of clouds and storms. Could I have done well without any mixture of sin, I might have hoped for entire health. But since I have interspersed my obedience with many sinful failings and enormities, why do I think much to interchange health with sickness? What I now feel I know; I am not worthy to know what I must feel. As my times so my measures are in the hands of a wise and good God. My comfort is that He that sends these evils proportions them. If they be sharp I am sure they are just; the most that I am capable to endure is the least part of what I have deserved to suffer. Nature would fain be at ease, but, Lord, whatever become of this carcass Thou hast reason to have respect to Thine own glory. I have sinned and must smart; it is the glory of Thy mercy to beat my body for the safety of my soul. The worst of sickness is pain and the worst of pain is but death. As for pain, if it be extreme it cannot be long; and if it be long (such is the difference of earthly and hellish torments) it cannot be extreme. As for death, it is both unavoidable and beneficial; there ends my misery and begins my glory. A few groans are well bestowed for a preface to an immortal joy. Howsoever, oh God, Thy messenger is worthy to be welcome; it is the Lord, let Him do whatsoever He will.

C

Upon the Challenge of a Promise

It is true an honest man's word must be his master. When I have promised I am indebted and debts may be claimed, must be paid. But yet, there is a great deal of difference in our engagements. Some things we promise because they are due; some things are only due because they are promised. These latter, which are but the mere engagements of courtesy, cannot so absolutely bind us that notwithstanding any intervention of unworthiness or misbehavior in the person expectant we are tied to make our word good though to the cutting of our own throats. All favorable promises presuppose a capacity in the receiver; where that palpably faileth, common equity sets us free. I promised to send a fair sword to my friend; he is since that time turned frantic.† Must I send it or be charged with unfaithfulness if I send it not? Oh God, Thy title is the God of truth [John 14:16]; Thou canst no more cease to be faithful than to be. How oft hast Thou promised that no good thing shall be wanting to Thine, and yet we know Thy dearest children have complained of want. Is Thy word therefore challengeable? Far, far be this wicked presumption from our thoughts! No, these Thy promises of outward favors are never but with a subintelligence of a condition: of our capableness, of our expedience. Thou seest that plenty or ease would be our bane; Thy love forbears to satisfy us with an harmful blessing. We are worthy to be plagued with prejudicial kindness if we do not acknowledge Thy wisdom and care in our want. It is enough for us that Thy best mercies are our dues because Thy promises. We cannot too much claim that which Thou hast absolutely engaged Thyself to give and in giving shalt make us eternally happy.

CI

Upon the Sight of Flies

When I look upon these flies and gnats and worms, I have reason to think, "What am I to my infinite Creator more then these?" And if these had my reason, why might they not expostulate with their Maker why they are but such, why they live to so little purpose and die without either notice or use? And if I had no more reason than they, I should be (as they) content with any condition. That reason which I have is not of my own giving; He that hath given me reason might as well have given it to them or have made me as reasonless as they. There is no cause why His greater gift should make me mutinous and malcontent. I will thank my God for what I am, for what I have, and never quarrel with Him for what I want.†

CII

Upon the Sight of a Fantastical Zealot†

It is not the intent of grace to mold our bodies anew but to make use of them as it finds us. The disposition of men much follows the temper of their bodily humours.† This mixture of humors wrought upon by grace causeth that strange variety which we see in professions pretendedly religious. When grace lights upon a sad melancholic spirit, nothing is effected but sullenness and extreme mortification and dislike even of lawful freedom, nothing but positions and practices of severe austerity; when, contrarily, upon the cheerful and lively, all draws towards liberty and joy. Those thoughts do now please best which enlarge the heart to mirth and contentation.† It is the greatest improvement of Christian wisdom to distinguish all professions betwixt grace and humor, to give God His own glory and men their own infirmities.

CIII

Upon the Sight of a Scavenger Working in the Channel

The wise providence of God hath fitted men with spirits answerable to their condition. If mean men should bear the minds of great lords, no servile work would be done; all would be commanders and none could live. If, contrarily, great persons had the low spirits of drudges, there could be no order, no obedience because there should be none to command. Now, out of this discord of dispositions God hath contrived an excellent harmony of government and peace, since the use which each sort must needs have of other binds them to maintain the quality of their own rank and to do those offices which are requisite for the preservation of themselves and the public. As inferiors, then, must bless God for the graces and authority of their betters, so must superiors no less bless Him for the humility and serviceableness of the meaner; and those which are of the mid-rank must bless Him for both.

CIIII

Upon a Pair of Spectacles

I look upon these not as objects but as helps; as not meaning that my sight should rest in them but pass through them and by their aid discern some other things which I desire to see. Many such glasses my soul hath and useth: I look through the glass of the creatures at the power and wisdom of their maker; I look through the glass of the Scriptures at the great mystery of redemption and the glory of an heavenly inheritance; I look through God's favors at His infinite mercy, through His judgments at His incomprehensible justice. But as these spectacles of mine presuppose a faculty in the eye and cannot give me sight when I want it but only clear that sight which I have, no more can these glasses of the creatures, of Scriptures, of favors and judgments enable me to apprehend those blessed objects except I have an eye of faith whereto they may be presented. These helps to an unbelieving man are but as spectacles to the blind. As the natural eyes, so the spiritual have their degrees of dimness, but I have ill improved my age if, as my natural eyes decay, my spiritual eye be not cleared and confirmed. But at my best I shall never but need spectacles till I come to see as I am seen [1 Cor. 13:12].

CV

Upon Motes in the Sun

How these little motes move up and down in the sun and never rest, whereas the great mountains stand ever still and move not but with an earthquake! Even so light and busy spirits are in continual agitation to little purpose, while great deep wits sit still and stir not but upon extreme occasions. Were the motion of those little atoms as useful as it is restless, I had rather be a mote than a mountain.

CVI

Upon the Sight of a Bladder

Everything must be taken in his meet time. Let this bladder alone till it be dry and all the wind in the world cannot raise it up, whereas now it is new and moist, the least breath fills and enlargeth it. It is no otherwise in ages and dispositions. Inform the child in precepts of learning and virtue while years make him capable, how pliably he yieldeth, how happily is he replenished with knowledge and goodness. Let him alone till time and ill example have hardened him, till he be settled in an habit of evil and contracted and clung together with sensual delights, now he becomes utterly indocible. Sooner may that bladder be broken than distended.

CVII

Upon a Man Sleeping

I do not more wonder at any man's art than at his who professes to think of nothing, to do nothing. And I do not a little marvel at that man who says he can sleep without a dream. For the mind of man is a restless thing, and though it give the body leave to repose itself as knowing it is a mortal and earthly piece, yet itself, being a spirit and therefore active and indefatigable, is ever in motion. Give me a sea that moves not, a sun that shines not, an open eye that sees not, and I shall yield there may be a reasonable soul that works not. It is possible that through a natural or accidental stupidity a man may not perceive his own thoughts (as sometimes the eye or ear may be distracted not to discern his own objects), but in the meantime he thinks that whereof he cannot give account, like as we many times dream when we cannot report our fancy. I should more easily put myself to school unto that man who undertakes the profession of thinking many things at once. Instant motions are more proper for a spirit than a dull rest. Since my mind will needs be ever working, it shall be my care that it may always be well employed.

CVIII

Upon the Sight of a Death's-head

I wonder at the practice of the ancient both Greeks and Romans whose use it was to bring up a deaths-head in the midst of their feasts on purpose to stir up their guests to drink harder and to frolic more; the sight whereof, one would think, should have rather abated their courage and have tempered their jollity. But however it was with them (who believed there was nothing after death, that the consideration of the short time of their pleasures and being spurred them on to a free and full fruition of that mirth and excess which they should not long live to enjoy), yet to us that are Christians and therefore know that this short life doth but make way for an eternity of joy or torment afterwards, and that after the feast we must account of a reckoning, there cannot be a greater cooler for the heat of our intemperate desires and rage of our appetites than the meditation of the shortness of life and the certainty of death. Who would over-pamper a body for worms? Who would be so mad as to let himself loose to that momentary pleasure of sin which, ere long, must cost him everlasting pain and misery? For me, methinks, this head speaks no other language than this: "Lose no time, thou art dying, do thy best, thou mayst do good but a while and shalt fare well for ever."

CIX

Upon the Sight of a Left-handed Man

It is both an old and easy observation that however the senses are alike strong and active on the right side and on the left, yet that the limbs on the right side are stronger than those on the left because they are more exercised than the other. Upon which self-same reason it must follow that a left-handed man hath more strength in his left arm than in his right. Neither is it otherwise in the soul; our intellectual parts grow vigorous with employment and languish with disuse. I have known excellent preachers and pregnant disputants that have lost those faculties with lack of action, and others but meanly qualified with natural gifts that have attained to a laudable measure of abilities by improvement of their little. I had rather lack good parts than that good parts should lack me. Not to have great gifts is no fault of mine; it is my fault not to use them.

CX

Upon the Sight of an Old Unthatched Cottage

There cannot be a truer emblem of crazy† old age: moldered and clay walls, a thin uncovered roof, bending studs, dark and broken windows, in short, an house ready to fall on the head of the in-dweller. The best body is but a cottage; if newer and better timbered yet such as age will equally impair and make thus ragged and ruinous, or before that, perhaps casualty of fire or tempest or violence of an enemy. One of the chief cares of man is to dwell well. Some build for themselves fair but not strong; others build for posterity, strong but not fair, not high; but happy is that man that builds for eternity as strong, as fair, as high as the glorious contignations† of heaven.

CXI

Upon the Sight of a Fair Pearl

What a pure and precious creature is this, which yet is taken out of the mud of the sea! Who can complain of a base original when he sees such excellencies so descended? These shellfishes that have no sexes[22] and therefore are made out of corruption, what glorious things they yield to adorn and make proud the greatest princesses! God's great work goes not by likelihoods. How easily can He fetch glory out of obscurity who brought all out of nothing!

CXII

Upon a Screen

Methinks that this screen that stands betwixt me and the fire is like some good friend at the Court which keeps from me the heat of the unjust displeasure of the great wherewith I might otherwise be causelessly scorched. But how happy am I if the interposition of my Saviour, my best friend in heaven, may screen me from the deserved wrath of that great God who is a consuming fire [Heb. 12:29; Deut. 4:24]!

CXIII

Upon a Bur-leaf

Neither the vine nor the oak nor the cedar nor any tree that I know within our climate yields so great a leaf as this weed, which yet after all expectation brings forth nothing but a bur, unprofitable, troublesome. So have I see none make greater profession of religion than an ignorant man whose indiscreet forwardness yields no fruit but a factious disturbance to the Church wherein he lives. Too much show is not so much better than none at all, as an ill fruit is worse than none at all.

CXIV

Upon the Singing of a Bird

It is probable that none of those creatures that want reason delight so much in pleasant sounds as a bird. Whence it is that both it spends so much time in singing and is more apt to imitate those modulations which it hears from men. Frequent practice (if it be voluntary) argues a delight in that which we do, and delight makes us more apt to practice and more capable of perfection in that we practice. Oh God, if I take pleasure in Thy Law, I shall meditate of it with comfort, speak of it with boldness, and practice it with cheerfulness.

CXV

Upon the Sight of a Man Yawning

It is a marvelous thing to see the real effects and strong operation of consent or sympathy, even where there is no bodily touch. So one man puts the whole company into dumps; so one man's yawning affects and stretches the jaws of many beholders; so the looking upon bleary eyes taints the eye with bleariness. From hence it is easy to see the ground of our Saviour's expostulation with his persecutor: "Saul, Saul, why persecutest thou me?" [Acts 26:14]. The Church is persecuted below; He feels it above and complains. So much as the person is more apprehensive must he needs be more affected. O Saviour, Thou canst not but be deeply sensible of all our miseries and necessities. If we do not feel Thy wrongs and the wants of our brethren, we have no part in Thee.

CXVI

Upon the Sight of a Tree Lopped

In the lopping of these trees experience and good husbandry hath taught men to leave one bough still growing in the top the better to draw up the sap from the root. The like wisdom is fit to be observed in censures which are intended altogether for reformation, not for destruction. So must they be inflicted that the patient be not utterly discouraged and stripped of hope and comfort, but that while he suffereth he may feel his good tendered and his amendment both aimed at and expected. Oh God, if Thou shouldest deal with me as I deserve, Thou shouldest not only shred my boughs but cut down my stock and stock up my root. And yet Thou dost but prune my superfluous branches and cherishest the rest. How unworthy am I of this mercy if, while Thou art thus indulgent unto me, I be severe and cruel to others perhaps less ill-deserving than myself!

CXVII

Upon a Scholar that Offered Violence to Himself

Had this man lain long under some eminent discontentment, it had been easy to find out the motive of his miscarriage. Weak nature is easily overlaid with impatience; it must be only the power of grace that can grapple with vehement evils and master them. But here the world cannot say what could be guilty of occasioning this violence. This man's hand was full, his fame untainted, his body no burden, his disposition (for ought we saw) fair, his life guiltless. Yet something did the Tempter find to aggravate unto his feeble thoughts and to represent worthy of a dispatch. What a poor thing is life whereof so slight occasions can make us weary! What impotent wretches are we when we are not sustained! One would think this the most impossible of all motions. Naturally every man loves himself and life is sweet, death abhorred. What is it that Satan can despair to persuade men unto if he can draw them to an unnatural abandoning of life and pursuit of death? Why should I doubt of prevailing with my own heart by the powerful overruling of God's spirit to contemn life and affect death for the sake of my Saviour (in exchange of a few miserable moments for eternity of joy) when I see men upon an unreasonable suggestion of that evil spirit cast away their lives for nothing and so hastening their temporal death that they hazard an eternal?

CXVIII

Upon the Coming in of the Judge

The construction of men and their actions is altogether according to the disposition of the lookers-on. The same face of the judge without any inward alteration is seen with terror by the guilty, with joy and confidence by the oppressed innocent, like as the same lips of the bridegroom drop both myrrh and honey at once [Cant. 5:13], honey to the well disposed heart, myrrh to the rebellious. And the same cup relishes well to the healthful and distastes the feverous; the same word is though a sweet yet a contrary savor to the different receivers, and the same sun comforts the strong sight, dazzles the weak. For a man to affect either to do or speak that which may be pleasing to all men is but a weak and idle ambition when we see Him that is infinitely good appear terrible to more than He appears lovely. Goodness is itself with whatever eyes it is looked upon. There can be no safety for that man that regards more the censure of men than the truth of being. He that seeks to win all hearts hath lost his own.

CXIX

Upon the Sight of an Heap of Stones

Under such a pile it was that the first martyr was buried [Acts 22:19-20]. None of all the ancient kings had so glorious a tomb; here were many stones and every one precious. Jacob leaned his head upon a stone and saw that heavenly vision of angels ascending and descending [Gen. 28:11]. Many stones light upon Steven's head in the instant of his seeing the heavens opened and Jesus standing at the right hand of God. Lo, Jacob, resting upon that one stone, saw but the angels; Steven, being to rest for once under those many stones, saw the Lord of the angels. Jacob saw the angels moving, Steven saw Jesus standing. As Jacob therefore afterwards according to his vow made there an altar to God, so Steven now in the present gathers these stones together, of which he erected an holy altar whereon he offered up himself a blessed sacrifice unto God. And if there be a time of gathering stones and a time of casting them away [Eccles. 3:5], this was the time wherein the Jews cast and Steven gathered up these stones for a monument of eternal glory. Oh blessed saint, thou didst not so clearly see heaven opened as heaven saw thee covered. Thou didst not so perfectly see thy Jesus standing as He saw thee lying patiently, courageously under that fatal heap. Do I mistake it or are those stones not flints and pebbles but diamonds and rubies and carbuncles to set upon thy crown of glory?

CXX

Upon Sight of a Bat and Owl

These night-birds are glad to hide their heads all day, and if by some violence they be unseasonably forced out of their secrecy, how are they followed and beaten by the birds of the day! With us men it is contrary: the sons of darkness do with all eagerness of malice pursue the children of the light [John 12:38; 1 Thess. 5:5] and drive them into corners and make a prey of them. The opposition is alike, but the advantage lies on the worse side. Is it for that the spiritual light is no less hateful to those children of darkness than the natural night is to those cheerful birds of the day? Or is it for that the sons of darkness, challenging no less propriety in the world than the fowls do in the lightsome air, abhor and wonder at the conscionable as strange and uncouth? Howsoever, as these bats and owls were made for the night, being accordingly shaped foul and ill-favored, so we know these vicious men (however they may please themselves) have in them a true deformity fit to be shrouded in darkness, and as they delight in the work of darkness so they are justly reserved to a state of darkness.

CXXI

Upon the Sight of a Well-fleeced Sheep

What a warm winter coat hath God provided for this quiet innocent creature, as indeed how wonderful is His wisdom and goodness in all His purveyances! Those creatures which are apter for motion and withal most fearful by nature hath He clad somewhat thinner and hath allotted them safe and warm burrows within the earth. Those that are fit for labor and use hath He furnished with a strong hide. And for man, whom He hath thought good to bring forth naked, tender, helpless He hath endued his parents and himself with that noble faculty of reason whereby he may provide all manner of helps for himself. Yet, again, so bountiful is God in His provisions that He is not lavish, so distributing His gifts that there is no more superfluity than want. Those creatures that have beaks have no teeth, and those that have shells without have no bones within. All have enough, nothing hath all. Neither is it otherwise in that one kind of man whom He meant for the lord of all. Variety of gifts is here mixed with a frugal dispensation; none hath cause to boast, none to complain. Every man is as free from an absolute defect as from perfection. I desire not to comprehend, oh Lord, teach me to do nothing but wonder.

CXXII

Upon the Hearing of Thunder

There is no grace whereof I find so general a want in myself and others as an awful fear of the infinite majesty of God. Men are ready to affect and profess a kind of familiarity with God out of a pretence of love, whereas if they knew Him aright they could not think of Him without dread nor name Him without trembling. Their narrow hearts strive to conceive of Him according to the scantling of their own strait and ignorant apprehension, whereas they should only desire to have their thoughts swallowed up with an adoring wonder of His divine incomprehensibleness. Though He thunder not always, He is always equally dreadful; there is none of His works which doth not betray omnipotency. I blush at the sauciness of vain men that will be circumscribing the powerful acts of the Almighty within the compass of natural causes, forbearing to wonder at what they profess to know. Nothing but ignorance can be guilty of this boldness. There is no divinity but in an humble faith, no philosophy but in a silent admiration.†

CXXIII

Upon the Sight of an Hedgehog

I marveled at the first reading what the Greeks meant by that proverb of theirs, "The fox knows many pretty wiles but the hedgehog knows one great one."[23] But when I considered the nature and practice of this creature, I easily found the reason of that speech grounded upon the care and shift that it makes for its preservation. While it is under cover it knows how to bar the fore-door against the cold northern and eastern blasts and to open the back-door for quieter and calmer air. When it is pursued, it knows how to roll up itself round within those thorns which nature hath environed it so as the dog, instead of a beast, finds now nothing but a ball of pricks to wound his jaws and goes away crying from so untoothsome a prey. He that sent the sluggard to school to the pismire† [Prov. 6:6], sends also in effect the careless and imprudent man to the hedgehog while he saith, "If thou be wise thou shalt be wise for thyself" [Prov. 9:12]. The main care of any creature is self-preservation; whatsoever doth that best is the wisest. These creatures that are all body have well improved the instincts of nature if they can provide for their bodily safety. Man, that is a reasonable soul, shall have done nothing if he make not sure work for the better part. Oh God, make me soul-wise. I shall never envy their craft that pity my simplicity.

CXXIV

Upon the Sight of a Goat

This creature is in an ill name. It is not for any good qualities that God hath made choice of the goat to resemble the wicked and reprobate soul [Lev. 16:20–22]. It is unruly and salacious and noisome. I cannot see one of them but I presently recall to my thoughts the woeful condition of those on the left hand whom God hath set aside to so fearful a damnation [Matt. 25:33]. They are here mixed with the flock. Their color differs nothing from the sheep, or if we do discern them by their rougher coat and odious scent we sever ourselves from them. But the time shall come when He shall sever them from us Who hath appointed our innocence to the fold and their harmfulness to an everlasting slaughter. Onwards if they climb higher than we and feed upon those craggy cliffs which we dare scarce reach to with our eyes, their boldness is not greater than their danger, neither is their ascent more perilous than their ruin deadly.

CXXV

Upon the Sight of the Blind and the Lame

Here is a true natural commerce of senses: the blind man hath legs, the lame man hath eyes. The lame man lends his eyes to the blind, the blind man lends his legs to the lame, and now both of them move where otherwise both must sit still and perish. It is hard to say whether is more beholden to other; the one gives strength, the other direction, both of them equally necessary to motion. Though it be not in other cases so sensible,† yet surely this very traffic of faculties is that whereby we live; neither could the world subsist without it. One man lends a brain, another an arm; one a tongue, another an hand. He that knows wherefore He made all hath taken order to improve every part to the benefit of the whole. What do I wish ought that is not useful? And if there be anything in me that may serve to the good of others, it is not mine but the Church's. I cannot live but by others; it were injurious if others should not likewise share with me.

CXXVI

Upon the Sight of a Map of the World

What a poor little spot is a country! A man may hide with his thumb the great territories of those that would be accounted monarchs. In vain should the great Cham, or the great Mogul, or Prester John seek here for his court.[24] It is well if he can find his kingdom amongst these parcels. And if we take all together these shreds of lands and these patches of continent, what a mere indivisible point they are in comparison of that vast circle of heaven wherewith they are encompassed! It is not easy for a man to be known to that whole land wherein he lives, but if he could be so famous the next country perhaps never hears of his name, and if he can attain to be talked of there yet the remoter parts cannot take notice that there is such a thing. And if they did all speak of nothing else, what were he the better? Oh the narrow bounds of earthly glory! Oh the vain affectation of human applause! Only that man is happily famous who is known and recorded in heaven.

CXXVII

Upon the Sight of Hemlock

There is no creature of itself evil; misapplication may make the best so and there is a good use to be made of the worst. This weed, which is too well approved to be poisonous, yet to the goat is medicinal as serving by the coldness of it to temper the feverous heat of that beast. So we see the marmoset eating of spiders both for the pleasure and cure. Our ignorance may not bring a scandal upon God's workmanship; or, if it do, His wisdom knows how to make a good use even of our injury. I cannot say but the very venom of the creatures is to excellent purpose. How much more their beneficial qualities! If ought hurt us the fault is ours in mistaking the evil for good. In the meantime we owe praise to the Maker and to the creature a just and thankful allowance.

CXXVIII

Upon a Fleur-de-lys

This flower is but unpleasingly fulsome for scent, but the root of it is so fragrant that the delicatest ladies are glad to put it into their sweet-bags. Contrarily, the rose-tree hath a sweet flower but a savorless root, and the saffron yields an odoriferous and cordial spire† while both the flower and the root are unpleasing. It is with vegetables as with metals: God never meant to have His best always in view, neither meant He to have all eminences concealed. He would have us to know Him to be both secretly rich and openly beautiful. If we do not use every grace in its own kind God loses the thanks and we the benefit.

CXXIX

Upon the Sight of Two Trees, One High, the Other Broad

Those trees that shoot up in height are seldom broad, as contrarily those trees that are spreading are seldom tall. It were too much ambition in that plant which would be both ways eminent. Thus it is with men. The covetous man that affects to spread in wealth seldom cares to aspire unto height of honor; the proud man, whose heart is set upon preferment, regards not (in comparison thereof) the growth of his wealth. There is a poor shrub in a valley that is neither tall nor broad nor cares to be either which speeds better than they both. The tall tree is cut down for timber; the broad tree is lopped for firewood, besides that the tempest hath power on them both; whereas the low shrub is neither envied by the wind nor threatened by the axe but fostered rather for that little shelter which it affords the shepherd. If there be glory in greatness, meanness hath security. Let me never envy their diet that had rather be unsafe than inglorious.

CXXX

Upon the Sight of a Drunken Man

Reason is an excellent faculty and indeed that which alone differenceth us from brute creatures, without which what is man but a two-legged beast? And as all precious things are tender and subject to miscarriage, so is this above others. The want of some little sleep, the violence of a fever, or one cup too much puts it into utter distemper. What can we make of this thing ("man" I cannot call him)? He hath shape, so hath a dead corpse as well as he. He hath life, so hath a beast as well as he. Reason, either for the time he hath not or if he have it he hath it so depraved and marred for the exercise of it that brutishness is much less ill-beseeming. Surely the natural bestiality is so much less odious than the moral, as there is difference in the causes of both. That is of God's making, this of our own. It is no shame to the beast that God hath made him so; it is a just shame to a man that he hath made himself a beast.

CXXXI

Upon the Whetting of a Scythe

Recreation is intended to the mind as whetting is to the scythe, to sharpen the edge of it which otherwise would grow dull and blunt. He therefore that spends his whole time in recreation is ever whetting, never mowing. His grass may grow and his steed starve. As contrarily he that always toils and never recreates is ever mowing, never whetting, laboring much to little purpose. As good no scythe as no edge! Then only doth the work go forward when the scythe is so seasonably and moderately whetted that it may cut and so cuts that it may have the help of sharpening. I would so interchange that I neither be dull with work nor idle and wanton with recreation.

CXXXII

Upon the Sight of a Looking Glass

When I look in another man's face, I see that man and that man sees me as I do him. But when I look in my glass, I do not see myself, I see only an image or representation of myself. Howsoever it is like me, yet it is not I. It is for an ignorant child to look behind the glass to find out the babe that he seeth. I know it is not there and that the resemblance varies according to the dimness or different fashion of the glass. At our best we do but thus see God here below; one sees Him more clearly, another more obscurely, but all in a glass [2 Cor.

3:18]. Hereafter we shall see Him not as He appears but as He is; so shall we see Him in the face as He sees us. The face of our glorified spirits shall see the glorious face of Him who is the God of spirits. In the meantime the proudest dame shall not more ply her glass to look upon that face of hers which she thinks beautiful than I shall gaze upon the clearest glass of my thoughts to see that face of God which I know to be infinitely fair and glorious.

CXXXIII

Upon the Shining of a Piece of Rotten Wood[25]

How bright doth this wood shine! When it is in the fire it will not so beam forth as it doth in this cold darkness. What an emblem is here of our future estate! This piece while it grew in the tree shone not at all; now that it is putrified it casts forth this pleasing lustre. Thus it is with us: while we live here we neither are nor seem other than miserable. When we are dead once then begins our glory, then doth the soul shine in the brightness of heavenly glory, then doth our good name shine upon earth in those beams which before envy had either held in or overcast.

Why are we so over-desirous of our growth when we may be thus advantaged by our rottenness?

CXXXIV

Upon an Ivy-tree

Behold a true emblem of false love; here are kind embracements but deadly. How close doth this weed cling unto that oak and seems to hug and shade it but in the meantime draws away the sap and at last kills it! Such is an harlot's love, such is a parasite's. Give me that love and friendship which is between the vine and the elm whereby the elm is no whit worse and the vine much the better. That wholesome and notable plant doth not so close wind itself about the tree that upholds it as to gall the bark or to suck away the moisture; and, again, the elm yields a beneficial supportation to the weak though generous plant. As God, so wise men know how to measure love not by profession and complement (which is commonly most high and vehement in the falsest) but by reality of performance. He is no enemy that hurts me not; I am not his friend whom I desire not to benefit.

CXXXV

Upon a Quartan Ague†

I have known when those things which have made an healthful man sick have been the means of making a sick man whole. The quartan hath of old been justly styled the shame of physicians. Yet I have more than once observed it to be cured by a surfeit. One devil is sometime used for the ejection of another. Thus have I also seen it in the sickness of the soul. The same God whose justice is wont to punish sin with sin, even His mercy doth so use the matter that He cures one sin by another. So have we known a proud man healed by the shame of his uncleanness, a furious man healed by a rash bloodshed. It matters not greatly what the medicine be while the Physician is infinitely powerful, infinitely skillful. What danger can there be of my safety when God shall heal me as well by evil as by good?

CXXXVI

Upon the Sight of a Loaded Cart

It is a passionate expression wherein God bemoans Himself of the sins of Israel: "Ye have pressed me as a cart is pressed with sheaves" [Amos 2:13]. An empty cart runs lightly away; but if it be soundly laden, it goes sadly, sets hard, groans under the weight, and makes deep impressions; the wheels creak and the axeltree bends and all the frame of it is put unto the utmost stress. He that is omnipotent can bear anything but too much sin. His justice will not let His mercy be over-strained. No marvel if a guilty soul say, "Mine iniquity is greater than I can bear" [Ps. 31:10] when the infinite God complains of the weight of men's sins! But let not vain men think that God complains out of the want of power but out of the abundance of mercy. He cannot be the worse for our sins, we are. It grieves Him to be over-provoked to our punishment; then doth He account the cart to crack, yea, to break, when he is urged to break forth into just vengeance. Oh saviour, the sins of the whole world lay upon Thee. Thou sweatest blood under the load. What would become of me if I should bear but one sheaf of that load, every ear whereof, yea, every grain of that ear were enough to press down my soul to the nethermost hell?

CXXXVII

Upon the Sight of a Dwarf

Amongst all the bounteous gifts of God what is it that He hath equally bestowed upon all except it be our very being while we are? He hath not given to all men the same stature of body, not the same strength of wit, not the same capacity of memory, not the same beauty of parts, not the same measure of wealth or honor. Thus hath He done also in matter of grace. There are spiritual dwarfs, there are giants, there are perfect men, children, babes, embryons. This inequality doth so much more praise the mercy and wisdom of the Giver and exercise the charity and thankfulness of the receiver. The essence of our humanity doth not consist in stature; he that is little of growth is as much man as he that is taller. Even so also spiritually, the quantity of grace doth not make the Christian but the truth of it. I shall be glad and ambitious to add cubits to my height [Matt. 6:27], but withal it shall comfort me to know that I cannot be so low of stature as not to reach unto heaven.

CXXXVIII

Upon an Importunate Beggar

It was a good rule of him that bade us learn to pray of beggars. With what zeal doth this man sue, with what feeling expressions, with how forceable importunity! When I meant to pass by him with silence, yet his clamor draws words from me. When I speak to him though with excuses, rebukes, denials, repulses, his obsecrations, his adjurations draw from me that alms which I meant not to give. How he uncovers his sores and shows his impotence that my eyes may help his tongue to plead! With what oratory doth he force my compassion so as it is scarce any thank to me that he prevails! Why do I not thus to my God? I am sure I want no less than the neediest; the danger of my want is greater; the alms that I crave is better; the store and mercy of the Giver is infinitely more. Why shouldst Thou give me, oh God, that which I care not to ask? Oh give me a true sense of my wants and then I cannot be cool in asking, Thou canst not be difficult in condescending.

CXXXIX

Upon a Medicinal Potion

How loathsome a draught is this, how offensive both to the eye and to the scent and to the taste! Yea, the very thought of it is a kind of sickness, and when it is once down my very disease is not so painful for the time as my remedy. How doth it turn the stomach and wring the entrails and work a worse distemper than that whereof I formerly complained! And yet it must be taken for health. Neither could it be so wholesome if it were less unpleasing; neither could it make me whole if it did not first make me sick.

Such are the chastisements of God and the reproofs of a friend, harsh troublesome, grievous; but in the end they yield the peaceable fruit of righteousness.

Why do I turn away my head and make faces and shut mine eyes and stop my nostrils and nauseate and abhor to take this harmless potion for my health when we have seen mountebanks to swallow dismembered toads and drink the poisonous broth after them only for a little ostentation and gain? It is only weakness and want of resolution that is guilty of this queasiness. Why do not I cheerfully take and quaff up that bitter cup of affliction [Mark 14:36; Luke 22:42] which my wise and good God hath mixed for the health of my soul?

CXL

Upon the Sight of a Wheel

The prophet meant it for no other than a fearful imprecation against God's enemies, "O my God, make them like unto a wheel" [Ps. 83:13], whereby what could he intend to signify but instability of condition and sudden violence of judgment? Those spokes of the wheel that are now up are, sooner than sight or thought, whirled down and are straight raised up again on purpose to be depressed. Neither can there be any motion so rapid and swift as the circular. It is a great favor of God that He takes leisure in His affliction, so punishing us that we have respites of repentance. There is life and hope in these degrees of suffering, but those hurrying and whirling judgments of God have nothing in them but wrath and confusion. Oh Lord, rebuke me not in Thine anger. I cannot deprecate Thy rebuke—my sins call for correction—but I deprecate Thine anger. Thou rebukest even where Thou lovest. So rebuke me that while I smart with Thy rod I may rejoice in Thy mercy.

*   *   *   *   *

FINIS

Notes

Notes to the Introduction

1. Of the many examples, Henry Bull's *Christian Prayer and Holy Meditation* (London, 1570) is typical. After a calendar and almanac for the Christian year, Bull gives an introduction in which he outlines "steps" in prayer: consider to whom you are praying, prepare yourself, be in love and charity with your neighbor, be aware of your own wretchedness, be persuaded of God's favor, etc. "Last of all [p. 32] they use the reading and saying of Psalmes & other good prayers, because they know that thereby peculiarly, besides the other Scriptures, there is no smal helpe as may appeare by Paule, Eph. 5. Col. 3 [Eph. 5:19; Col. 3:16] where he willeth the congregation to use psalmes, hymns, & spirituell songs, so that in the hart we would sing & say them." There follows a phrase-by-phrase meditation on the Lord's Prayer.

2. Etienne Gilson, *The Philosophy of St Bonaventura*, trans. Dom. Illtyd Trethowan and F. J. Sheed (New York: Sheed & Ward, 1938), pp. 96–97; quoted by permission.

3. Louis Martz, *The Paradise Within: Studies in Vaughan, Traherne, and Milton* (New Haven: Yale University Press, 1964), pp. 22–23; quoted by permission.

4. Roland Bainton, *Here I Stand* (New York: Mentor Books, 1955), p. 31.

5. I am much indebted here to Barbara Kiefer Lewalski, *Donne's Anniversaries and the Poetry of Praise: The Creation of a Symbolic Mode* (Princeton: Princeton University Press, 1973), Chap. 3, "Protestant Meditation and the Protestant Sermon."

6. George Lewis, *Life of Joseph Hall, D.D.* (London, 1886), p. 32.

7. *Religio Medici*, pt. 1, sect.25.

8. Owen Feltham, *Resolves: A Duple Century*, 4th ed. (London, 1631), 2nd cent. no. 68.

9. Louis L. Martz, *The Paradise Within*, p. 30.

10. *The Collected Poems of Joseph Hall*, ed. Arnold Davenport (Liverpool, 1949), p. 127.

11. *The Sermons of John Donne*, ed. Evelyn M. Simpson and George R. Potter (Berkeley, Cal., 1953–62), 8:220.

12. *The Works of Joseph Hall, D.D.*, ed. Philip Wynter, 10 vols. (Oxford, 1863), 6:530–31; reprinted AMS (Holland), 1969. Hereafter references to

this standard edition will be parenthetically incorporated by volume and page number.

13. 1653, part 4, p. 233; quoted by U. Milo Kaufmann, *The Pilgrim's Progress and Traditions in Puritan Meditation* (New Haven: Yale University Press, 1966), p. 171.

14. 1680, p. 31; quoted by Kaufmann, p. 119. The place of publication of all English 17th-century books is London, unless specified otherwise.

15. "Observations of Some Specialities of God's Providence in the Life of Joseph Hall, Bishop of Norwich, Written with his Own Hand," the basis for any life of Hall; reprinted in Wynter, vol. 1.

16. Cf. E. S. Schuckburgh, *History of Emmanuel College* (Cambridge, 1904); M.M.Knappen, *Tudor Puritanism* (Chicago, 1939), chap. 26; S. E. Lehmberg, *Sir Walter Mildmay and Tudor Government* (Austin, Tex., 1964), chap. 14; and Gordon Rupp, *William Bedell, 1571-1642* (Cambridge, 1971).

17. "Some Specialities," Wynter, 1:xxiii.

18. *Palladis Tamia*, ed. D. C. Allen (New York, 1938), p. 283 v.

19. *The Discovery of a New World (Mundus Alter et Idem)*, ed. Huntington Brown (Cambridge, Mass., 1937).

20. Cf. F. Huntley, *Bishop Joseph Hall, 1574-1656: A Biographical and Critical Study* (Cambridge: D.S.Brewer Ltd., 1979), chap. 3.

21. Leonard D. Tourney, *Joseph Hall* (Boston: Twayne, 1979), "Chronology," [p. 11].

22. The poem is entitled "The King's Prophecy, or Weeping Joy," commemorating the death of Elizabeth and the accession of James.

23. Rudolf Kirk, ed., *Joseph Hall, D.D.: Heaven upon Earth and Characters of Vertues and Vices* (New Brunswick, N.J., 1948), p. 86.

24. Huntley, *Hall* (1979), Chap. 4.

25. Ibid., chap. 9.

26. Ibid.

27. *Books & Bookmen* 24 (June, 1979):15.

28. Details of this trip appear in Hall's epistle to Sir Thomas Challoner, Prince Henry's Chamberlain, published in 1608, Wynter, 6:138-43.

29. Meditation no. 34 of the third "Century," Wynter, 7:500

30. The year 1606, as the Gunpowder traitors were tried and executed, was the climax of anti-Jesuitism in England. The Jesuits may not have been responsible for attempting to blow up King James and Parliament on Nov. 5, 1605, but the important fact is that almost every Englishman believed that they were. Cf. F. Huntley, "*Macbeth* and the Background of Jesuitical Equivocation," *PMLA* 79 (1964):390-400.

31. Hall's *Poems*, ed. Davenport, p. 123.

32. "Pharisaism and Christianity," Wynter, 5:21.

33. Reproduced from the edition by Kirk (1948).

34. Kaufmann, p. 123.

35. It is natural for Hall to omit his running *exemplum* from chapters XVI and XVII, the rejection of Mauburnus' scale on the "Understanding" and "premonitions" concerning the "Understanding."

36. Hall was called "Bernard" by one admirer, "Ro. Lo.," in the 1625 *Collected Works of Joseph Hall, D.D.* There is no doubt that Bernard was Hall's favorite "father." The following passage from the saint's Sermon no. 37 on "The Song of Songs" could have been written by the seventeenth-century divine: "In this land of my pilgrimage I have accustomed myself to nourish my soul on the Law and the Prophets, and on the Psalms which speak so beautifully to you; I have run through the pleasant fields of the Gospels and I have sat at the feet of the Apostles." Tr. Kiliant Walsh, Cistercian Fathers Series, No. 4 (Spencer, Mass., 1971), quoted in Introduction, p. xvi.

37. Cf. Anne Louise Masson, *Jean Gerson: sa vie, son temps, ses oeuvres* (Lyon, 1894) and James L. Connolly, *John Gerson: Reformer and Mystic* (Louvain, 1928).

38. For example, "that worthy Chancellor of Paris" (chap. 5); "ascend this Mount of Contemplation" (chap. 6), translating Gerson's title.

39. Louis L. Martz, *The Poetry of Meditation: A Study in English Religious Literature of the Seventeenth Century* (New Haven, 1954), p. 331.

40. I have not seen this book, and until further fascicles of the *Gesamtkatalog der Wiegendrücke* appear must be content with less detailed descriptions. One of the best is in J.E.G.De Montmorency, *Thomas à Kempis: His Age and Book* (London, 1906), p. 131. Hain describes as no. 9103 in *Reportorium Bibliographicum*, 2:121, a copy which he examined in the Hof- und Staatsbibliothek in Munich. Augustin de Backer, *Essai Bibliographique sur le Livre De l'Imitatione Christi* (Liége, 1864), no. 40, quotes Hain. The British Museum has a 1518 octavo edition of the same combination, an anonymous *De Imitatione Christi* with *De meditatione cordis ab I. de Gersonne*, printed, significantly enough, in Antwerp (H. Eckert). My thanks go to Dr. Harriet Jameson, Head of The Rare Book Room, Graduate library, University of Michigan at Ann Arbor.

41. Pierre Debongnie, *Jean Mombaer de Bruxelles*, . . . Univ. de Louvain: Conférences d'Histoire et de Philologie, 2nd series (1928), no. 11, p. 207.

42. Trans. by Leo Sherley-Price (London, 1952; Baltimore: Penguin Books, 1954), I, 20, p. 50. Further allusions to this translation will be documented within my text.

43. Samuel Kettlewell, *Thomas à Kempis and the Brothers of the Common Life* (London, 1887), 1:422.

44. *Natural Magic* (Oxford, 1965), p. 12.

45. 1680, p. 9; quoted by Kaufmann, p. 190.

46. Published under the following title. *Susurrium | cum | Deo. | Soliloquies: | or, | Holy Self-Conferences of | the Devout Soul, upon | sundry choice Oc-*

204

casions, | *With Humble Addresses to the* | *Throne of Grace.* [rule]*Together with* | *the Souls Farewell To Earth,* | *and* | *Approaches to Heaven.* | [rule] | *By Jos. Hall, B. Norwich.*

47. *The Soules Farewell to Earth,* 1651, pp. 391–92 (Wynter, 8:107).

48. Cf. Robert Bozanich, "Donne and Ecclesiastes," *PMLA* 90 (Mar. 1975), 270–75.

49. Joan Webber, *The Eloquent "I": Style and Self in Seventeenth-Century Prose* (Madison, Wis., 1968), p. 210.

50. Roberta F. Brinkley, ed., *Coleridge on the Seventeenth-Century* (Durham, N.C., 1955), p. 371.

51. Cf. H. Fisch, "Bishop Hall's Meditations," *RES* 25 (1941), 210–21.

52. Kaufmann, pp. 124ff.

53. This engraving of the Bishop at the age of fifty became the original for the oil painting in Emmanuel College. The background of folio volumes and heraldic devices is omitted but the large gold medal given to Hall by the Synod of Dort shows in prominent detail; Hall wore it to the end of his days, the sacred side (mountain, temple, Tetragrammaton) next to his heart, the obverse (the Synod in session) showing.

54. Text: 1619, Epigram no. 78 of the "Third Book."

55. *The Poetical Works of Robert Herrick,* ed. L. C. Martin (Oxford, 1956), p. 64.

56. The Hon. Robert Boyle, *Occasional Reflections upon Several Subjects, with a Discourse about such Kind of Thoughts* (Oxford, 1848), p. xiii.

57. *Tristram Shandy,* bk. 1, chap. 22.

58. Kaufmann, pp. 120–21.

59. Ibid., p. 137.

60. Text: 1650, p. 705. Hereafter the page references to this 1650 edition of Baxter will be incorporated.

61. Baxter quotes (on page 809) eight lines from the second day of the first week beginning "Th' Empyreal Pallace, where th'Eternal Treasures / Of Nectar flows," from page 67 of the 1605 Sylvester, and on page 815, Baxter quotes ten lines from the seventh day of the first week beginning "With cloudy cares th'one's muffled up somewhiles," which appear on page 246 of the 1605 Sylvester.

62. *The Works of George Herbert,* ed. F. E. Hutchinson (Oxford, 1945), p. 172.

63. All editions of *The Temple* differ from this wording and indentation; here I use Baxter's quotations.

64. Hutchinson, pp. 107–9.

65. *Worthies of England,* ed. J. Nichols (London, 1811), 1:566.

66. *Susurrium cum Deo,* 1651, p. 58.

67. Sir Sydney Lee, "The Beginnings of French Translation from the English," *Transactions of the Bibliographical Society,* 8:97–106.

Notes to The Art of Divine Meditation

1. *Dedication:* I regret that I am unable to identify this gentleman whose family spelled its name variously as Lee, Lea, Leigh, Ley, and Legh.

2. *sudden meditations:* the very successful *Meditations and Vowes, Two Centuries,* published the preceding year.

3. *Junius:* François du Jon (1545–1602), the author of theological and ecclesiastical treatises under the name of Franciscus Junius. He was a French Huguenot scholar, like Casaubon and du Moulin, greatly admired in England.

4. *Augustine's brook:* I have looked in vain for this reference.

5. *our late Estye:* Thomas Este or East (1540–), musician, composer, and father of the famous madrigalist.

6. *reverend Deering:* Edward Dering (1540?–1576), famous Cambridge divine.

7. *unmoveable:* regular

8. *Chancellor of Paris:* Gerson (1362–1429), one of Hall's major sources.

9. *blessed Monica:* in his autobiography, written in the Tower when he was sixty-seven years old, Hall compared his own mother, in her Christian piety, with Monica, the saintly mother of Augustine.

10. *The Council of Constance, 1414-18:* naturally Hall would disagree with Gerson's part in the condemnation at the Council of Constance of the doctrines of the "early Protestant" Huss. On the whole, Hall treats Gerson as an authority because "our adversaries" (the Jesuits) "disclaim him for theirs."

11. Apparently in Bernard's sermon "The Canticles of Canticles," chap. 14, "The Manner in which the Spouse, that is the Church, desires to be drawn to her beloved." *Saint Bernard on the Love of God,* tr. by the Rev. T.L. Connolly, S.J. (Westminster, Md, 1951).

12. *Jerome . . . Roman dames:* the famous translator of the Bible into the Latin *Vulgate* (405 A.D.) confesses this in *Letters,* no. 22, "To Eustachius."

13. *Gugli, Paris:* several worthies have gone by the name of Guillaume de Paris. Hall probably refers to the famous mystic of the Dominican convent of Jacques de Paris at the beginning of the 14th century [*Dict. de Theologie Catholique* (1920), vol. 6, 1978].

14. *Dionys. Carthus:* Denys of the Grande Chartreuse (d. 1471).

15. *kindly:* of its true kind, typical.

16. *according to Bernard:* I cannot find this allusion.

17. *twins:* seems to be true of every set of twins in story from Plautus' *Menaechmi* on. *Turtles* means turtledoves.

18. *Material and Formal Causes:* two of Aristotle's four secondary causes. For example, the material cause of a chair is wood or iron or aluminum; its formal cause is four legs, a seat, and a back.

19. The sentence reminds one of Dante's line "Nessun maggior dolore / che ricordarsi del tempo felice / nella miseria" (1.5.121–22).

20. St. Paul. Cf. 2 Cor. 21:4.

21. There is an echo here of 2 Peter 3:8. Is this Bernard, Augustine, Bonaventura?

22. *learned father . . . translation:* probably St. Jerome.

Textual Notes to The Art of Divine Meditation

Dedication
different: a correct reading from early editions; 1634 mistakenly has *indif-ferent.*
examples: made plural in 1614–34 to accommodate Hall's added example "On Death."

Chap. I
cloisterers: from 1606; 1634 mistakenly has *cloysters*

Chap. VII
[title.] 1617 inadvertently omits the final phrase but all other editions have it.
thy lets: from 1606; other editions have *the* instead of *thy.*
neglect of duty: 1634 substitutes *or* for the *of* in earlier editions.
their lines: all texts have *his line*; I correct the grammar.

Chap. VIII
hearth: 1634 corrects the *heart* of earlier editions
strange metal: as in 1606; later editions, including 1634, have *strong metal.*
in settling: 1634 omits the *in* of earlier editions

Chap. IX
the body: 1634 omits the article of earlier editions.
call in the mind: after 1617 the *in* was omitted. The earlier reading is a nice colloquialism.

Chap. XII
[title.] The initial *Of* was added in 1634.

Chap. XVII
disposition: 1634's correction for earlier *disquisition.*

Chap. XIX
there may be degrees: the earlier reading makes better sense than 1634's *here.*
none envieth him: 1634 corrects the idiom of earlier *envieth at him.*

Chap. XX
fullness of joy: earlier editions inserted *the* before *fullness.* 1634 follows the King James version.

Chap. XXI
our voices to theirs: 1634 has *in theirs*; I adopt the reading from 1606 to 1624.

Chap. XXII

yet wert Thou: 1606 inserts *then* before *wert*, later omitted.

Chap. XXIII

more blessed: 1606–24 omits *more;* 1634 inserts it in obvious parallelism with *less.*

Chap. XXIV

one of these evil: in 1634; earlier editions have *these evils.*

And if all the world: 1634 alone inadvertently omits *if.*

thou consultest: 1634's clear correction of earlier *insultest.*

of more estimation: from earlier editions; 1634 has *of mere estimation,* a mistake.

Chap. XXV

they were affected: from earlier editions is more exact and more in keeping with Hall's emphasis upon the *affections* than 1634's *they were afflicted.*

than in sovereignty: 1634 omits *then* of earlier editions.

Chap. XXVI

meditation, which: 1606–17 have *on which:* 1634 follows 1621.

Chap. XXVII

Witness: singular in 1634; plural previously.

Chap. XXXII

requesting at His hands that which: most of the editions, including 1634, have *requesting that at his hands which.* For greater clarity I change the position of *that.*

Chap. XXXVI

desiring from 1634 and 1621; earlier, *resolving.*

Chap. XXXVII

we Christians; I omit 1634's extra *that* before *we Christians.*

End of treatise

1606–1609 had here *Deo soli gloria,* omitted from 1614 forward in order to accommodate the added example "On Death."

'On Death"

Of more recent composition and obviously subjected to better scrutiny, this part has relatively few textual irregularities.

Sect. IV

they complain not: 1624, 1628, 1634 inadvertently omit *not.*

Sect. XV

loosed from their racks but chose: all texts have *and chose;* I think *but* makes better sense.

Notes to the Occasional Meditations

1. Sulpicius Severus, whose Saint's Day is Jan. 29, was a sixth-century bishop of Bourges and author of a biography of St. Martin (Nov. 9), fourth-century bishop of Tours. He was called "Severus" to distinguish him from Sulpicius "Pius," a later bishop of Bourges. See note no. 16.

2. Gliding stars were popularly thought to be a bad omen but Hall pays no attention to the superstition. He does, however, subscribe to the common view that nothing in God's creation can "fall" until the final destruction at God's command. Hence falling stars are not stars at all but merely sparks blown off from a heavenly fire.

3. Robert Hues of Oxford described the first globes made in England in his *Tractatus de Globis et eorum usu* (London, 1594), dedicated to Sir Walter Raleigh. When Hall wrote this essay, a globe was a very rare and costly tool of science.

4. *Plato's Republic eaten by mice*: I have come upon this quaint portent elsewhere before but cannot track it down.

5. On grounds of sense-data and Psalm 93:1, most of Europe rejected the soliocentric theory of the universe for at least a century and a half after Copernicus.

6. It was commonly believed that all of nature was affected by the Fall. See Donne's "First Anniversary" and Milton, *Par. Lost*, 9. 780–82: "her rash hand in evil hour / Forth reaching to the Fruit, she pluck't, she eat: / Earth felt the wound."

7. *want* does not mean *desire*; it means *lack*. Here I call attention to the accompanying glossary of unfamiliar terms.

8. Hall's exegesis, which he had worked out in *Solomon's Divine Arts* (1609), stems from the traditional interpretation of Solomon's great love poem as an allegory of the marriage between Christ and the Church. In Acts 3:22–23, Peter quotes Deut. 18:18–19 as prophesying Christ. Hence Christ, "the true Moses," marries the Church, who is "black and comely." Hall was very fond of the Canticles. Cf. *Oc. Med.* LXXIV.

9. This seems to be a version of the game of Cherry-pit, in which contestants throw a handful of cherry-pits towards a small hole to see how many "stones" come nearest it or knock the opponent's "stones" away.

10. William Gilbert, Elizabethan England's foremost scientist, published his *De Magnete* in 1600, and minor experiments became popular. Pieces of jet and especially amber, rubbed on the sleeve, picked up various substances;

hence in 1646 Dr. Thomas Browne coined the word *electricity* from *elektron*, Greek for amber.

11. Had this earthquake been more than a rumor we might have been able to date this essay, but there has never been an earthquake anywhere near Lime (present-day Lyme Regis, on the southern coast of England).

12. The great library was probably the Bodleian at Oxford, through the kind offices of its librarian Thomas James (1573?-1629). In 1606 Hall had Christianized the moral philosophy of the Stoics in *Heaven upon Earth*. Thomas James in 1598 had published *The Moral Philosophy of the Stoics*, a translation from the French of Guillaume Du Vair, Bishop of Lisieux, *La Philosophie Morale des Stoiques*. That Hall knew James as the Bodleian's librarian is shown by a letter to him on Oct. 17, 1608 (Wynter, 6:236).

13. *brazen serpent:* In religious painting Moses' raised staff on which the brazen serpent is lifted is sometimes depicted in the shape of a cross.

14. *ruined abbey:* Hall's initial impression could have come from Bury St. Edmund's, where, from nearby Hawsted, he often visited his friend William Bedell; or from Waltham Abbey, where at the time of writing he was chaplain to Lords Denny and Doncaster. England's abbeys were destroyed by Henry VIII in his zeal to stamp out Roman Catholicism. Though in his own zeal Hall castigates the former Roman Catholics who lived in this abbey, he does not completely exonerate Henry VIII.

15. Here Hall joins the long Christian tradition of *ars moriendi*, the "craft of dying."

16. Marginal quotation: "If Christ could suffer Judas, why should not I tolerate Brictio?" In chapter 15 of Sulpicius' dialogue of St. Martin (see note no. 1), Brictio, an unregenerate priest, is egged on by demons to heap imprecations upon St. Martin. With these quoted words, the saint pardoned the man [Mary Caroline Watt, *St. Martin of Tours: The Chronicle of Sulpicius Severus done into English from the French of Paul Monçeaux . . .* (New York, n.d.), p. 256]. Thanks to Sylvia H. Horowitz, State University of New York at Binghamton.

17. This prodigious eater is probably Gargantua. Hall had very likely read Rabelais while a student at Cambridge, for his satirical *voyage imaginaire, Mundus alter et idem* (1605) bears many a resemblance to Pantagruel's voyage to Utopia around the Cape of Good Hope.

18. In both 1630 and 1631 this title was followed with the phrase "By way of conclusion." When the next edition added forty-nine meditations, the phrase was omitted.

19. The story of Empedocles is told by Laertius, 8.51-73.

20. For the comet of 1618 and the 'wars' see the introduction on the dating of *Occasional Meditations*.

21. The texts have the word "die," an obvious error for "cry."

22. *sex in shellfish:* embryogenesis, particularly in crustacea, was a late

development in the history of biology, the fairly recent J. Vaughan Thompson (1779–1847) being practically a pioneer. Before him it was commonly believed that oysters were born in slime by parthenogenesis.

23. *Greek proverb:* in Erasmus' *Adagia.* An emblem for wiliness, the hedgehog, being prickly himself, proverbially takes refuge in thornbushes.

24. Three fabled rich conquerors: "Cham," probably Kubla Khan; "Mogul," for Mongolian; "Prester John," a non-existent medieval monk who is supposed to have ruled over a rich kingdom in Asia or Africa.

25. The phenomenon of slow oxidation known as "fox-fire," the glowing of living organisms, at low temperatures, in certain substances that have previously been exposed to light or other radiation.

Glossary of Unfamiliar Words in Both Texts

accumbent: a seated person.
admiration: wonder.
aliened: alienated.
angell: gold coin worth about ten shillings, so called from device of
   St. Michael and the angel.
appendances: adjuncts, something that goes along with something
   else.

barrator: a hired bully, a brawler.
brave, bravery: ostentation, particularly in clothes.

careful: full of cares, anxious.
cater: caterer.
challenge: engage in.
colors: in rhetoric figures of speech, stylistic ornament.
commons: the common folk.
conceit: a thought, a mental conception.
consulted: counselled.
contentation: the fact of being satisfied.
contignation: in building, the joining together of beams.
corn of sand: a small grain.
curious, curiosity: intricate, artfully detailed.
crazie: crackled, used of glass or chinaware.

during: enduring.

earnest: down payment.

fanning of corn: winnowing of wheat.
fantastical men: possessing wild ideas.
fly: an actual fly or any insect such as a moth, etc.
frantic: phrenetic, insane.

gleeds: burning coals, embers.
gracious: full of Christian grace.
gyves: ankle-chains.

hangby: a dependent, a hanger-on.
humor: moisture, disposition, temperament.

inchoation: beginning, origin.
incurious: plain, not fancy.
innocent: harmless.
insensible: not observable by the senses.
insultation: the act of insulting.
invention: in rhetoric, the finding of appropriate arguments.

Laodicean: a lukewarm person.
lets (v., n.): hindrance, to hinder, as a "let-ball" in tennis.
limed: a method of catching small birds for eating by smearing a sticky substance on the places where they alight.
live-load: livelihood.
lodestone: a variety of magnetite.

mast: fruit of forest trees like beach, oak, chestnut, etc.
mewed and mured: cooped up in a small place.
monster: a defective child, formerly thought to be sub-human.
mulcted: punished, deprived of.

natural (n.): an idiot, congenitally insane person.
niceness: finickyness.

occaecation: blindness, act of blinding.
overly: haughty, supercilious.

painful: careful.
passenger: a person passing by.
passing-bell: rung before a coffin in procession.
pieces: firearms.
pismire: an ant.
places: in rhetoric, the *topoi*, or commonplaces.

professor: not a college teacher but any one who professes something.

quartan ague: a fever that reaches to paroxysm every fourth day.

recepit: recipe.
reins: kidneys.
reluctation: opposition, resistance.
rivality: rivalry.
rush candle: a candle of feeble power made by dipping the pith of a reed in grease.

sacre (verb), **sacred** (past tense): to cause something to be sacred.
sensible: perceivable by the senses.
silly: innocent.
simples: herbs, medicinal plants.
spire: a sprout or shoot.
stablish: establish.
starve with cold: to die in sub-zero weather.
straited us: short-changed us.
style: a name, a title.
subduction: taking something away from some one.
surityship: in law a mortgage falling due.
sustentation: sustenance.

teston: a silver coin worth less than a shilling, the first coin to bear the portrait of a king (French *tête*, Latin *testus*, head).
tractation: treatment of discussion of a subject.
turtles: turtledoves.

ure: "in ure," to put into use (NED 2).

venditation: act of selling.
venial: a venial sin is not as heinous as a "mortal" sin.

want (n., v.): a lack, to lack something.

zealot: a religious fanatic, described further in *Oc. Med.*,CXIII

A Table of the Biblical Story of Creation
Indexed to Hall's Occasional Meditations

The *Occasional Meditations* has merely a table of all one hundred and forty, not a helpful scheme for finding a particular one. An alphabetical index would be helpful but awkward. I have furnished this table as being both helpful and significant in view of the background of interest in the Genesis story and the many attempts to write hebdomadal or hexaemeral poetry. Most important for Hall was the publication in 1578 of Guillaume Salluste du Bartas' *Première Sepmaine ou Crèation du Monde*, adapted and translated by Hall's friend Joshua Sylvester in 1605 as *Divine Weeks and Works*. King James was a personal friend of du Bartas, and Sylvester's adaptation became vastly popular.

The titles within each category of "creatures" are alphabetized by their key-words, here italicized.

I. The Heavens
(Gen. 1:8 – "And God called the firmament heaven.")

VII. Upon a *Cloud*

III. Upon the Sight of an *Eclipse* of the Sun

I. Upon the Sight of the *Heavens* Moving

XIII. Upon the View of the *Heaven* and the Earth

CV. Upon *Motes* in the Sun

IV. Upon the Sight of a Gliding *Star*

XXXIX. Upon the Small *Stars* in the Galaxy, or Milky Circle in the Firmament.

XCVI. Upon Sight of a Bright Sky Full of *Stars*

CXXII. Upon the Hearing of *Thunder*

LXXXVIII.Upon the View of the *World*

II. The Earth and the Waters
(Gen. 1:9–10 – "and let the dry land appear . . .
and the gathering together of the waters.")

XXXVII. Upon a *Coal* Covered with Ashes

LX. Upon the First Rumor of the *Earthquake* at Lyme, wherein a

III. The Grass, Flowers, Shrubs, and Trees

(Gen. 1:11–12 – "let the earth bring forth grass, the herb yielding seed, and the fruit tree yielding fruit.")

IV. The Birds

(Gen. 1:20 – "and fowl that fly above the earth.")

V. The Animals
(Gen. 1:24 – "and the beast of the earth after his kind.")

VI. The Insects
(Gen. 1:25 – "and everything that creepeth upon the earth.")

VII. Man

(Gen. 1:26 – "Let us make man in our own image
. . . and let him have dominion.")

LXVI. Upon an *Arm* Benumbed

CXXXVIII. Upon an Importunate *Beggar*

XXVII. Upon the Sight of an Humble and Patient *Beggar*

CVI. Upon the Sight of a *Bladder* (education)

XXXVIII. Upon the Sight of a *Blackamoor*

XCIV. Upon a Cancelled *Bond*

LVII. Upon the Sight of a *Blind* Man

CXXV. Upon the Sight of the *Blind* and the Lame

XL. Upon the Sight of *Boys* Playing

XCVIII. Upon a *Child* Crying

LXX. Upon the Putting on of his *Clothes*

CVIII. Upon the Sight of a *Death's-head*

LXXIX. Upon a *Defamation* Dispersed

CXXX. Upon the Sight of a *Drunken Man*

CXXXVII Upon the Sight of a *Dwarf*

LXXXIX. Upon the Arraignment of a *Felon*

VIII. Upon the Sight of a *Grave* Digged Up

XCII. Upon the Sight of an *Harlot* Carted

CXVIII. Upon the Coming in of the *Judge*

CIX. Upon the Sight of a *Left-handed* Man

XXV. Upon his *Lying* down to Rest

LXXXIV. Upon a Penitent *Malefactor*

LXXIV. Upon the Sight of a *Marriage*

CXXXIX. Upon a *Medicinal* Potion

XLII. Upon the Sight of a *Natural*

LXXVIII. Upon the Tolling of a *Passing-bell*

C. Upon the Challenge of a *Promise*

CXXXV. Upon a *Quartan* Ague

LXXII. Upon the *Red Cross* on a Door

CIII. Upon the Sight of a *Scavenger* Working in the Channel

CXVII. Upon a *Scholar* that Offered Violence to Himself

L. Upon the *Shutting* of One Eye

XCIX. Upon the Beginning of a *Sickness*

CVII. Upon a Man *Sleeping*

XXX. Upon the Hearing of the *Street-cries* in London

XII. Upon the Report of a Man Suddenly *Struck Dead* in his Sin
XCI. Upon the Variety of *Thoughts*
XCVII. Upon the Rumors of *Wars*
LXXIII. Upon the Change of *Weather*
CXV. Upon the Sight of a Man *Yawning*
CII. Upon the Sight of a Fantastical *Zealot*

VIII. Man-made Objects
(Gen. 4:22 – "Tubal-cain, an instructor in every artifice.")

LXXVI. Upon the Ruins of an *Abbey*
LVI. Upon the Sound of a Cracked *Bell*
LXXX. Upon a Ring of *Bells*
CXXXVI. Upon the Sight of a Loaded *Cart*
CX. Upon the Sight of an Old Unthatched *Cottage*
II. Upon the Sight of a *Dial*
LXXXI. Upon the Sight of a Full Table at a *Feast*
XXII. Upon the Blowing of the *Fire*
XXVI. Upon the Kindling of a Charcoal *Fire*
VI. Upon the frame of a *Globe* Casually Broken
XXXII. Upon the Sight of a Dark *Lantern*
LXXI Upon the Sight of a Great *Library*
XX. Upon Occasion of the *Lights* Brought In
XXI. Upon the Same Occasion
CXXXII. Upon the Sight of a *Looking glass*
LXXXII. Upon the Hearing of a *Lute* Well Played On
CXXVI. Upon the Sight of a *Map* of the World
LIX. Upon the Sight of a Piece of *Money* under the Water
XLIV. Upon the Hearing of *Music* by Night
LXXVII. Upon the Discharging of a *Piece*
X. Upon the Sight of a *Pitcher* Carried
XLVII. Upon the Quenching of *Iron* in Water
CXII. Upon a *Screen*
CXXXI. Upon the Whetting of a *Scythe*
LXVII. Upon the *Sparks* Flying Upward
CIV. Upon a Pair of *Spectacles*
CXL. Upon the Sight of a *Wheel*

Note: *In view of the belief that God gave man dominion within the creation, it is interesting that out of 140 meditations almost one-half (68) are devoted to man and his artifacts.*

Bishop Joseph Hall and Protestant Meditation... provides the fullest account to date of the distinctly Protestant mode of meditation in England in the seventeenth century. Dr. Huntley analyzes and explores the five characteristics of meditation — its psychology, theology, philosophy, its public rather than private orientation, and the rich variety of Protestant meditation emerging from "the three books" in which one reads about God. Finally, Dr. Huntley places Hall in the literary and religious contexts of his time. The texts of *The Art of Divine Meditation* and *Occasional Meditations* are here edited for the first time in over a century. The latter, only occasionally noted by critics and scholars, is an important part of the seventeenth-century tradition.

Frank Livingstone Huntley is Emeritus Professor of English at the University of Michigan, and has held a Fulbright lectureship in Japan, a visiting professorship at Heidelberg University, as well as fellowships at the Folger Library and the Clark Memorial Library. He is best known for the major studies, *Jeremy Taylor and the Great Rebellion* (Univ. of Michigan Press, 1970), *Sir Thomas Browne: A Biographical and Critical Study* (Univ. of Michigan Press, 1962, 1968), and *Bishop Joseph Hall (1574-1656): A Biographical and Critical Study* (Cambridge, 1979). He also has written a book on Dryden's "Essay of Dramatic Poesy" (Univ. of Michigan Press, 1951, 1968) as well as over 75 articles on seventeenth-century English and Japanese literature, many of which have been reprinted in collections.

mRts

medieval & renaissance texts & studies is a research program and publication program of CEMERS, the Center for Medieval and Early Renaissance Studies at the State University of New York at Binghamton. The main mRts series emphasizes texts, translations, and major research tools. From time to time distinguished monographs and reprints will also be published. mRts is also engaged in the adaptation of modern technology for scholarly purposes and in fostering new approaches to scholarly publication.